DISCARD

DISCARD

5/02

Emma's World

Emma's World

An Intimate Look At Lives Touched By The Civil War Era

Shirley Blotnick Moskow

NEW HORIZON PRESS
Far Hills, New Jersey

Copyright © 1990 by Shirley Blotnick Moskow
All rights reserved. No part of this book may be reproduced or transmitted in any form whatsoever, including electronic, mechanical, or any information storage or retrieval system, except as may be expressly permitted by the 1976 Copyright Act or in writing from the publisher. Requests for permission should be addressed to New Horizon Press, P.O. Box 669, Far Hills, New Jersey 07931.

Library of Congress Cataloging Card Number: 90-60916

Shirley Blotnick Moskow
   Emma's World

ISBN: 0-88282-059-1
New Horizon Press

*In memory of Eric,
and times past*

AUTHOR'S NOTE

These letters have been transcribed as faithfully as possible. All original grammar, punctuation, and spelling have been retained to preserve individual and regional differences of correspondents.

Acknowledgments

*M*y father-in-law Max J. Moskow is an inveterate collector and his purchase of a bundle of old letters unwittingly set in motion events that culminate with publication of *EMMA'S WORLD*. It is just one of many things for which I thank him.

Still, I would not have embarked upon the adventure that is this book without the encouragement of Ruth Diengott and my mother-in-law, the late Goldie Fram Moskow. They introduced me to Emma.

With unflagging good humor, my husband, Richard, listened to countless stories about Emma. Indeed, her name surfaced at the dinner table so often that he came to think of her as one of the family. Our sons, Jeffrey and Neal, grew up with Emma, and our daughters-in-law, Laurie and Tina, are on intimate terms with her. I am grateful to all of them for their patience and for putting up with my lapses into the nineteenth century.

For numerous kindnesses in sharing family history and his considerable research into Barbour/Evans geneology, I owe thanks to Emma's great grandnephew, Robert M. Howes. He put me in touch with other family members, including his great aunt, Julia Evans, whom I interviewed in her ninety-sixth year, and cousin Marian B. Patch, who made available her grandfather Alfred Barbour's letters and papers. Alice Pepper, whose husband John is a Barbour descendent, provided family photographs.

Finally, I can never repay the special debt of gratitude due other writers who took time from their own work to help me with this project: Myrna Kaye, Joan Lautman, Roberta Leviton, Barbara Mende, Sabra Morton, Doris Pullen, Geri Quinzio, Janet Tassel, and Molly Turner. Their care and intelligence inform every page of *EMMA'S WORLD*.

Contents

Foreword   xiii

Part One: Emma's Family and Friends

1. (1854–1856)   3
2. (1857)   14
3. (1858–1859)   22
4. (1860–1861)   41

Part Two: Emma's Country

5. (1861)   61
6. (1861)   84
7. (1862)   105
8. (1863)   135
9. (1863)   169
10. (1864)   188
11. (1865)   213

Part Three: Emma's World

12. (1865)   229
13. (1866)   252
14. (1867)   269
15. (1868)   284

Epilogue   289

You may forget but
Let me tell you
this; someone in some future time
will think of us

—Sappho

Foreword

*E*mma Barbour's brother, Ned, was nineteen years old when he breakfasted at Harper's Ferry in November 1859, a few weeks after John Brown, the abolitionist, led his attack on the West Virginia arsenal. The young Northerner, mindful of Brown's rebellion and curious about the site, decided to explore a bit. Where the melée had taken place, he discerned large blood stains dappling the floor. Investigating further, he examined splintered gashes in the armory door, made by a ladder used in battering it down. And all the while he poked and pried, he felt the guards' Southern eyes scrutinizing him.

Later in the day, his train stopped at Charles Town, West Virginia, where the insurrectionists were tried and executed. Having heard that two Northerners had been asked to leave town the day before, Ned decided against disembarking. He felt that the locals regarded him as a "suspicious northerner." And, indeed, when he arrived in Winchester, Virginia, where he was staying, his landlady told him that the mayor wanted to see him at once. His Honor's concerns were assuaged only after Ned opened his large trunks to reveal the merchandise he was peddling.

We know about Ned's uneasiness—the feelings of a Northerner traveling in the South prior to the Civil War—because, weary and far from family in Cambridge, Massachusetts, he felt homesick and wrote to his sister on her sixteenth birthday. Emma saved his letters, along with others she had begun squirreling away five years earlier. Altogether, she left behind fourteen years' worth of letters when she married. The neat packet of small envelopes was stowed away in a little leather trunk, such a one as a lady might carry on her lap during a long stagecoach ride. Perhaps it is the trunk Emma carried as a young girl when she went visiting. It is quite worn and probably did not suit her trousseau, so was replaced. No one knows.

A philatelist exhumed the letters from under a blanket of dust in 1951, when he inspected the shoebox-sized trunk at an antiques show. He purchased it for the stamps on the envelopes. Then he returned home and his wife, noticing the postmark "Cambridge," where she had been born, began reading the letters. She was intrigued by them, but the ink was faded, the spidery handwriting often illegible, and there was so much interlining that she became discouraged by the tediousness of the task.

I learned about the Barbour Collection when I married the philatelist's son. My mother-in-law's descriptions of the contents of the letters tempted me to transcribe some of the yellowed pages. The task begun, I became fascinated with Emma and her friends. Although I was dismayed at first because none of the letters were from Emma, I came to know her by extrapolating bits of information from the comments her correspondents wrote to their trusted confidante, my own search of private and public records, and ultimately through interviews with Barbour family descendants who shared old correspondence and family documents.

Emma Sargent Barbour was born on November 20, 1843, the fifth child, second daughter, of Susan Sargent and John Nathaniel Barbour, who recently had moved from Boston, across the Charles River, to Cambridgeport, Massachusetts. During her lifetime, she blazed no frontier in geography or science, penned no great book, inspired no immortal art or cause. She grew up, married and died

Foreword

within a few city blocks of the house in which she had been born. Emma, in short, was like most of us.

However, the brush of time paints even the commonplace with an exotic tint. Epic events and heroic figures often bear an antiseptic similarity one to another when they are memorialized in books and films, and purge the past of human proportions. That is why, more than one hundred years after Emma's death, her world, with its hoop skirts, frequent train collisions, parlour games, and a country at war with itself, seems at once foreign and familiar.

John Tyler, tenth President of the United States, was in office when Emma was born, and a few Cambridge people still remembered parties hosted by General George Washington at his military headquarters on Brattle Street during the Revolutionary War. She was a toddler when gold was discovered in California; she was a schoolgirl, already saving letters, when Harriet Beecher Stowe published *Uncle Tom's Cabin;* and a young woman of eighteen when Abraham Lincoln delivered his Emancipation Proclamation. The first professional baseball club, the Cincinnati Red Stockings, was organized the year she married, and George Westinghouse manufactured an electric motor the year she died.

The Emma we meet in these letters was slim, in an age whose standard of beauty was the well-padded woman. She had dark hair and black eyes and at seventeen looked mature. She was evidently at the top of her class in school and popular with other students. She made lifelong attachments among the girls with whom she shared adolescent confidences at church, sewing circle, and Sunday school. Young men invited her to play croquet and to stroll under the elms on Cambridge Common in summer. In winter, they requested the honor of her company at ice skating parties and for sleigh rides. A crush on one young fellow apparently ended unhappily because he preferred someone else. Later, she fell in love with a soldier who went off to war, and married him after he returned.

The Civil War, its prelude, and aftermath, is the historic landscape of Emma's letter collection, which furnishes a detailed account of civilian life during the middle of our nation's first century. It reconstructs a unique moment in time with unusual vitality and fidelity. Emma's correspondents attempted to understand their turbulent times as well as themselves when they focused on intimate details. They were schoolgirls chatting about "beaus," lessons, and fashion; her brothers and sister offering advice while sharing confidences; her parents giving guidance; and her betrothed reassuring her when she confessed to pre-nuptial jitters. Their letters yield a rich social history.

In addition, the letters are a testimony of life's perpetual celebrations and sorrows. Their messages are poignant, unselfconscious confessions and observations flashed intact across decades of change. They come from the heart of the Confederacy in Mobile, Alabama, and the capital of the Union; from the Western frontier and from the backwoods of Maine. They shed light on the roles of men and women in their domestic lives, touching on child rearing, housekeeping, education, farming, manners, folk medicine and politics. And in so doing, they voice the ethos of that age, a belief in the perfectibility of people, the strong motivation for self-improvement exemplified by vocabulary-building evenings devoted to word games, filled-to-capacity lecture halls, and school themes with such titles as "Employment Essential to Human Happiness."

Letters from Emma's young friends also embrace a ubiquitous religious theme. It was a popular pastime to compare and share sermons by different ministers. Church was the community center, concert hall, and theatre to which these Christians went for their society, intellectual sustenance, and entertainment. A young woman friend, having moved to a nearby city wrote, "I want to ask one little favor of you . . . get me a card containing the lessons for the year . . . Each Sunday I can read over the lesson for that day and think of you and the girls and wonder what you would be saying about the lesson."

Then, too, like other Victorians, Emma's friends were preoccupied with the concept of romantic death. After complaining about her teacher and her homework assignments, an eleven-year-old schoolgirl continued, "Did you go to Eddy Page's funeral and does Doris dress in black all the time. I felt bad when I heard of his death and read that piece of Poetry about him and how bad that Hovey boy must have felt when he saw that dear little Eddy drop down dead and how bad Mr. Page's folks must have felt when they saw their dear son brought home dead." Then, "When you write tell me all about it." From Mobile, Cousin Elizabeth Horton wrote that her high school classmate had died. "I knew nothing of it until the worst was past. I mourned for her as one who had gone unprepared to meet her God. But when I heard the particulars of her death, I rejoiced that she had gone. She died a most happy death, exalting in her Saviour. Her last words to a brother were, 'I see Jesus coming with a sceptre in one hand and a crown in the other.'"

The politics of slavery also concerned Emma's cousin, Elizabeth. In a letter dated Mobile, November 15, 1860, she wrote, "Lin-

Foreword

coln never will be president of the United States, though he may be of the 'Free States.'" She continued, "Until recently I have been for 'A union of hearts, a union of hands, and a union of States, none can sever,' but since the worst must come to the worst, I have to omit the last kind of union. The S-O-U-T-H will not have a 'Black Republican' for a ruler, nor a part negro for a Vice-President." Regaining her composure, Elizabeth concluded, "I do not suppose that Politics can interfere with our correspondence; at least, I hope not."

Not long after the war started, Maria Morse's father applied for a post in the Capital, and Maria soon began writing to Emma from Washington, D.C. Her first letter included a detailed narrative of her trip from Cambridge, with a diagram of her steamship stateroom. She described the nation's capital as a "busy country town" that had more pigs than cats. Subsequent messages were full of news about the school in which she taught, a parade of 1500 Confederate prisoners of war, and how a tribunal of churchmen came to judge her sister insane. Once, she observed, "I see so much art and cunning that I suspect almost everyone until I know better." and, about the First Lady's well-known extravagances, she commented, "Last night the President and Mrs. Lincoln held a levee. I could not go but have heard that there was a great crowd and much dress and show. How foolish and wicked in these times. I am ashamed of our American women."

It was not an easy life for most women, certainly not for Emma's sister Susan, who wrote most of the letters Emma stashed away. On her twenty-fifth birthday, Susan married a divinity student, William Henry Evans. He had been born in England and brought up as an Episcopalian; however, in order to win Susan's hand, he abandoned the Church of England and became a Baptist. His family was resentful, but he was very much in love with Susan, an intelligent woman with city-bred manners and sophisticated tastes.

After their marriage, his first parish was in China, Maine, where Susan felt like an outsider among country folk. She wrote letters about her efforts to find friends and then raise a family in the backwoods. They chronicle the transformation of a happy young bride to an overweight, care-burdened, and work-worn wife and mother. Overwhelmed with chores, she frantically scribbled long, newsy letters in the snatches of time between nursing a baby and drawing water from the cistern, or between mending clothes and baking bread. She poured out her feelings, writing, "I am thankful, [to be able to] express myself to some unfettered by any restraint. I regard it as a great privilege."

She groused and gossiped about her neighbors, yet was grateful for every kindness they extended to her. "You don't know how hard it is to feel like an exile," she wrote. And, when her husband was assigned to a new church, she confided, "To go among strangers again is discouraging . . . people do act so strangely here I can't for my life find out what they mean, or who is friendly and who is not . . ." But move she did. She enclosed swatches of wallpaper in her letters and told about putting down rugs that didn't fit. She made up beds of husk mattresses, cooked on a temperamental wood stove, welcomed itinerant peddlers who came to her door offering a few luxury items, sewed by hand, and shopped, thriftly counting out each penny from her meager store, for she dearly loved nice clothes and good food. And, in spite of her complaints, she sympathised with the demands of her husband's calling and encouraged him to be the best minister that he could.

Her letters quoted Shakespeare and included French expressions she had learned in school, and they told how she missed the lyceum, books, and stimulating conversation, pleasures she had grown accustomed to in Cambridge. Without them, her spirit became becalmed, then sagged. "I feel like an ignoramus," she wrote after a while. "I would like to borrow books if I could but this is not a reading public." And, another time, "Send the Chronicle, Harper, or something." Desperately, she explained, "I must sometimes write nonsense to keep off the blues." Once, when children and husband were all sick, she spilled out her thoughts in a long letter. "Of course I am tired sleepy, and would like to be fussy if I dared, but it won't do for me. I must keep the rest up." Some nights Susan was so exhausted that she dropped into bed with her clothes on, plaintively reflecting, "I do wish it took as long to make dirt as to clean it up."

Small wonder that, when Emma wrote of her engagement, Susan warned, "you see what you will come to if you get married. If I had known all beforehand, I shouldn't have thought I could live through it, but I did, you see and managed to be pretty comfortable part of the time."

In one letter, there is an inkling that Susan may have had some regrets about her marriage. In January, 1865, she wrote, "I do really hope if you like W.H.W., you will not commit yourself to anyone else if there is the least prospect of anything . . . Remember my experience and profit thereby. I have felt very sad at times thinking about the past." As in this instance, she often used her experience as an example for Emma, saying, "I think a word or so may help others over the places where I myself have stumbled."

Foreword

Whenever Emma visited Susan or stayed with friends, she received mail from Cambridge. Her father wrote often. His letters sometimes began in a stilted literary style, but soon relaxed to reveal an intelligent, loving man, devoted to his family. "We do miss you very much," he wrote, looking back wistfully to the happy times when all of his children were at home. He was generous with parental advice, but not self-important, referring to himself as "an old fogie." In a letter responding to Susan's concern that she may have offended him, he explained to Emma, "I wrote her a free unbending letter and she in reply one full of sympathy . . . as I should expect from her warm true generous womanly sympathies that bind genial and congenial hearts together." Another time, asking Emma to return home, he added, "You need not consider this an imperative order, but use the judgment for which you are accountable."

John Barbour was a merchant and, during the war, he served as Deputy Collector for the United States Internal Revenue Office in Cambridge. A member of the First Baptist Church, where he taught Sunday School, he was a religious man, as familiar with the Old and New Testaments as he was with his newspaper, *The Cambridge Chronicle.* In discussing politics at the time of Lincoln's Proclamation of Freedom, he compared the plight of the slaves with the predicament of Jews in the days of Ashavarius. He wrote, "I might consent that certain rebels might hang on an institution—as high as Haman did."

Nevertheless, he cautiously avoided advising his sons about going to war. Possibly influenced by Thoreau, he wrote to Emma, "When our government acts upon a principle in direct opposition to the law of God . . . we cannot have that deep pervading sense of duty, to induce our loved ones to offer their lives as we should if duty and conscience and opinion coincided. I have no doubt that God will work out the destruction of slavery, though our Gov't deny their participation, yet I prefer to work with than against God."

No aspect of his behavior was exempt from ethical consideration. When the call to jury duty came at an inconvenient time, he served, noting, it was one of "the responsibilities of life from which I must in no wise shirk." Having promised to enclose a piece of mail for her prospective sister-in-law in the letter he wrote to Emma, he added a postscript. "On reflection I remember that it is illegal to enclose in one envelope letters to different persons so I sent two separate."

There are fewer letters from Emma's mother. Very often her Father concluded letters his wife began. She penned chatty messages about home and church, about conversations with friends, about her garden, and, once, about dashing from street to street in a futile attempt to greet a returning regiment. Although she wrote infrequently, she urged Emma's friends to write, and they did.

Friends shared the latest tidings; who was engaged, married, had a baby, or died, and later, who was serving in the army, and where. They enjoyed teasing and relating accounts of their pranks, like the mock funeral for a book, conducted by the graduating class after they completed Cicero. "Piper came first. he had on an old black beaver with the number '62' in large white letters . . . some false mustachios of black wool . . . eyeglasses . . . a white sash . . . a large stand up collar and a great white choker, white streamers on his arms . . . Dodge was dressed to represent President Felton as he dresses at Commencement . . . they marched into the schoolyard and burried (sic) the Corpse . . . held in a square of black cloth edged with white and lowered into the grave by four boys . . . Dodge made quite a speech, consisting of Latin nonsense composed for the occasion . . . It was quite killing."

For many in the graduating class, make-believe funerals were too soon followed by the sad reality in wartime. Older brothers already had answered the call to colors and the *Cambridge Chronicle* listed the names of the dead. Letters to Emma record the changes. "I hope Gus Smart will find William's body though of course it would be little comfort except to know he was buried at home." And, "I see by the papers that the Feds are thinking of calling at Mobile," followed a few lines further by, "John Tucker's brother is dead . . . there was a military funeral here this week, a young man who was wounded at Gettysburg died at Washington and was brought home."

After the war, like many young men, Emma's brothers, Alfred and Ned, went West. (Another brother, William, was a farmer in Massachusetts.) Ned, whose health had never been robust, settled briefly in Cleveland, then Columbus, and was living in Cincinnati when he became seriously ill and went to live with Alfred in Tremont, Illinois. Determined to be independent, Ned set off again as soon as he felt better. This time, he headed farther West, towards a remote settlement in Minnesota, where he found a job as bookkeeper in a lumber camp.

The last letter in the Emma Barbour collection is dated January 30, 1868, from Aunt Harriet in New Jersey, expressing delight about Emma's proposed bridal visit. Emma married William Henry Whitney in the living room of her parents' home on February 18, 1868. When they returned from their wedding tour, she went to live nearby

Foreword

in the Auburn Court cottage he had prepared for her. She left behind her bundle of letters, most likely in her old bedroom under the eaves of the house where she grew up.

Emma's letters, despite their faded penmanship, vividly preserve the passions and problems, the fads, fun, and frustrations of Americans who lived in the middle of the nineteenth century. By documenting the stories of ordinary lives during an extraordinary period in history, they offer charmingly authentic evidence of the drama in social history. These letters are spontaneous and intimate; through their words we are privileged to enter and experience a very private world.

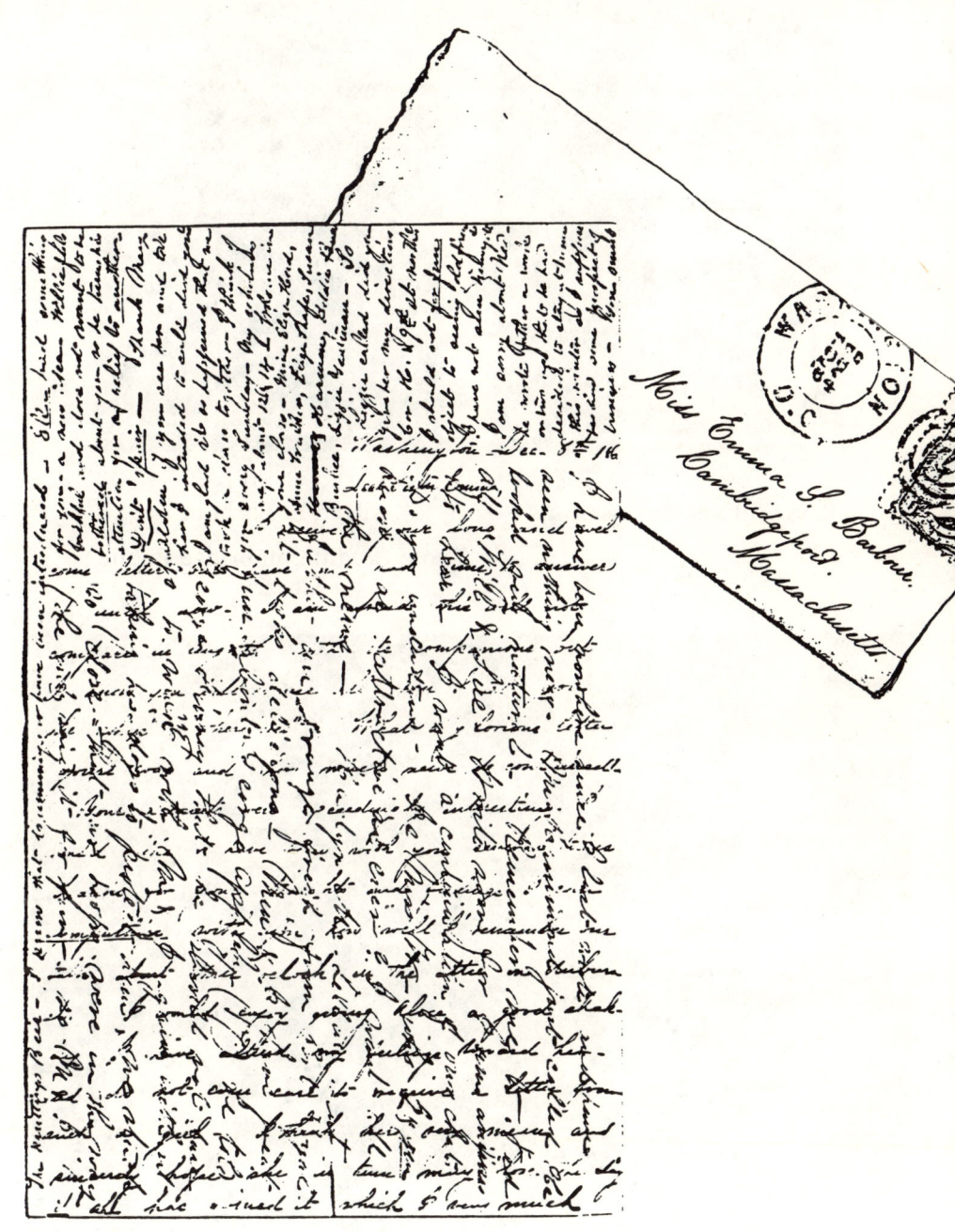

A Letter From Maria Morse

Rev. William Henry Evans   Alfred L. Barbour

Photo Credit: Cambridge Public Library

Aunt Lovica and Uncle James Barbour

Part One
Emma's Family and Friends: Portrait of An Era

"The candlestick set in a low place has given light as faithfully, where it was needed, as that upon a hill."
Margaret Fuller

1
(1854–1856)

*B*y the time Emma Sargent Barbour was born in 1843, a national consciousness was forged, one that thrived on change. The first generation of Americans had converted their currency from pounds to dollars and their allegiance from the Old World to the New. Settlers no longer thought of themselves as colonists or Englishmen, but as citizens of The United States of America.

Change was the country's most dramatic feature, and Emma's letters recreate the climate of a society in flux. Frontier wilderness was transformed into civilized settlements. Foreigners crossed the Atlantic and Pacific oceans and became Americans. Railroads altered the speed with which people traveled distances, just as the telegraph changed the way they communicated. And a press, unfettered by government, refashioned the meaning of news.

Then the Industrial Revolution changed how and where goods were produced, as well as how and where people lived. Once women and children went to work in factories, family life was reshaped. Born in the 1830s of the factory system, and nurtured by the humanitarian efforts of the 1840s, the woman suffrage movement, under the leadership of Lucy Stone, held its first national convocation, the Woman's Rights Convention, in 1850 in Worcester, Massachusetts.

Massachusetts figured prominently in reform movements of the nineteenth century, and scores of propaganda pamphlets and newspapers were published there, no doubt because of the state's many literate citizens. A schoolhouse in every village had been provided for in the original charter for the Commonwealth, and, in 1852, Massachusetts put into effect the county's first compulsory school attendance law. Mill towns often grew prosperous by exploiting child labor; therefore, the Commonwealth required all children between the ages of eight and fourteen to attend school at least twelve weeks a year, six of which had to be consecutive. The emphasis on universal public education distinguished the United States from other countries, and its importance can be seen in the letters of Emma's correspondents.

Chiseled by their unique experiences and fortified by an embracing religious revival, Americans at mid-century exemplified a new national character—independent, self-confident, resourceful, and optimistic. These were the qualities necessary to survive and prosper in the emerging nation where dreams could be translated into opportunity by Emma's brothers and others prepared to take advantage of the changes. No challenge seemed overly great. To adjust to so different a perspective as required by Herbert Spencer's theory of evolution and Charles Darwin's thesis of the origin of the species, a new concept developed: Americans were part of a divine plan. The New World was Eden.

Europeans called it arrogance. America, they predicted, would be the graveyard of culture. Confronted by the boastful claims of brash Americans, Europeans were offended by rude clothes and rude manners. Above all, they disdained the Americans who, having come from a society based on order and an appreciation of class structure, established an extraordinarily egalitarian society.

The irony was that Americans founded the first democratic government in the modern world, yet sanctioned slavery of the black

(1854–1856)

race. To condone the institution, they cited historical precedent in the Bible, and later even postulated a separate origin theory of the white race. And therein lay the seeds of their heartbreak. Slowly but inexorably, the weed took hold, flourished, and threatened to overrun Eden until, in order to uproot it, in the middle of the nineteenth century, the nation risked ruin to redefine what it meant to be an American.

These were the issues and events that concerned Emma's parents in 1854, when she started saving letters, but they could have little interest or meaning to a child. She was eleven and her correspondence reflected youthful matters—the difficulty of getting established in a new school, the sadness of separation from old friends. These first letters came from Elvira, who went to live sixty-five miles west of Cambridge in Palmer Depot, a community tucked in the valley of the Cedar Mountains on the banks of the Quabaug River. Once a sluggish farming village, Palmer was typical of the New England mill towns that enjoyed a fling with prosperity in the middle of the century.

With Elvira's letter in hand, Emma could imagine what Palmer was like, quite different from Cambridge, a highly sophisticated community. Charles Eliot, son of a Harvard president, recalled "Longfellow and Lowell were writing their poems, . . . Peabody preached and Agassiz lectured and Asa Gray botanized and William James philosophized, . . . John Fiske was writing histories and Thomas Wentworth Higginson essays, . . . John Bartlett compiled 'Familiar Quotations' and John Holmes dashed off letters bubbling with fun. There too John K. Paine was composing an opera and Henry Dexter fashioning statues and Alvan Clark polishing unsurpassed lenses for telescopes and the famous firms of Mason & Hamlin and Ivers & Pond building fine organs and pianos." Book publishing and the manufacturing of bricks, confectionery, soap, furniture, tinware, glassware, and metal goods rounded out the list of Cambridge's primary industries.

It is likely that Elvira's family moved because her father found employment in the rough and hustling village. Palmer's mills were the first to use short staple cotton and wool to weave quality fabrics —thanks to Joseph Brown of Rhode Island, who devised the cheap spindles and machinery. Four mills employed 505 men and 541 women. Among other commercial enterprises were six blacksmith shops, a saddle and harness manufactory, a hat manufactory, a carriage manufactory, a soap and candle work, a tinware manufactory, and a lumberyard. Railroads came, tying the busy town to markets from Boston to New York. Between 1840 and 1855, the village's population doubled to 4000.

As befitted its importance, Palmer participated in the hotel building boom that was sweeping the country and boasted two fine hotels as well as a guest house. Six taverns offered fellowship and cheer to the tired foot soldiers of the Industrial Revolution and to the neighboring farmers who coaxed a harvest from rocky fields.

Moreover, the town had a public laundry. A local businessman followed the lead of a California miner named Davis who, in 1849, found it more profitable to set up the first public laundry in America than to pan for gold. This advertisement in *The Palmer Journal* ran weekly: "Girls Wanted: A dozen girls to work in a laundry at Palmer Depot. Good smart girls can earn from $3 to $5 a week in the establishment. Enquire of M.C. Munger."

Like other newspapers, *The Palmer Journal,* Gorden M. Fisk editor and publisher, also carried advertisements for a popular sex manual, ***The Married Woman's Private Medical Companion,*** by Dr. A. M. Mauriceau, and anti-Catholic propaganda with such headlines as "Irish girl burning church," "Catholic priest arrested for assault on hunchback boy," and "Another Catholic outrage," about a bookburning of "poisonous materials" in an Albany, New York, almshouse.

Palmer had six churches, including the one Elvira attended, the "orthodox," which was the Orthodox Congregational Church.

Emma may have been mourning Elvira's departure when this letter arrived. It could have been the first letter she ever received that was addressed to her, or from someone her own age. Perhaps that is why she treasured it.

Palmer Depot July 1854

My dear Friend

Mother and Hattie have gone to the laundry and Sarah and I are here alone. Sarah is writing to a friend of hers and as I had nothing in particular to do I thought I would write to you. We started from Cambridge about half past six a week ago last Friday morning and arrived at the depot about half an hour before the cars started and arrived here about half past eleven. We went directly to the hotel where we stayed until the next morning when we came here to this house and have been here ever since but I hope we shall not be here much longer. I am real homesick here it is such a dreary place. I went to meeting

(1854–1856)

Sunday all day in the morning. I went to the Baptist and in the afternoon I went to the Orthodox and neither of them have settled Pastors. Those two are all there are in the place and such meetings I never saw. There are two schools in the place a school for rather large children and a school for rather small children. George Frank and I go to the large school. George and I study Greenliefs National Arthithmetic, Mitchells Geography, Webster's spelling book, Welds Grammar and Swan's district school reader. I believe that is all but we have to study pretty hard so as to get up with the class. Frank studies Colburns Arthithmetic, Mitchells Geography, Websters spelling book and Gramm school reader but he has to study about as hard as I do. George and I are going into the high school next term but it does not keep only two terms in a year so I shall have all the rest of the time for vacation we have the month of August here the same as they do down to Cambridge. There are just thirty scholars in the school now but before we went there were only twenty-seven. I do not think that is many compared with Dr. Smiths school did it seem a great many to you it keeps every Wednesday all day and every other Saturday we have to carry our dinner as the school is about one mile from the house and begins at nine and leaves off at twelve at noon. I asked Herbert what he wanted me to tell you and he said send love. Tell Dr. Smith mother says she hopes she shall see the time that I shall come there to his school and she says she should feel more contented if the schools were better I guess I shall come down there next spring and then we shall have nice times shant we playing I cannot stop to write any more.

Goodby from your affectionate
friend Elvira

P.S. Write as soon as possible.

Emma wrote back, but it was autumn before she heard from her pen pal again. Elvira sorely missed Cambridge, especially Master Elbridge Smith's school, where she had learned to write in the Duntonian style.

Beautiful handwriting was an important social grace, and the fluid strokes of the Duntonian style were greatly admired. According to an obituary in *The Boston Transcript* "Mr. Alvin R. Dunton, professor of penmanship, died at his residence in Camden, Maine, yesterday (October 6, 1891), aged 79 years. Mr. Dunton was the author of the Dunton System of penmanship and had been a professor of penmanship since his early manhood. He had taught penmanship in nearly every state in the Union." In his teacher's manual, Dunton emphasized that public school education eschewed private instruction. He urged teachers to have all pupils work on the same assignment at one time. To manage the penmanship class, he recommended, after students picked up their pens, that teachers count: "one, elbow on desk; two, dip pen; three, lift pen; four, position pen on paper." Thereafter, "one," "two," "three," "four" were cues for the up and down strokes of the pen as letters were formed.

Elvira dramatically downgraded everything in Palmer. Yet her teacher, Henry L. Boltwood, a Phi Beta Kappa graduate of Amherst College, Class of '53, went on to become an outstanding educator. After the Civil War, he settled in Illinois, where he is remembered as the "father of the Township School." He founded two. The first in the state, Princeton, organized in 1867, was so successful that it attracted pupils from abroad, at one time as many as ninety. In 1878, he founded a similar school at Ottawa. He also served on the state board of education, was president of the state teachers' association, and wrote five textbooks.

Although he came from a prominent Amherst, Massachusetts, family—a street in the town is named Boltwood—and had enjoyed an elitist education, Elvira's teacher was a staunch democrat and an outspoken critic of two educational trends of his time: the glorification of college athletics and secret societies in high schools. In a speech widely reported in newspapers, he complained that school athletics often was accorded more interest than academics, noting, "Five columns of newspaper glory to a game between Yale and Harvard, twenty lines to an intercollegiate debate." And, about public schools, he wrote, "Everything that tends to interfere with the idea that all the pupils of a school are absolutely on an equal footing and are equally wards of the taxpaying public, to be educated for a citizenship which acknowledges no class distinctions whatever, has an evil tendency."

Palmer Depot, October 1854
Palmer, Ms.

Dear Emma,

I received your kind letter and was very much pleased with it. I suppose you think that I did not get it, but you are mistaken for

(1854–1856)

I did. I go to the high school which is not much higher than Dr. Smiths School. I am in the lowest class, which is the fourth. Our Masters name is Mr. Boltwood and mother says he deserves that name for he bolts ahead and does not stop for anything but he is a very good teacher after all although he is not so good a one as Dr. Smith. Oh Emma you do not know how much I miss the Cambridge schools, here our master is very strict and gives such long lessons that I have to study a little harder than I did down there. We do not have any assistant teachers nor anything else that is worth mentioning. We have to write Compositions every other week but the boys have to write Compositions one week and Declaim the next so you see they have a pretty hard task to accomplish to what the girls do. How do the girls get along in their studies down there? If you see Hatty Webber please tell her I want her to write to me and not wait for me to write first. Did you go to Eddy Page's funeral and does Doris dress in black all the time, I felt bad when I heard of his death and read that piece of Poetry about him and how bad that Hovey boy must have felt when he saw that dear little Eddy drop down dead and how bad Mr. Page's folks must have felt when they saw their dear son brought home dead. When you write tell me all about it. I look forward to the time next spring when I shall be once more in that pleasant place Cambridge and Emma if we should never meet again on this earth may we meet in that happy land where "studies and farewells are a sound unknown.

May I but meet thee on that peaceful shore the parting word shall pass my lips no more." Tell Mr. Smith I have almost forgotten how to write in the Duntonion system so you must excuse me. George tends at a book store and he has to go through the cars to sell papers and the other day as he was going through them he saw Martha Bray and her father they were going to Detroit I guess. I heard that Addy Cox had moved in the house that we used to live in and I was very glad to hear it. I must close now for it is getting late.

P.S. Give my love to all the girls and other folks that I am acquainted with and especially Addy Cox. Excuse bad writing and mistakes and write soon.

Goodby from your still loving and
affectionate friend Elvira

In spite of Elvira's disparaging comments, Palmer appears to have been committed to supporting public education. The village appropriated $525 annually for maintaining its thirteen schools. Elvira attended the public high school, which held four sessions a year, each in a different place: Palmer Center, Three Rivers, Depot Village, and Thorndike.

Within the month, Elvira revised her opinion of her school. She was happier once she began to make friends. She mentions a classmate named Merrick, whose father was foreman at one of the mills. Elvira's letters, particularly this one, highlight the importance of school to girls. (Coeducation is an American word; schools in Europe were for boys.)

Palmer Depot
Nov. 5, 1854
Sunday Afternoon

Dear Emma,

When I wrote to you last I told you that the Master was very strict, but he is not so much so as he was then and does not give quite so long lessons as he did then and I am very glad for then I did not have time to get my lessons very perfect. Mr. Boltwood our teacher preached at the Baptist Church this morning but I missed hearing him for I could not go. I felt very sorry for I wanted to hear him very much. George has been amusing Herbert but he has gone off so I suppose I shall have to take care of him now. I was very glad to hear of that little girl but I believe she was there when I was there was she not but I believe she did not have to lie on an inclined plane all of the time did she isn't her name Knights I guess you told me about her when I was there didn't you. We do not have to write Compositions now because most of us have Journals in which we have to write an account of the day we have not begun yet but we are going to begin Monday which is tomorrow but those that do not have Journals have to write Compositions I have not written but three yet and am glad I have not got to write any more. I suppose you have Sabbath school Concerts down there. We have had one here since we came and that began at five o'clock I miss them very much. I have not felt very well for sometime but I have not said anything about it to mother nor any of the rest of the folks because I am afraid she will not let me go to school for the school is a mile from our house and therefore it makes me very tired to walk which I have to do. I have not told you anything about the girls here for there is but one girl that I care anything about and her name is Merrick every time I see her she reminds me of you. As I wrote you so long a letter before that I have not much to say now so I must bid you farewell till next time.

Goodbye from your ever affectionate
friend Elvira

P.S. Give my love to all your folks and excuse bad writing and spelling and write as soon as possible.

Elvira suffered quietly the symptoms of her unknown malady—confiding only in Emma—rather than tell her mother of her discomfort and risk being kept at home. School was more than an educational obligation, it was a social opportunity. In the restricted society in which these proper young women were reared, access to female friendships was severely limited to school, the formalized custom of visiting, and church. Elvira's remarks about the Knight girl suggest that the youngster was suffering from a hiatus hernia or heart disease, since the treatment for both conditions included lying on an inclined plane with the head raised.

Mr. Boltwood, her teacher, whose preaching she had missed, would ten years later be ordained chaplain of the 67th Regiment, United States Cavalry Troops. On April 9, 1865, the day Robert E. Lee surrendered, Boltwood was present at the capture of Fort Blakely, opposite Mobile, Alabama, when the last battle of the war was fought.

We do not know whether Emma answered this letter, the last from Elvira. The next letter Emma saved came to her several months later, when she was staying with her Sullivan cousins—her paternal great-grandmother was a Sullivan—in Woburn Center, about ten miles west of Cambridge.

Girls visiting and staying at each other's homes for days or weeks was a practical nineteenth-century institution that bonded female friendships and helped young women meet prospective husbands among the relatives and neighbors of their hostesses. It was also an informal apprenticeship. Guests were expected to assist with household chores, so that they enhanced their knowledge of and practiced housewifely skills.

The letter Emma received at her cousins' was from her sister, Susan. Most of Emma's letters are from her. Although Emma was ten years her sister's junior, the girls enjoyed an intimate and affectionate relationship. Susan, born in 1833, was the second oldest of the five Barbour children. Not coincidentally, in Emma's absence, Susan had a friend stay with her, too.

Cambridge Port Friday Aug 25

Dear Emma:

Mother was busy and so I thought I would answer your letter. We did not get it till last night. We were glad to hear that you were well and enjoying yourself so much. We want to see you at home for we miss you very much, but we hope you will stay as long as you want to, and be sure not to come home without bringing some of them with you. Emily has been here since you have been away so that I have had company but she is going home this afternoon so I expect to be pretty lonesome tonight. I had a great mind to come out to Woburn to stay over Sunday, but concluded not to as there is a man going to preach that I want to hear. Willie got home on Monday from Asabet, he had a splendid time. Alf is going to Groton with Emily to stay till Monday and is going to bring Ned home. Father Mother Wm. Henry and I went to Chelsea Beach Wednesday. We had a nice time but I got cold and have not been well since. Aunt Elisa and Sara Eliot and Uncle William came out and spent the day yesterday. We are pretty lonesome at home and shall be glad when the children get back. Addie is gone to Waltham. I went in the factory to see them make candy this morning. Give our love to Mrs. Sullivan & family and tell her to be sure and let Louisa come. I shall expect Rebecca & Mattie next week. It is time for me to close now, as I am in a great hurry please excuse the looks of this letter, get some one to help you if you cannot read it yourself.

Goodbye dear—from sister,
Susan

It is my birthday today
22 years old—

As she often did, Susan wrote in haste. Afterwards, perusing the scrawl-filled page, she apparently doubted that a child would be able to decipher it. Of course, to benefit from her advice—"get someone to help you if you cannot read it yourself"—Emma had to complete the letter.

Susan mentions a trip to Chelsea Beach. On Massachusetts' North Shore, Chelsea was the closest saltwater beach from Boston, accessible by either steamer or railroad. A day at the beach was a popular leisure activity, but women rarely ventured into the water. Their swimming outfits—cloth cap, tunic, drawers, stockings, bathing shoes, and undergarments—made it virtually impossible for them to stay afloat. Further, it would have been outrageous for a woman to be seen in wet clothes that hugged her body.

2
(1857)

*E*mma's extended family included relatives in the South. Cousin Elizabeth (Eliza) Horton, the daughter of Emma's mother's sister, was a passionate letter writer, often underlining words and phrases for emphasis. A few days younger than Emma, Elizabeth was enthralled by politics. In her girlish chit-chat, the observation on handwriting gives evidence that a separation between North and South has taken place in her thinking, though it is more than four years before the Civil War. Elizabeth briefly attended school in the North, but her parents lived in Mobile, Alabama, where her father operated a branch of the Barbour family's shipping business. This

(1857)

letter to Emma came to Father Barbour's Boston business address, 55 Cornhill Street.

Mobile June 22, 1857

Dear Emma,

I received your letter two weeks ago, today, but have delayed writing, in order to send you an account of our examinations, which I anticipated would be next Thursday; but I am much afraid now, that it will not be before next week.

Last week there was quite a change in the weather. Friday morning was as cold as a Fall morning in Boston. Notwithstanding it is turning pleasant again.

I suppose you had a grand time, last Wednesday, the 17th of June, but you know that day is nothing here.

(You remember Charley, who I told you about. Well, he went up the country to school last October, and got back here last Friday week. He has been here twice during that time, but I was out both times. So, as yet, I have not seen him. Is it not too bad?

The girls here wear brown hats some, but I think they wear shakers here the most. Young ladies, even wear them (that is shakers).

If you want to Hear real good singing, you must come to our school. You will hear pretty tunes, and good singing, if you exclude me.

I hardly think you could believe, by my writing, that I took writing lessons, in the winter. I really think you write very well; and I will pay the Yankees one compliment, that is, as a general thing, they write very well. Most of the girls here write a pretty hand, but not as plain as Yankees do.

Last night, when a lady and her nephew, a young boy, were riding home from church, in a buggy, the horse ran away and threw the lady out on the side-walk. Her face was badly bruised, but whether or not she was hurt more, I have not ascertained.

I am thinking, from the appearance of the clouds, that we will have a storm to-night, anyhow we are greatly in need of rain.

Do you have any mosquitoes at the North? They are awful here. We cannot think of sleeping, except under a mosquito bar.

I am drawing a piece to show at the examination. I can assure you it is nothing great, as it is my first piece out of a drawing book. Our school is a great place for drawing. During

15

the winter we only drew once a week; but now we draw most every day.

I have finished my composition, except copying it. It is a dialogue with another girl. I am <u>mighty</u> glad of it.

Dear Emma, I wish you would <u>come</u> spend the winter with me. Please ask your father. I will send you home as fat as a butter ball, if I can. Please come.

June 25th 1857

For the two days past, I really have not had time to write. Yesterday I went to the examination of the Grammar School which Hattie attends. It rained most all day, but notwithstanding there were a great number present. Today I went to the same of the Grammar School George attends. Our School went too. Lately we have had considerable rain, but <u>I</u> believe we are going to have pleasant weather now.

All our family continue in good health. Willie sometimes has a bad cold, which makes him a little cross.

Carry is working Julia such a pretty dress, now. It is a pink lawn & double skirt. Each skirt the sleeves, belt, band, and ruffle around the neck are worked. It is so pretty.

Well! it is raining again. I am so tired of seeing it rain I don't know what to do.

We are having an iron railing balcony, put all around the Temperance Hall. It is a great improvement.

I am very glad you have had the pleasure of seeing Earl Brewer so lately.

Times are so dull now, that I have nothing more to say.

Give <u>our</u> love to <u>all</u>. Answer soon.

Believe me ever <u>Your</u> affectionate cousin,

Eliza

Elizabeth flits from topic to topic. First, she lights on the 17th of June, Bunker Hill Day, which commemorates the first major battle of the American Revolution and was never observed beyond a few counties in Massachusetts. Then she comments on bonnets called "shakers," which were styled after those worn by sisters of the religious sect Shakers, also known as The United Society of Believers in the Second Coming of Christ. Finally, she mentions the Temperance Hall. In the ante-bellum period, the North spawned a

THE CAMBRIDGE & BOSTON HORSE CAR

Lizzie Wellington suggested that she and Emma take the horsecar from Porter's (August 21, 1857)

Photo Credit: Cambridge Historical Commission

host of reform movements, but only prohibition gained a following in the South.

Emma's father, John Nathaniel Barbour was a pioneer temperance advocate and helped to publish some of the earliest temperance newspapers in the Bay State. Because of his efforts to abolish the rum traffic, his life and property were threatened.

During the difficult days leading up to the Civil War, he was a strong peace advocate, although he aided the anti-slavery movement, and his home was a refuge for fugitive slaves. A family history, written around the turn of the century, recounts that one night, while a couple of slave owners waited on a Boston wharf to take their slaves South, Barbour, with Judge Russell and Wendell Phillips, chartered a tug, smuggled two slaves off a vessel in the harbor, and spirited them to Canada. Such deeds won him the friendship of Henry Wilson, John Greenlief Whittier and Charles Sumner.

John Barbour was quite familiar with the Boston waterfront. One of six children of an English tailor, he was born and educated in Boston's North End and had been employed by his brother James' firm, Barbour & Son, on Central Wharf, Boston. He and James had changed the spelling of their surname from Barber to Barbour, perhaps in response to pro-French sentiment in Boston after the War of 1812. Barbour & Son engaged in the shipping trade to the West Indies, Mediterranean, and Sandwich Islands. Their ship, the *Robin Hood,* was commanded by Captain Francis D. Hardy of Cambridge.

Before Emma was born, the Barbours moved to Cambridge, where her father leased a house from his brother, James, and operated a wholesale grocery business, Sullivan & Barbour, with his cousins.

He wrote the following letter to Emma, when she was in Groton Center, Massachusetts, about thirty miles northwest of Cambridge, addressing it c/o A. F. Hildreth, Esq.

Boston August 21, 1857

Dear Emma,

Your letter to Susan was received yesterday. You did not say in it, when you intended to return home—I do not know that there is anything of much interest to write to you about. We are all at home except Alf, who is still on the Mount Auburn Carr. and comes home on Saturday evening—Last Sunday Mr. Henry preached at West Cambridge for Dr. Swain—He is to preach for Mr. Mason next Sabbath—all day, he is rather <u>dreading</u> it and of course, Sue feels pretty badly. I think however they will (both of them) get over it, without much real damage—Mr. Mason is off on his vacation, I have a fine class of young ladies in the Mission School on Sunday—There are a good many persons absent from our meetings now,—they will probably soon return—We eat, drink and sleep, at home pretty much the same as ever, nothing of any great importance happening to vary the scene of home life—I am glad to hear that you are enjoying yourself and hope, that in so doing—you are also making yourself useful to Aunt Hildreth, as you are now abundantly capable of doing, if you are willing. —Sue misses you a great deal, and in fact we all miss you, at times—Mr. Morse told me about the sad fate of the poor dog—he feared, that the little fellow would run mad and he deemed it his duty to kill him, but he had hardnesse to "screw up his courage to the striking point" as the confiding creature looked up in his face with so much affectionate attachment that his heart failed him—and he would have gladly avoided the fatal act, but he was compelled to do it-and so "he hardened his heart" and the poor fellow died—

I believe that Susan wrote you not to make any particular, arrangement to meet Lizzie Wellington but to make your return home, depend more upon the convenience of Uncle & Aunt, than upon other things—I send you some paper enclosed in this, which will probably be enough for your needed correspondence. We are all well, and send love to all the folks. Yours truly & affectionately

Father

The "Mr. Henry" Father Barbour mentions in passing is William Henry Evans, Susan's future husband, who is going to preach. John Barbour also observes that prayer meetings were not well attended; many residents left Cambridge during the summer. Although Louis Pasteur had not yet developed his germ theory, folk wisdom prescribed that people should not stay in crowded cities during hot weather, when experience showed that epidemics of disease were most likely to occur.

Emma's classmate Lizzie Wellington was in the country, vacationing in Lancaster, approximately 30 miles west of Cambridge, when she wrote about her interest in the Shakers. The sect had established several communes around the country, including one in Harvard, Massachusetts, the town east of Lancaster. Visiting the Shakers was fashionable and a tourist attraction, included on the itinerary of Charles Dickens and the Prince of Wales when they came to the United States. Like the Grand Tour of Europe, such excursions were undertaken as much for enlightenment as for pleasure.

The Shakers, an offshoot of the Quakers, first emigrated to the United States from England in 1794. Their communities, in which all property was held in common, are sometimes called the first experiments in commune living in the New World. The sect was unusual in that it relied entirely on converts to perpetuate itself; men and women were celibate and lived in separate dormitories. Their credo, "hearts to God and hands to work," inspired industry among the Shakers, who were the first producers of commercial seed in the United States, as well as the inventors of the first air-tight woodburning stove, the circular saw, cut nails, a washing machine, flat brooms and the first metal pen points. During the nineteenth century, many idealistic communities were founded in the United States, but none was more unusual or successful than the Shakers.

Lizzie suggested that she and Emma meet on their way home at Porter's, the train depot in North Cambridge, which took its name from Porter's Hotel, which claimed to have originated the cut of meat known as Porterhouse steak, a breakfast favorite with the drovers taking cattle to market down Massachusetts Avenue.

Lancaster (Ms.) Aug. 21, 1857

Dear Emma,

As I date my letter, I see that in ten more short days, we shall commence our luck in the "Cambridge High School." However, I think I shall be ready. I have had a very pleasant time this vacation, thus far, and think I shall be prepared by that time, to recommence my studies. The only thing I am provoked about is my per cent. You must not forget the resolutions we made; about laughing at certain "things". I am afraid you will think I have. Since I wrote last, the aspect of affairs has changed somewhat, I am happy to say. You know, I told you, I was going home either Friday or Saturday. Instead of that, I am not going until Wednesday, which I suppose will suit us both better. Some acquaintances of our family are coming to Boston, Wednesday, and I am going with them. If it rains Wednesday, we shall not go, but I shall wait and go the first pleasant day. We shall go in the noon train, which leaves Lancaster at quarter past twelve. Now, Emma, I shall expect to see you Wednesday noon, if it does not rain. I should not want to get to "Porters", and not go to Boston. If you have a trunk, they will take it down on the horse cars, by paying five cents extra. I have always done so, when I have had a trunk, but I took a carpet bag this time. I hope you will write me a letter, and tell me your plans about going home, and if mine are agreeable to you.

Please write so as to send it Monday, and you might direct it to "Lancaster" instead of "South Lancaster" as I told you before, as it is more convenient. (Care of Miss Thayer). I suppose you are most tired of hearing about going home.

I took a lovely ride this morning to the top of "Whittemore Hill." Aunt Abby went home today. Have you been yet to see the "Harvard Shakers"?

"Miss Rice," and Sarah Magoun have been making a visit to Lancaster beside Dr. Smith with his wife, and Carrie. I have not seen any of them. I don't wonder they want to visit Lancaster, it is such a beautiful place. I believe I told you we started to go to the "Industrial School" Monday morning; but it commenced to rain, and we were obliged to come back. I will bid you Good Bye.

Accept this from your

"Affectionate Schoolmate"
Lizzie

The lazy days of summer drew to an end and Emma entered her first year of high school, a privilege enjoyed by only about ten percent of the country's girls. Schoolgirls had special status. Because they were required to do homework, they often were excused from household chores. Also, during the time they walked back and forth and were in school, they escaped hours of parental supervision. As a result, they had an uncommon amount of freedom.

3
(1858–1859)

*E*mma continued her correspondence with Cousin Elizabeth in Mobile, telling her about such Cambridge happenings as the parades, fireworks, public orations, and collations that marked February 1, 1858. The festivities celebrated what The Cambridge Chronicle called "one of the Greatest surprises ever known . . . West Boston and canal or Craigie Bridges were from that time and henceforth and forever forward to be free public thoroughfares." Formerly toll roads, these bridges would now provide Cambridge with free access to Boston, a major mercantile center.

Mobile, Feb. 15, 1858

Dear Emma:

I received your letter, which I have been expecting for a long, long time, to-day. I beg your pardon, but almost positively I answered your last letter; and if you did not receive it, it was the fault of the mail, rather than my fault. But since you have such a high opinion of me, I will not correct you, more than to say that among the gentlemen, which I suppose you allude to, were Mr. Hall and an other married gentleman. If your duties were such as mine, you would not have any more time than I for seeing gentlemen. (My occupations are not laborious, but they take up considerable of my time.) I have said too much on this subject, I am afraid. I am not angry, but very much excited.

I am taking music lessons now, and have been for a short-time since, "Hazel Dell," or "Whitney Loved so long," was about one of the first pieces I have learned.

Why was the 1st of Feb. so much celebrated? Ma thinks that it is because the bridges were made free; but I told her that I did not understand you in that way.

How can you find time to write in school hours? It is against the rule, in all the Public Schools here, to write anything that does not relate to our lessons, unless, of course, in a copybook. Even were it not prohibited, few would find the time to write letters the length of yours.

The winter here has been remarkably mild. We have had a few days, most-as cold I expect, as you have North.

As Mrs. Hurter's family live quite near here, we are over there very often; in fact, her boys are over here every day. A short time since Mrs. H. gave a tea party. Ma & Pa, Mary Frank & Gustavus were invited. Sister was away, making a visit in Aberdeen, Miss., & therefore she was not invited. All, I understand had a delightful time. At present Mr. Hurter is in New Orleans.

A gentleman by the name of W.F. Hunter, or the "children's friend", has been lecturing in this city, in the cause of Sabbath Schools. Perhaps you have heard him, as he has been in Boston. All his meetings are delightful; and if ever he comes to Boston again, I would advise you to go hear him.

How are the girls? and if it is proper, how are the boys? Do you & Addy still keep your Telegraph wire a going? I suppose it is of little use to ask if Sue is yet married; for I expect to see it in several papers, when the grand event takes place.

I am very glad to hear that grandmother is so much better, and I hope she may continue that, during the remainder of the winter.

Remember me kindly to all friends and acquaintances in Cambridgeport & other places. Write soon.

       Believe me ever
       your true and sincere Cousin,
       Elizabeth J. Horton

P.S. Please excuse mistakes, since it is very late. E.J.M.

Elizabeth asks about the forthcoming wedding of Emma's sister. Susan Elizabeth Barbour married William Henry Evans, twenty-six, on her twenty-fifth birthday, August 25, 1858. Eight months later, the couple left Cambridge for rural Maine and the bridegroom's first ministry.

The fledgling minister and his wife were self-conscious in their new surroundings. They tried hard to affect dignity and to assume a correct, mature demeanor. While they waited for the arrival of a merchant ship to bring "Matilda," a Victorian euphemism for bedding, the newlyweds boarded with a parishioner. Susan suffered the lack of privacy, particularly during intimate moments, and apparently, even behind closed doors, the young couple muffled their giggling. Susan's letters home were a precious escape. They helped her to maintain close family ties and gave her an oppportunity to voice her feelings.

          China (Me.) April 4, 1859

Dear Emma:

I sat down today to write to mother and thought as it was a confidential letter I would direct it to you and you could hand it to her without saying anything to anybody. I've been thinking about you a great deal lately and much as I like W.H.'s company, have thought that I should not object to sleeping with you a night or two in our own little room (mine no longer.) You don't know how bad it is to feel like an exile, as I sometimes do. I hope you will not very soon. How should you like the arrangement I spoke of? I need not ask I am sure. Perhaps it may come to pass if our plans work right. There is going to be a State Convention here the middle of June at Biddeford near Portland, which W.H. thinks of attending. Now we think some of starting from here together and he to stop and attend the Conv. while I keep on to Boston with the baggage. In that case, I should arrive two or three days sooner. We shall not certainly come home

(1858–1859)

before then except for something very special. This is only a kind of air-castle we have been making, it may all fall through. If I ever live to come home again, I shall not visit any other place any more than I can help. We have had an awful time with the freshets carrying away bridges and tracks. Last week the track in Vassalborough just this side of Getchels Corner was washed away and not being informed in time the passenger train from Boston pitched into the breach, smashed up the locomotive, and the conductor's arm got broken. The passengers escaped injury. We have not had any train up or down since but the mail comes up on a hand car every day. There is an old lady lying dead here, whose friends in Mass. have been sent for, but we don't expect them very soon unless the road is repaired which we hope will be completed this week. What a time they had about the Cochituate at Boston. W.H. has two funerals this week to attend, perhaps three. They are all old persons and have been sick a long time. One is a Miss Mann who is cousin to Hon. Horace Mann. W.H. is going to take me to ride this P.M. I have not been for a good while the travelling has been so bad. The weather is mild and it is getting to look quite like spring here. What should you think if I told you that we have two dogs here where we board? It is a fact. They are both little dogs. —one is an old one which they are expecting and hoping will die every day. The other is a cunning little puppy—which they had given to them. One of them will probably be disposed of before long. I will send you their portraits. 🐕 Pinky 🐖 Jenny. The last one looks something between a pig and a rabbit. I have made that collar at last and am doing one now like the first one you worked. Sarah Evans had one like it you know. By the way where is that girl? Tell her to write me a letter. As for Mary Sargent I have given her up as hopeless and don't expect anything. It was not you who gave me bad accounts of her, you did not say anything bad at all. I should admire to see Maria and Addie & Albertine and the others. How are the Richers? I have been thinking a great deal about Sarah Colby. How thankful it ought to make us that we are spared to each other yet. I think that we always loved each other dearly although we were different in age and other things. Do you ever get to the Saturday meetings. Remember me to all who inquire. I got a letter directed by Bill but found the inside was from Abby Lewis. I was

Emma's World

disappointed that it was not from him though I was happy to hear from her of course. May Callender I think much more about. O dear, I should like to see the Cambridge folks. I suppose the new meeting house won't be done when I come home. When I get to keeping house, you can come & make me a visit maybe. I should advise you to come in warm weather. I hope you try to help all you can about the work. Mother must get very tired with so much to do. I watch the papers every day to see if the Radius or Diameter or Circumference, come in from Nova Scotia freighted with Matilda, but I am afraid after all she won't come. W.H. and I find a good many things to laugh at in spite of all our troubles, but we have to do all our laughing to ourselves and keep pretty still about it. How is Willie Lothrop and the rest of your Beaux, Charlie Nelson & etc? What is new?

I shall have to close this letter now though I would like to write more but it is time for me to be going. We think of discontinuing the Daily Journal next year, it is too expensive. We shall take the semi-weekly. When the folks have read the March Harper & Atlantic we would like it. I sent Ned some stamps to pay the postage of them. I suppose I shall think of a dosen more things after I have sent this, but I must let it go. —goodbye— Love to all.

Sue—

P.S. I received a wedding <u>invite</u>—from Boston. If our folks go please present my regrets <u>etc.</u> I will try to call on them next summer—Thank Emily for her letter, I will remember it—Once more goodbye. Sue

With her letter, Susan enclosed the following newspaper clipping:

RAILROAD ACCIDENT IN MAINE—Narrow Escape. . We learn from the "Eastern Express Company", that an accident upon the Somerset and Kennebec Railroad occurred on Wednesday night last, which providentially was not attended with fatal consequences, yet the escape of so many passengers from destruction was quite remarkable. The recent heavy rains had caused a slide on the road, carrying away about forty feet of the track at Vassalboro and as the passenger train from Boston approached the spot, the break was observed by the engineer in time to "break up" and check the speed of the train considerably. The

(1858–1859)

engine and baggage car were thrown off and badly smashed. The engineer and fireman saving themselves by jumping off in season, but the conductor who was on the engine, was seriously but not fatally injured. The breaking up of snow and ice by the recent heavy rains has caused much trouble to travel, both on railroad and highways in the State of Maine.

The reverse side of the clipping bears the following notices:

First Night Ball A Social Party, under the management of Prof. C.M. Brown will be given at Essex Hall on Thursday Evening April 7, 1859. Ticket $1. Music —Potter's Quadrille Band

---

Dancing. S.H. Spaulding respectfully gives notice that his Spring Term for Young Ladies and Misses will commence at Union Hall on Wednesday, April 6, at 3 o' clock. For particulars apply at [page torn at this point]

The Exhibition of Paintings And Statuary at The Boston Atheneum will be open on Tuesday. April 5. The collection of Paintings will comprise a large number of pictures which have never been on public exhibition.

Probably because officiating at funerals provided the Rev. Mr. Evans with additional income, Susan mentions the deaths of several old people, strangers to Emma. Among them is a cousin of Horace Mann. Emma may have known the "Father of Public Schools," who left the practice of law in 1837 to become secretary of the newly established Massachusetts State Board of Education, which was in Cambridge. An anti-slavery Whig, he later served in the United States House of Representatives and as president of Antioch College in Ohio.

The dramatic train accident Susan describes was not unusual. To accommodate the demands of the rapidly expanding country, American railroads were constructed quickly—between 1850 and

1854 approximately 10,000 miles of track were laid—too often without adequate concern for safety. Accidents were routine.

By horse, rail and boat, Americans were clearly on the move. Cousin Elizabeth begins the next letter with a description of her recent trip to Mobile Bay, the busy seaport at the Mobile River delta. Yet, most of the letter is concerned with religious matters, a topic close to the hearts of Emma's friends, who grew up during the great religious revival that began in the 1830s. Evangelical Protestantism viewed Manifest Destiny in the New World as an extension of Christianity; temperance, prison reform, education, and other humanitarian causes were moral crusades. Perhaps because church leaders preached a fundamentalist interpretation of St. Paul's demand that women be silent (I Cor. 14:34), Emma's pious friends, like the majority of women, take no notice of the efforts of the pioneer feminists of their day.

>Mobile, May 16, 1859
>
>My dear Emma: 'Tis beautiful moonlight evening. Mother & Frank are on the Gallery with Mr. and Mrs. Hurter; Pa has gone to the Temperance Lodge: Mary, to the Musical Association of which she & Carrie are members; the baby is in bed; & the rest of the children are playing in the back Yard with Lizzie, Martha & Mary Ann Hurter. Carrie has been in New Orleans since last Wednesday. Thus are we all enjoying the evening, though I am writing.
>
>I had such a delightful trip last Saturday in company with a lady, gentleman, & children. We left home Friday evening about eight o'clock, went on board a Bay-boat, & about ten o'clock retired to our berths, and in the morning found ourselves about twenty-five miles down the bay, amongst the shipping. Here we staid all day, watching them put cotton on ships bound for Liverpool. We went on board one of the ships, the *Sam Dunning*, where I saw a healthy, rosey-cheeked Yankee boy, very much like one of my escourts from Boston to Mobile. It was half-past-eight Saturday night before I got back home, & you cannot imagine how delightful it was coming home on the water, with the moon shining brightly over us.
>
>This is the week for our Encampment, & it is a time that I generally look forward to with the greatest pleasure, but this year I have no desire to go, besides being very much occupied

with my books. I do not know when I have before had so much to do.

I do sincerely wish that we had some prayer meetings to attend. We have one in our Church every Friday night, held at the house of the members; but they are very thinly attended, & there is little interesting. I do love to attend them, especially when held in the day-time, as I am seldom bright—after dark. I feel & I know that I lack a great deal of interest which I ought to feel. I find it difficult to do always what I know is exactly right, most especially at school, where I see so much deception continually practiced; but I do hope, dear Emma, to become a strictly consistent Christian, & I trust that I do try to be one. I have no young friend to whom I might confide my thoughts & feeling. I know one who though considerable older than my self, would take a great pleasure in encouraging me, were she always here. That one is my darling Miss Ginnie, who staid through the winter with us; but who is now in Talledega. She is without exception, as near perfect as I ever saw anyone. We are all very much attached to her, & will always claim her when she comes to Mobile. I wish that you knew her. You would soon without doubt love her as dearly as a sister. I have a dear friend who is a mute, & she always seems happy to hear of any one's uniting with the church, but having been a mute since her first birthday, she has few correct ideas, I should judge, concerning her soul & religion. I talk with her on one hand only, & we can generally carry on a conversation very rapidly. I wish also that you knew her, as she takes great interest in all my friends, as well as in my health & happiness. Examination comes after a while. I have my subject for composition all ready. We cannot tell our subjects to each other, or to anyone out of the school; but as you will probably neither be here, nor see any one who will, it does not make any difference if I tell you. It is "Employment Essential to Human Happiness."

I guess it will be splendiferous. The alarm has just rung for nine, and notwithstanding the noise & confusion, I scarce keep my eyes open to finish this. So Good-night. Write soon again to your most affectionate cousin,

Elizabeth Horton

Like Elizabeth, Susan wrote to Emma about her trips. Emma was visiting the Sullivans in Woburn when her sister told about a sojourn to Waterville, a distance of some fifteen miles, which was delayed a day because of rain. Travel in an open carriage depended upon the whims of the weather, since wheels easily mired in soft, rutted roads, and clothing, which represented a substantial investment of money and time, might be spoiled. Few ready-made clothes were available, and those that were were fit poorly, since it was not until the Civil War, when thousands of men were measured for uniforms, that clothes were sized properly. Although Isaac Singer and A.B. Wilson had improved the sewing machine patented by Elias Howe of Cambridge, many women continued to sew by hand. From Susan's next letter, it is understandable how the name "sewing bee" evolved.

To Susan, Waterville was a welcome respite from China. The pace was faster and the people more sophisticated. There was a circus in town the day she arrived and she writes that in Maine even religious people attended. She no doubt remembered that in Cambridge, as in many other places, some citizens held such entertainments in low esteem as a waste of time. One critic argued that the money spent for circus tickets could better be used to recruit a good lecture series. Nevertheless, menageries were generally popular, and several circus caravans had regular routes along the Atlantic seaboard. Since there were no zoos or other collections of animals, circuses claimed to be educational, exhibiting the first camel, leopard, lion, orangutang and elephant on this continent, usually carting them from town to town by wagon.

In an effort to bring respectability to the circus, some shows would not admit a woman to a performance unless she was accompanied by a gentleman. Others presented only all male troupes. One company advertised in Portland, Maine: "The Manager pledges himself that his exhibition shall be of a strictly moral character, and free from the many objections frequently made to entertainments of this description."

It is noteworthy that the show in Waterville boasted a calliope. The new instrument, patented in 1855 by J.C. Stoddard of Worcester, Massachusetts, was comprised of a set of steam whistles with a keyboard and pin drum, similar to a music box.

China (Me.) June 16, 1859

Dear Emma

I made up my mind not to write another letter before I came home, but I remember that I was indebted to you, and besides that I wrote a very blue letter to Pa the first of the week, so I concluded to try and see if I couldn't improve upon it this time. I feel a great deal better than I did, in fact about as well as ever Time has passed rapidly with me this week & I have enjoyed myself very much. When I wrote to father I was just about starting for Waterville I went up Street, and got as far as Mr. Hunnewell's where our team was, when the clouds looked so threatening we gave it up. I wished very much to go and was quite disappointed, but it soon began to rain in torrents and continued all the P.M. As I could not go there Mrs. Shaw came over & invited us over to tea so we went & had a very pleasant visit. Mrs. Hunnewell has a daughter getting ready to be married & she was making up clothes, and tore from a piece of cotton enough for a pair of pillow cases & gave me I took it to Mrs. Shaw's to work on & Mrs. Kendall who is stopping there, offered to hem & stitch the end with the machine, which I was glad to accept. I returned in the eve. (the rain having ceased) and made several calls on the way. The next day I went over to Waterville & I tell you it seemed like breathing a Home atmosphere. The place reminds me of Cambridgeport though it is not so large, it seemed so good to see something stirring, there was more than usual that day, for they had a great Circus over there with six elephants, zebra & Calliope—also a 700 pound woman & a boa-constrictor. Most everybody goes to Circus here, whether they are religious folks or not, some of the folks asked us if we were going. When they had one here in China the minister led the crowd . . . We visited Mr. Wood the Baptist minister he has a very pleasant family, several young ladies, also some students from the College board there, it seemed like old times to get among such company again. I wish I could get over oftener to W. but it costs 40 cents every time we go there are two toll bridges 10 cents each. I enjoyed enough there to last a good while, it is so dull here, it seems as if I could not stay a minute. Mrs. Wood said she should die if she had to live in China. She is a very nice intelligent lady rather gay, however. Mr. Wood is a good deal like W.H. in many respects—though he is older & of course a better preacher. W.H. & he had a grand time, they went up to the college & saw the Faculty & students. There was quite a smart shower, the wagon got pretty wet, I wore my blue silk and got considerable mud on it from the wheels, but it all rubbed off & left no mark to be noticed. These wagons are horrid for spoiling clothes. Yesterday, the S. Circle met here, and as the work did not come in which they expected, they offered to work for me, which I was glad enough of, you may be sure. I had been put back on account of not being well the week before. One lady gathered the skirt of my borage dress and hemmed the bottom another finished a stocking for W. H. which I was toeing and heeling, two others sewed up the pillowcases, two more made the sleeves of my gingham dress one let out the blue muslin, so I got a great deal of help you see. If I had only had the waist of my gingham cut, I should have got it most done, but I had not had time to cut it. I have been at it today, shall not get it finished before I come home however. We had a very pleasant circle indeed and I enjoyed it. I had a letter from Kate Foster last week. She feels very bad about changing her resident. She says she hopes she shall never have to part from another people. They have taken a little boy to bring up 5 years old from the Orphan Asylum. I should think she had enough to do without that. I dont see how some folks manage to get along with so much to do.

I was very glad to get mothers letter, & sorry that she lost her porte monnaie, glad it was no worse. I shall be very careful of mine as I haven't so much that I want to lose any—The other piece of intelligence in her letter caused me much grief as well as surprise, I didn't know how to believe it.

What kind of ribbon are you going to have on your neapolitan? I am going to have my bonnet colored for a second best. I'll get a new one as mine looks rather pasee.

How do you like Cicero? Really Miss B. you are getting along smart, I expect to find you very learned—I don't know but you will think you know more than I do by this time. All is if you do don't apply to me to help you. There are some hard knots in Cicero as I know by experience.

How do you like the prospect of having my pink striped dress? I hate to give it up but it must be so. I have worn it but very little. You must prepare to see an <u>elephant</u> or mammoth when I arrive. Tell mother to lay up <u>stores for one</u>. W.H. does not weigh any more than he did when he came, he has lost considerable flesh lately—I tell him I shall make him go home every night, and I shall stay & sleep with you. He says, "O go off" —But it is time to stop both the nonsense and the letter. give my love to all I long to see you Pray that I may come & meet you all in safety goodbye till we meet. **As ever**

your affec. Sister

(1858–1859)

P.S. I have got on my summer clothes at last. Its roasting hot. Thunder storm this P.M. We have given away Pinky and have another little black dog also called Pinky.
Rosa is going to lay eggs again very soon.

Susan realized her desire to visit Cambridge during the summer, and her mother accompanied her back to Maine. When Father Barbour wrote, he was at home with only his eldest son, Alfred. Emma was in Woburn with the Sullivans.

Boston Aug 10, 1859

My dear Emma

Your letter has been received just now. I had a letter from Mother yesterday, she arrived in good order except being wet a little, as she was caught in the shower, about half way from Getchels Corner to house—We had a letter from Edwin this morning, and I think I may go up to Wolfborough and stay a few days, he is not quite so well as he was—
 The morning after you left home Alfred took down the cage and found one of the young birds dead, how it happened we do not now know and can have no idea—but this we know, we cannot help it, the others all appear well—In the evening after you had gone, Mrs. Munroe & Mrs. Clark came into the house to see if I was very sick, and if they could do any thing for me—So you see I am well cared for—I do not think I shall come to Woburn till I return from Wolfborough—Give my respects to Mrs. Sullivan and the rest of the family—we enjoyed Mattie's visit very much. Capt. Phinney called in at the store yesterday, he said Mary was enjoying herself very much in Falmouth, as full of fun and play as ever

Yours truly
Father

 Please hand the $3 to Mrs. Sullivan I will explain when I come to Woburn.

Father Barbour mentions the death of Emma's pet bird. In a previous letter, he told of a dog that had to be destroyed. Partly, his letters reflect the Victorian fascination with death; however, it was fashionable on the continent as well as in America at this time to bring animals, birds, and plants into houses. Some contemporary observers suggested that urban sprawl at mid-century inspired the introduction of these natural decorative elements into households. Others wrote that pets and plants were meant to reinforce in women the priority of their nurturing role.

Although his father expressed concern about Edwin's health, apparently Emma's youngest brother— "Ned" to his brothers and sisters—recovered sufficiently by fall to undertake an extended business trip South, peddling his homemade beauty preparations and elixirs. He wrote to Emma on her sixteenth birthday.

> Winchester Va.
> Nov. 20, 59

Dear Emma,

Your kind came to me so long ago, that I have almost forgotten when it was, and I must beg to [be] excused for not having answered it before this, but in traveling about so I have as much as I can do to keep the business straight and but little time to write, I assure you not half so much as I could wish so what I have has to be apportioned off. Such sentiments as fill your letter can come only from a heart filled with the love of God, and a true devotion to his cause, how I wish I had some of the same love, but I fear it is not for me, such love and such appreciation of God's goodnes to us I cannot comprehend.

Your letter is full of precious and undying truths but I cannot yet feel that they apply to me tho I believe them but what I mean is, I do not feel their weight in my heart.

I wrote to Father on Thursday last, stating to him that I went through and dined at Harper's Ferry. I have since thought it a wonder they didn't have something to say to us for we had five very heavy trunks, and while we remained there (about an hour) were sticking our noses into every nook and corner of the place. We saw the engine house where Brown and his party were captured. The building remains in the same condition as it was at that time, there are large stains of blood on the walls and floor and great holes in the door made by the ladder used in battering it down, also post holes in the walls of the house, which is brick, from which the "parties" inside had fired, also shots in the houses about the government buildings. There were soldiers on guard but they said nothing to us or we to them. The place is very romantically situated. The railroad runs along the bank of the river on one side, and on the other you see huge

Winslow Homer's Christmas Belles
Photo Credit: Boston Public Library

piles of rock hundreds of feet high almost directly over your head. I couldn't help thinking when we were inching along what havoc one of those great rocks would make should it fall while a train is passing.

We breakfasted (after having riden all night from Fredricksberg) at the Relay House, which is at the junction of Washington & B. & O. R.R. and as we had some little time to spare, looked about the place, there is an immense viaduct which crosses the river there, it is a immense piece of masonary built of granite, of which a person can have but a faint idea without seeing it after leaving there, (as have said) we passed through Harper's Ferry, also through Charlestown [West] Va. where the insurrectionists have been tried and sentenced, as two Northern men had been directed to leave the place a day or two previous to this, we concluded to go on our way and not stop at Charlestown. I have no doubt before we were half way to Winchester the mayor of the City had received telegraphic despatches that "suspicious Northerners" were on their way to this place with suspicious looking baggage and to look out for them for directly after we arrived we received a despatch by the lady of the house from the Mayor, inquiring our business, but we soon put their fears to rest by opening our trunks and telling them our business and have been treated ever since like gentlemen. have had good sales which have been attended by the best people of the place.

We are very pleasantly situated as regards board, we are boarding at the house of a widow lady who has three daughters at home who are nice young ladies, and help to drive away that worst of all diseases homesicknes, which I assure you I have felt before this. The Southern people so far as my appearance has gone are a very cordial and kind hearted people, all the boarders at the house take a lively interest in our welfare and in fact every body in the place (for we are pretty well known here by this time) treats us with respect, and as Southerners always treat persons who mind their own concerns you need have no fears at home for my safety for there is no danger, as I have nothing to do with politics or slavery. My love to all at home, and write me as soon as convenient, for it is possible without letters I might get homesick and you ever have the thanks of your affectionate Bro.

Ned

(1858–1859)

About fifty-five miles northwest of Washington, D.C., Harper's Ferry is wedged into a gorge of the Blue Ridge Mountains, where the Potomac and Shenandoah rivers converge. Only a month before Ned's visit, the United States arsenal there had been raided by John Brown, the abolitionist. Brown and twenty-one of the twenty-two men with him—one escaped—were either killed that day or later hanged.

The great-grandnephew of President George Washington, a slave owner and a hostage at Harper's Ferry, described his captor as "the coolest and firmest man . . . in defying danger and death. With one son dead by his side, and another shot through, he felt the pulse of his dying son with one hand, and held his rifle with the other . . . His lips were like the lips of fate, and yet they met together as lightly as rose petals."

There had been slave uprisings since colonial times—the earliest in Virginia in 1663—but Brown was a charismatic figure; his bloody insurgency served the anti-slavery cause well, long after his body lay "a mouldering in the grave."

While in the South, Ned intended to pay his respects to his cousins in Mobile, and Elizabeth wrote that they were impatient for his visit.

Mobile, Nov. 22, 1859

My Dear Emma:

After several fruitless attempts to write you a long letter, I have made up my mind to content myself with writing a short one, and commence, accordingly, to-night, having finished my studies a little earlier than usual.

Mr. and Mrs. Hurter and Lizzie are in the parlor & Mary and Carrie have company besides, and they are now having a pleasant time with the Guitar and Piano; but I am not permitted to go in the parlor to see company this Winter, but very seldom. I find that by imposing such restrictions on myself I get along better with my studying, and do not regret that I made a promise to the effect to a very dear friend of mine.

This year is my last year as a school-girl, and I therefore have much to occupy my time both when in and when out of school. I am reading now the middle part of the twelfth book of Virgil, and expect to finish it, so as to commence Cicero the first of December—My class commences Trigonometry to-morrow. We are studying Haven's Mental Philosophy & Famison's Rhetoric, and expect to commence Astronomy soon. I have taken French again under a new teacher; and we use Fasgnelle's Napoleon, in connection with Ollendorf's Grammar. We have to write compositions, at home, every Saturday, & impromptu ones, in school, almost every Monday morning. We always have to read them aloud before the whole class; and think it a very great favor if anything happens to prevent it.

Bro. Frank received a letter from Ned, postmarked Richmond, Va., a week ago last Saturday, in which he said he thought it would be March before he could come to Mobile. Bro. Gus. writes that he hopes Ned will come by way of New Orleans, while he is South. It seems a long time to look forward to; but March wil be here before we are aware; for time fairly flies in this part of the country.

My vacation was spent very pleasantly, indeed. Mary & I passed a month together over the Bay, in two very pleasant, hospitable families, both of which were Baptist. We formed many very pleasant acquaintances. I wish you could have been here to enjoy it with us, but I suppose that could not have been. Of course, sweethearts & beaux were about. By the bye, how are Willie Russell, Whitney, etc? I have not forgotton them by any means.

I have nothing of so much interest as you have to tell respecting religious matters. It does seem to me that I am very cold & indifferent, but at the same time, I perform my religious duties no less regularly, and like as much as ever to attend divine services. I hope to have an interview with my pastor when he returns from Presbytery. He is such a good man, an earnest Christian. Prayer meetings are kept up here, but being always in the evening I cannot attend them; but if they were in the afternoon, it would afford me the greatest pleasure to attend them. One of my most intimate friends & school-mates is a member of the Baptist Church, and Bro. Frank & I sometimes go with her to her church & prayer meetings. Sunday week, Mr. Meikle being away, I went there and heard a fine sermon. I am truly happy to hear such good news from Ned, & hope that more & more of my relations may yet be brought into the Great Sheep-Fold. Pa received a letter from Cousin Mellie Horton, To-day, in which he speaks of a great change which has lately come over him. Would that Bro. Frank would come out & profess himself, before the world as a follower of Christ!

It seems to me, also, dear Emma, that a talk between us,

would do both us good. I find, too, that my thoughts wander in every direction when I attempt to pray even the most earnestly. Oh! if I could only live a consistent Christian through the whole of my life, I feel as if I could not want anything more. I feel little more reluctant than I used to about speaking to the unconverted. In the family where we spent half the time this summer, there are two young boys, the one twenty-one, and the other almost nineteen, both of whom are very fine boys, and have the greatest respect for religion; but they are neither of them Christians, I.E. professing ones. I hope they may become such. I spoke a little to the youngest one day, while over there.

Give my kindest wishes to Maria Morse, for her success in finding those things which we hope she is earnestly seeking for. Love to Addie, Lizzie, and all other friends. George is studying a speech, and every little while he stops and asks me to hear him recite a paragraph or so.

I have not been able to distinguish the lines on this paper so my letter is written in a very crooked manner. Write as often as you can, for it gives me great pleasure to read your letters; but don't tax yourself to answer mine as soon as they are received.

You were sixteen day before yesterday, and I will be the same age, on next Tuesday. I feel as old as that now, as I am very large, I think, and have domestic cares devolving on me, which make me feel very consequential. Ideas are giving out, so I must retire. I was up at five, this morning. Good-night. Eliza. Day after to-morrow is Thanksgiving day. Surely we have much to be thankful for, as a family, and so has this community. E.J.H.

Cousin Elizabeth asked about Whitney. This is the first mention of William Whitney, the man Emma eventually will marry, but Elizabeth is mostly interested in confiding her religious concerns to Emma. Religion during the Great Awakening, which held each person responsible for his or her own salvation, found different expression in the North and South.

Two Connecticut natives, the Bible-toting abolitionist John Brown and the Rev. Henry Ward Beecher, who used his pulpit to enlist aid and rifles (called "Beecher's Bibles") for the bloody fight over whether Kansas would be a free or slave state, exemplified the Northern morality. Southerners, on the contrary, were more apt to subscribe to the official position Presbyterians adopted in 1849, that slavery was a civil institution better governed by legislators than churchmen. Ultimately, polarization along these divergent viewpoints created regional schisms among the Baptists, Methodists, and Presbyterians.

As Cousin Elizabeth had long been aware, slavery was inextricably bound up not only with religion, but with politics. Meeting early in the summer in Charleston, South Carolina, the Democratic National Convention adopted a platform based on Senator Stephen A. Douglas's principle of popular sovereignty, which critics lampooned as "squatter's sovereignty" because it allowed each new territory to decide for itself whether to permit slavery. The platform caused the party to split. The Northern faction, which was forced to move to Baltimore, nominated Douglas for President. The Southern Democrats nominated a strong pro-slavery and states' rights advocate, Vice President John C. Breckenridge of Kentucky. This division within the Democratic party assured the Presidency to the man the Republicans nominated on their third ballot, Abraham Lincoln.

4
(1860–1861)

Nine years before the first legislature, in Wyoming territory, gave women the right to vote, and sixty years before the Nineteenth Amendment made full woman's suffrage the law of the land, Cousin Elizabeth showed herself to be an impassioned political partisan, concluding an otherwise intimate letter to Emma with a rousing "Douglas for ever!"

Mobile, Aug. 2nd, 1860

Dear Emma:

Your very welcome letter was received on Monday morning, and would have been answered on Tuesday, but for <u>want of</u>

time. I am going over the Bay, Saturday evening, and will probably be gone a month. Frank is going over with me, and Hattie is coming out on Monday. While, on Sunday, you are made happy by the Baptism of Whitney and others, I will be happy with my dear friend, Mary Hawkins. My happiness will be of a kind vastly inferior to yours. Oh! "would I were with thee." The state of religion in Mobile is very dull. Those female prayer meetings, which I so loved to attend, have been broken up for a long time. Our pastor's health is not very good, and we have only one service through the week, which is on Sunday mornings. There is only one other Presbyterian Church open in the city: but, notwithstanding the congregations are very small. How I long to be where I can attend regular prayer-meetings! I think—I know that my soul would be benefitted. it would cause great rejoicing to all our hearts to see Bro. Frank converted. He is such a good boy in every other respect. I think that he is a perfect darling. If he were only a Christian, I should be so happy. I wish that Ned would write to him on the subject. I rejoice to hear of "W's" conversion. I wish that all my friends were followers of the meek and lowly Jesus.

Many a sad heart has been lately made, in our community, by the death of Bessie Strang—one of my class, who graduated on the 26th of June, and entered her "heavenly home" on the 18th of July. Oh! Emma, you cannot imagine how great grief it has caused me. There were eight in the graduating class. Bessie had the valedictory, and took the highest honor. She was the liveliest in the class, & the healthiest, very pretty, and a favorite with the whole school. Her valedictory was very touching. I would have sent you a paper in which it was published, but I could not get any, except one copy for myself. On the 29th of June, we received our diplomas; and went to a Lunch given by the High School Boys. She was looking very well, and just as pretty as could be. I sat by her while eating. I saw her twice afterwards, and the last thing (almost) that she told me was that she was coming to see me soon. In the course of two weeks she sickened and died; and I knew nothing of it until the worst was past. I mourned for her as one who had gone unprepared, to meet her God. But when I heard the particulars of her death, I rejoiced that she had gone. She died a most happy death, exalting in her Saviour, her last words to a brother were, "I see Jesus coming, with a sceptre in one hand, and a crown in the other." Our families have been acquainted for twenty years. The sympathy of the whole city was excited. I never lost a friend or companion before, and scarcely knew, at first, how to bear it. But I found, I trust, great relief in prayer.

You will not have the pleasure of seeing any of my sisters this summer. Mary has gone up country, and it is five weeks today since she left. She is having a splendid time, and does not say a word about coming home. It is possible but not at all probable, that I will come on, summer after next.

Yes, indeed I have had something done to my teeth. I had them examined last Fall, and in less than a month, I had three large jaw teeth pulled. I could not tell how many cavities I have had filled. I intend to go to the Dentist again in October, and have them examined. It runs in our family to have awful poor teeth. It is fun to me, to have teeth pulled, except eye-teeth. I have a perfect horror of having one of those extracted, and hope that there will never be any occasion for it.

I do not believe that you can hate compositions more than I always did, before last session. Then, I began to like them, but never will love them. I am out of school now, and as most persons style me, "a young lady," I assure you, Emma, that I am no more a young lady than I always was. In fact, I feel more like a child, than ever; I.e., I have sweethearts & beaux, just as I did when North. I sometimes feel like laughing at the idea of my being out of school. Next winter, I intend to teach. I try now, but in vain, to be dignified. There is not a bit of dignity in me. Mary is quite dignified in school but not out of it, she is just like a school-girl. I am going to send my ambrotype (an excellent one) on North by Mr. Hurter. You can see it, if you go to Grandmother's. Ma says that it must stay with those which Pa brought on last summer.

We are all very well indeed, except colds. Aunt Betsee has been very sick for almost two weeks. Never before, during the twenty years Pa has moved has she been sick enough to have a doctor; but she is very old now, and her symptoms alarmed Pa so much, that he called in the doctor. She is much better now, but she does nothing in the working line, yet. Eddie is sitting down near me, writing a letter to Mary, on the slate, so as not to blot his paper all up. Martha Hurter is North this summer. I hope you will see [her].

We have had a terrible drought in the South. It did not rain in Mobile for more than a month. The weather has been and is now very hot. The streets have been very dusty. I am sitting now without a dress. You just might [smile] to see me cleaning up the house, in the mornings. I have to do housework, and get down on my knees with a little hand brush, & sweep away as mice. I keep busy all the time, and seldom find time to read and write. I have several garments to fix, finish, and make, before Saturday evening.

I am very glad to hear of Maria's conversion. How are Addie, & Lizzie Wellington? Remember me kindly to all the boys, and my best love to all the girls, and to all your family. I guess that all the folks send love; but I am too lazy to find out. One question, if you please. Is your father for Douglas? I say, "Douglas for ever!" I have done as you desired; answered your letter as soon as it deserved. Please tell me when you expect to graduate. Write soon & excuse the length of this. Your ever affec. cousin E

Elizabeth graphically describes her dental work. Although dentistry has been practiced since before the time of the ancient Greeks, it did not become a profession until 1840, when the world's first dental school was organized in Baltimore, Maryland. On December 11, 1844, a dentist, Dr. Horace Wells (1815–1848) took nitrous oxide (laughing gas) before having a tooth extracted and is credited with discovering the use of anaesthesia for dentistry. Elizabeth undoubtedly thinks that having teeth extracted is "fun" because of the laughing gas.

Father Barbour forwarded Elizabeth's letter when he mailed his own to Emma, who was visiting her brother William's fiancée, Julia, in Greenfield. His letter, and the following two, report on a fire in Cambridge caused by a lightning storm.

Boston   August 10, 1860

Dear Emma

I have received a letter from Elisa Jane (I suppose) which I now enclose with one from Bro. to Julia—I suppose they will both of them be acceptable—We are all well at home, nothing very unusual has happened there, except a very severe thunder lightning rain storm, which did very great damage in its extent—The Counting Room and Barn of M.E. Smith was struck by lightning—But I suppose Willie has written the particulars to Julia—You may judge the effects produced upon poor Sue—She was much affected—She suffers terribly—I deeply sympathize with her, though I do not like to have her know how much—You should be thankful to him who constituted you differently, so that you are not liable to such sensations—it is something beyond her control & should not be ridiculed or treated lightly I always try to show her, dependence upon him in whose hands are thunder lightning and all other sources of our dread and fear, let us fear to offend him, but put implicit confidence in his overuling providence. Aunt Margaret, Harriet, Rebecca and Uncle William were out with us during the severity of the storm. The rain that fell, was "torrentlike" as well as copious I saw Mr. Morse at meeting Wednesday evening & he said "Well Emma is gone, and Maria is almost gone" Last (Thursday) evening I was at the "neighborhood meeting" at his house—Maria said after meeting was over. "Oh how I do miss Emma. I feel real lonesome. I wish I was with her" We do miss you very much from home so we do Alfred. We have not of course, heard yet from any of you—The weather has been very warm, even hot. Last night was somewhat comfortable & today is the anniversary of the visit of meteors or falling stars—Why they should appear on the 9 & 10 of August can not be accounted for—I watched from our Southern window last night from 11½ to 1 o'clock the whole aspect was quiet—and the falling of the "Mildewed Catawba grapes" was so loud in the perfect stillness of night, as to be almost startling the section I saw was about one quarter of the heavens in the time I saw 10 meteors—which if continued through the night & as fully in other parts of the sky will give some 200 to 300 for the night—how wonderful how glorious. I however became sleepy and ingloriously retired to the Arms of Morphias (not morphy!) I shall send you a paper today if I don't forget it because perhaps you have no chance to read the news —My friend Mr. G.D. Richardson keeps store in Greenfield—if you should happen to be where he is my name would be a passport to his kindness—I was also many years ago acquainted with Mr. Elliot who then traded with our firm "Sullivan & Barbour" he would doubtless be pleased to see a daughter of mine, if visiting in his beautiful village—but it is so long ago that he may be among the departed ones—We Old fogies are apt to forget how fast time flies.

My love to Julia, I hope you will both enjoy yourselves & have a pleasant time.

Yours truly,
Father

On reflection I remember that it is illegal to enclose in one envelope letters to different persons, so sent the two separate.

Father Barbour wrote often about his observations and thoughts on scientific phenomena. His excitement over the spectacular meteor shower is understandable. The study of meteors didn't begin until 1833, when one night a brilliant shower rained more than 200,000 shooting stars over eastern North America. During the 1800s, the earth passed through especially thick swarms of meteors every thirty-three years, and several brilliant displays occurred. Father Barbour's citing, however, is of the Perseid meteor shower, an annual event in mid-August.

This was an age of scientific inquiry and discovery, encompassing exploration of primitive terrain on the uncharted continents of Africa and South America as well as archaeological excavations in the Mid-East. In the United States, too, exploration of the Western frontier uncovered new animal and plant species. Religious people interpreted these findings as revelatory of God's truth, which was consistent with their belief in nature as a manifestation of God's divine plan. On every frontier—social, political, industrial, religious, and scientific—the world view was changing dramatically.

Emma's friend Maria Morse, at whose house Father Barbour had attended a neighborhood meeting, writes with an explanation for the electrical storm fire.

> Cambridgeport Aug. 11th 1860
> Saturday Evening

Very Dear Emma,

Oh! I am so lonely! I have just finished a letter to Hattie Allen and cannot let the opportunity go by and not write. Nothing has happened since you went away scarcely and I am destitute of news as well as (every thing else now) Wednesday afternoon at one o'clock there was a tremendous thunder shower and I felt bad enough, although I am happy to say I was much calmer than usual. The lightning was very vivid and it struck the barn, house and office of Mr. M.L. Smith. Their girl was scrubbing the knives which attracted the lightning, her face was scorched a little, no other injury. The office was partially destroyed by fire —The Orthodox church in Old Cambridge also received an electric shock, no damage. The wind blew the rain and hail against the window glass so hard that we feared for it. The first shower passed over and I had begun to feel a little like myself when another came equally as violent at half past two. I wondered if you were safe at Greenfield out of the shower a great many times. I went to the meeting in the evening but Mr. Mason was gone and all my friends excepting Albertine & Alice—They had a very good meeting however—Mr. Eustice sat in front of me and was very much affected I hope he may decide in favor of Christ—Dear Emma, I do not feel as I think I ought, I have not faith it seems to me and yet I <u>know</u> Christ is true, I <u>cannot</u> doubt <u>Him</u>, but I want to feel <u>his</u> presence. I am not <u>happy</u> without it; <u>do pray</u> for me! I know you will especially. Thursday I had plenty to do and did not miss you much as I expected but when evening came I had to sit alone in the meeting (no one to lean on etc) and I began to realize my loneliness. They had a beautiful meeting; that Mr. Allen & his wife & little boy were here, he said he had just received a letter from a country town where his little daughter was visiting, stating that she was very sick with the scarlet fever, they were both in great distress as they had buried three little children before. That little boy and this girl are the only children I do not blame Mrs. Allen for thinking so much of them. Your father and mother were present. Yesterday afternoon & evening I spent with Albertine and had a very pleasant time. Today I have worked considerably and I saw Take Notice this morning which cheered me up a little. I wish I could have a regular talk with you—By the way Mrs. Fanny Whitmore has a little son; so somebody is not alone. I am so tired I must bid you Goodnight.

Monday Evening—I intended to have sent this letter this morning but thought I might get some more news by waiting until evening. I have just returned from the Young People's Meeting & I feel decidedly lonely, if it would do <u>any</u> good to cry I believe I would try it.

The meeting was quite thin and not particularly interesting (however the fault may be in me). The wind is blowing quite hard, the crickets are singing & everything seems dreary—OH! Dear!!!—Yesterday Dr. Cushman preached for us his sermons were both <u>excellent</u> but he wore a "surplus" into the pulpit which took the attention of the people, as father says for about ten minutes: (he also adds, '150 lbs. of pride') The evening meeting was <u>very</u> interesting, it was the S. school Concert. There was a gentleman from Baltimore, I should presume who gave an interesting account of the S. School of Dr. Ling's Church also several anecdotes relating to the mission school.

When I arrived home I found Mr. Follett there and had a very pleasant conversation which cheered me a little—I shall probably go to Weston tomorrow with the rest of our family—About twenty or thirty are going to Sandy Pond to spend the day. I shall take my bathing dress and hope I shall have a pleasant time. We shall not go to the Pond until Wednesday. You must remember me.

Sarah Colby has gone to Pittsfield with the <u>Wilson</u> family and Grandfather, Uncle Emery & wife will go to Medway tomorrow —(I am deserted) I have given up my visit to Concord for the present as it is not convenient for me to go—Your picnic friend has gone I expect as I do not see him anywhere—I saw Reed tonight and you hardly would know him he is so changed.

Quite a variety on this page—

I really wish you could see me now, perched upon a chair, clad in a spotless nightrobe except where I wiped some ink from my face. With a looking glass on my <u>knee</u> on the back of which I am writing—

It really frightens me to look at the last page & I must hurry and cover it up hoping it will be invisible to all eyes but two black ones, which I would <u>love</u> to see—

Albertine sends her love to you—<u>also</u> I

Your lonely friend,
Airam
Esrom

The thought just came to me how wicked I was to spoil your pleasure by this letter with its dreariness but do not let it mar your happiness in the least—Enjoy yourself while you are going.

Apparently, the looking glass on her lap inspired Maria Morse to sign this letter in mirror code.

The experience of the Allen family, whose young daughter was seriously ill and who already had buried three children, was not uncommon. Between 1860 and 1864, almost fifteen of every one hundred babies born in Massachusetts died before their first birthday (the federal government census had not yet begun to compile such statistics). Of those who survived the first year, many had their lives snuffed out in childhood by epidemics of cholera, diphtheria, typhoid, typhus, and—in the South—yellow fever, as well as by mumps, smallpox, and measles, which also left many blind victims. A child born in 1860 had a life expectancy of approximately forty-one years. Because of the dangers in childbirth, however, a girl who grew up, married, and bore children had a life expectancy of less than thirty-nine years. Most mothers did not live to see their youngest child leave home.

Maria also mentions a mission school. Beginning in the seventeenth century, Protestant missionaries proselytized among native Americans, educating them as well as converting them. By the nineteenth century, along with religion, missions exported democracy, capitalism, and education, logically extending the concept of the promised land by spreading the gospel. In 1844 several families had left the First Baptist Church in Cambridge to organize Old Cambridge Baptist Church, which sponsored missionaries to China, and in 1860, First Baptist Church began its own Mission Sabbath School.

Susan also wrote to Emma about the summer storm. She was in Cambridge awaiting the birth of her first child. A son was born September 12, 1860, and named Alfred Henry for her brother, pointing out once again the closeness of the Barbour family ties.

Cambridge Aug. 14th 1860

Dear Emma

I received your letter on Saturday & read it with much pleasure. I am glad to hear that you arrived safely and had a pleasant journey. it was so very warm that day I feared you might be uncomfortable but Bill said you would not feel the heat as much as we did—I don't wonder you are not in love with stage-riding. I should call that riding under aggravated circumstances. When I went up to Kate's house from the Depot there was twelve inside but some of them were babies. I should think that you & Julia would have had your skeletons mashed, and your bones well shaken up. But I suppose it did not last long. I am glad you like your stopping place so well and hope you will continue to do so & be happy & come home refreshed. Hope you will have plenty of work and rides and find lots of flowers to analyze I am glad the place is truly rural enough for you. I should admire to be there if I could, and also down to Harpswell, but I am anchored here for the present not very unwillingly for I consider it a great privilege to be at home so long after having been away so much—I hope you will learn how to get out of bed & fix it in the most approved style so that you may impart the knowledge to me when you come home. I fear however that I shall not prove a very apt scholar, but continue to tumble out pell-mell as I am used to. What is the object, pray, of turning the clothes half over I am glad that I am not particular. I guess you will stand as fair a chance as the rest of the girls to get married. Miss Nash's views on the subject of old maids probably dont coincide with yours. I can sympathise with her in her task of "making things out of nothing" I have had some experience in the business myself—

I should think you would smother to lie on a feather bed. I am sure I should. Mother says she did not think a "civilized being" now a days thought of using one. How much torture Julia must have endured sleeping here. I dont wonder she dont like to stay over night—Only think too how much she must have been shocked at my manner of getting out of and fixing the bed. (You now I suppose can easily fall in with her way.) I told Bill about the feather bed and he says he would rather sleep on the floor anytime. I told him when he got married he would have to have a patent bed half mattress & half feather, but he says "don't worry perhaps Julia & I may quit." No danger I guess. That was a great Sewing Circle I should think what was the object of it. The China people used to go at one o'clock.

There is not much news from Cambridge to relate. We had a letter from Alf last week. He was enjoying himself very much indeed. Bill is at work on the Railroad. he has got William Ackerson for a new boy. Ned is still at the store working hard, we have John to dinner every day. I dare say Ned would like to go there and show you round if he could. Pa was sick yesterday and did not go to Boston. He is some better today but not very smart. I had a letter from the dear man the day you went away but have heard nothing since—I dont know what has become of him. I miss you very much and so do we all. I do not sleep much nights it is so warm & the mosquitoes bite so. Last night I was awake from 1 till 5 o'clock, all the time. It is a dreary business I can tell you. Hannah says she is glad you have a family to take up your attention. The old cat mopes round as usual and the kitten is under everybodys feet. Mother trod on her yesterday. The weather is dreadful warm. The day you went away it was awful. We had company from Boston all day. There was a dreadful thunder storm at noon and another in the evening. M.L. Smith's house and office were struck, also Dr. Albro's

"Any Thing For Me, If You Please!" by Winslow Homer

church and two dwelling houses in O[ld]. Cambridge. No very serious damage. I was very much frightened.

The "big hoot" has gone off with an awful groan ever since you left, and the serenades are unabated in vigor and frequency. Yesterday I sat in your chamber because it was cooler, and lo & behold I had a serenade from that direction. Whether the performer was "hidden" or not I cant say It certainly was in one sense of the word, but the music? was not concealed by any means.

Dr. Cushman preached all day last Sunday. He wore a gown. His afternoon sermon was the best from the text "If any man thirst etc." Morning text was "Take no thought for the morrow etc." We had a very interesting S.S. Concert in the evening, but it kept too long from 7 till 20 minutes of 9. I shall not go again till Mr. Mason is there to "shut down the gate" There was a N.Y. man who spoke finely—I did not see Maria Sunday but Mother did & gave her your message. I believe she is not going away. I tried to see her at the evening meeting but missed her somehow or other.

Hannah says she hopes you will come back this week and we all want to see you but hope you will stay your visit out and feel content & rested by the change we shall all be glad to see you back again I will try to send you some Troches You must excuse the looks of this for I dont feel very bright or like taking much pains. Bill says tell Julia she may expect a letter when she gets one. I think she will get one Thursday however. You need not give my love to her. Yes, you may I will return good for evil. I guess Pa will write in this letter & tell you what news I have left out. I must now bid you goodbye from your aff. Sue

At home with family in Cambridge, Susan is in a playful mood as she writes about the "big hoot," possibly Will Whitney or another of Emma's boyfriends. The expression was used to describe someone who was amusing in a silly or noisy way.

Blissfully awaiting the birth of her baby, Susan takes no notice of bitter political debates raging around her. When the election of 1860 was held, one-third of the country's 31,500,000 people lived in the South. But fewer than five percent of white Southerners owned slaves. Half a million votes, primarily in the South, were cast for conservative leader John Bell of Tennessee and his Constitutional Union Party, which stood for "no political principle other than the Constitution of the country, the union of the states, and the enforcement of the laws." When Tennessee joined the Confederacy, Bell, who had served for more than 20 years in Washington, went home. Nevertheless, he took no part in the war.

Unlike Susan, Cousin Elizabeth could think of little else but politics. She spent her wrath on the "fire-eaters," William Lowndes Yancey and Leroy Pope (Percy) Walker. Yancey was known as "The Orator of Secession" because of the Alabama Platform, his proposal demanding that Southerners have the right to take their slaves into Western territories. Walker, a leading Alabama secessionist, was the first Confederate secretary of war and is credited with much of the Southern armies' successes during the first year of hostilities.

Just as the North gave currency to spurious stories of slave owners, the South was rife with pejorative rumors about Northerners. Elizabeth refers to two, a Yankee schoolteacher who took advantage of "Southern hospitality," and the political libel that Hannibal Hamlin of Maine was "part Negro." The Charleston (South Carolina) Mercury had reported on July 9, 1860, that Hamlin was part Negro, and the news was carried by The Chicago Democrat on June 4, 1861, although it seems without foundation in fact.

Shortly after Lincoln was elected President, and Hamlin, Vice president, Cousin Elizabeth fired off this letter to Emma, expressing the frustration of ordinary Americans caught in the events careening towards war.

Mobile, Nov. 15th, 1860

Dear Emma:

Your very acceptable letter reached me, in due season, a few minutes after I was taken sick, & had gone to bed. It is hard for me to realize it, but I have been very sick, keeping my bed for eight days, & being unable, during most of the time, to turn over in my bed. The Dr. pronounced it Bone fever accompanied with jaundice, but some think that it must have been Yellow fever. However, a merciful and kind Providence watched over me through it all; and now, by the same mercy, I am restored to my usual health. My fever was very high, and continued, almost without ceasing, for about 72 hours, coming back at intervals. Though I did not like to do so, I got Annie to read your letter to me; but none of the rest saw it. You would probably recognize an ambrotype taken of me as I look now; for I have had all my hair cut off, since my fever, and look exactly as I used to do. (of course I can't compliment myself) If I do say it, the ambrotype Ma sent on, of me, was acknowledged to be excellent.

I am glad you & "W" are such good friends; and I hope that you will conclude to "make it up" between you. I never thought of it before, but now I think that it would make a nice match. If you conclude to do so, I hope that your bridal tour will be to Mobile. How I wish I could tell you all, about those initials I gave you. I never built such a beautiful aircastle before, but the foundation was not strong enough and it has fallen down. I do not like to regard labor (building) of more than a year as entirely lost; but circumstances compel me to do so. When I build another, the foundation shall be stronger, even through the building itself be less beautiful. It would be a great relief to me to tell you the history of my acquaintance, i.e., with S.C.S. Jr. It was not my fault, Emma. Pshaw! What nonsense! But you can appreciate me. Do not show this for anything, unless to "W".

The news about Sue, was not news to us. We had heard of it a long time previouslly. Tell Sue that she should not think of naming him anything else but Abraham Lincoln, although it may not help him to be Lincoln's successor. But if she does not wish him forever ashamed of the name, she had better not give it to him. Lincoln never will be President of the United States, though he may be of the "Free States." Until recently I have been for "A union of hearts, a union of hands, and a union of States, none can sever", but since the worst must come to the worst, I have to omit the last kind of union. The S-O-U-T-H will not have a "Black Republican" for a ruler, nor a part negro for a Vice-President. My feelings have been so wrought up, that I can scarcely contain myself. I have discussed Politics "like everything" this fall. I am indignant at Lincoln's election and give all my Breckinridge friends a "blowing up" for helping to elect him; for the Breck. party did elect him. Please understand that I mean nothing personal; for my own brother voted for Breckinridge. I still side with Douglas, & will continue to do so. If the United States are not dissolved before that time, I believe he will be our next President; and that when he once gets in, he will keep the chair for eight years. I am afraid that I am going beyond bounds; but I can hardly help it. There is a meeting in town, to-night, of all opposed to—I have forgotten what; and I cannot find a paper with the notice of it, or I would cut it out and send you.

Alabama has two of the most hot-headed Breckinridgites to

(1860–1861)

be found: Percy Walker, and Wm L. Yancey. I am down on them, and on all the "fire-eaters" in their crowd. I am for Bell; next to Douglas. If Lincoln resigns his place, after he is inaugurated, and Bell be put in his place, then, there, will be no occasion for dissolving our now "glorious Union"! but such intense excitement prevails here, that I fear, if such a thing is ever to be, it will be before the time of the Inauguration. Dear me! there is no stopping me. Talk of "southern hospitality" and "Yankee Schoolteachers". Frank told me of a school teacher who came to Mobile. He stole away two negroes, and then ran off without paying a widow lady for his board. So for Ned, he had no opportunity for testing "our hospitality". He could not have chosen a more untimely season for coming South. I hope he and all of you will take a favorable time, & test it. Frank has been up into Mississippi, and has just returned. Gus has been over to make us a visit. I get along finely at school. I am assistant in one of the Primary Schools for boys. I have the names of forty eight boys on my book, who are intrusted to my special care. The Principal of the Department is an excellent lady, a member of the Baptist church, and a pious, consistent Christian. She is a fine teacher, and an excellent disciplinarian. I consider myself highly favored, in having gotten under such a nice lady. I knew her before, though not as intimately as I do now.

The state of religion here, now. We have procured a minister for six months, for our church. he will preach his first sermon, next Sunday. I suppose our night meetings will commence next week. I hope so, for we can then feel somewhat settled. Our former pastor left us last Spring, and is now settled at Dobbs' Ferry, N.Y., on the Hudson River.

Ma is now writing to Aunt Sarah Woodman. Cousin Phillie Woodman has lately become a Christian, and has united with a Baptist Church in Charleston. Nearly all my female cousins are now "followers of the Lamb." Would that all were! I must apologize for the looks of this letter, as I have not written so much before my sickness, and my hand gets very tired, and makes my writing nothing but a scrawl. Write soon! I do not suppose that Politics can interfere with our correspondence; at least, I hope not. In my next, I will try not to be so severe on the Yankees. Give my love to my cousin, in prospection, and to all the girls. Accept much from your ever affec. Cousin Eliz.

P.S. Love to all the family. E.

Elizabeth saw her prophesy come true. On December 20, 1860, South Carolina passed an Ordinance of Secession declaring the Union dissolved and, before Lincoln's inauguration, Alabama, Mississippi, Florida, Georgia, and Louisiana followed suit. Altogether, eleven states joined the Southern nation, the Confederate States of America, and Montgomery, Alabama's capital, became the Confederacy's first capital. Here Jefferson Davis was elected president and the Confederate constitution was drafted. Modeled after the Constitution of the United States, with important differences, the Confederate document sanctioned slavery, but ended foreign slave trade.

"Southern Confederacy"
Mobile, April 2nd, 1861

My dear Emma:

I made two desperate efforts one evening, to write to you; but as they both failed, I am now making a third one. If your letter had not reached me as soon as it did, you would most surely, have received one from me long since. Being almost certain that you was offended with my last letter, (which was extremely impudent) I was just on the point of writing a letter of apology, which the reception of your's relieved me from all fear on that score.

I do not think that I [have] written to you since our new brother has been admitted into the family; and as the encomiums which I invariably bestow upon him have by this time become quite stale, I forbear repeating them. He is a splendid, & splendid-looking fellow (gentleman) and very lively. But as is the case with most young men at the present day, he wants the "one thing needful." I know that many and fervent prayers ascend to Heaven's Throne of Grace for his conversion. Many, also, are poured forth for our dear brother Frank, who is still out of the "ark of safety." Our Church has been supplied, this winter, with a very able, earnest & solemn pastor; but his health has compelled him to leave us. He was from Pennsylvania. We now have a minister from South Carolina. He has only preached for us one Sunday, and we are hardly able to judge him, yet. The state of religion, in our midst, is very dull; as you may imagine in these "troublous times." Yes, dear Emma, times are indeed troublous, when our city is so flooded with soldiers, thirsting for the blood of those whom they consider their enemies, that it is sometimes hardly safe for ladies to go down

(1860–1861)

town alone. I suppose there are nearly four thousand (country) troops in our city, who, while waiting the orders of our president, are abandoning themselves to every species of vice. Our own troops are numerous. My fervent prayer is that not a drop of blood may be shed, on either side. Our party and your's, too, are both desperate; your party, if either, will be the one to commence war; our's by a sacrifice of comfort, and of mental & physical health, as one is attended upon the other, is striving to prevent it. But enough or this will be as impudent as my last letter.

I heard through a letter which Ma received from your mother, of the death of Mrs. Morse. It must indeed have been a great affliction to Maria to lose her mother. No doubt she is resigned to it, regarding it as a wise decree of Heaven. Give her my best love, and kindest sympathy. We have had considerable sickness in our family this season, but nothing very serious, since my sickness last October. It is something so very unusual to have sickness in the family, that unless it becomes serious, we almost forget about it. All are well now. How are you and "W" progressing? I would give a "pretty" to see him. Tell him so, please. How are all the girls? My special friends are all well. I should write about two of them, but it is growing dark, and I must be closing. With much love to all of our mutual friends, Addie, Lissie, "W", etc., and much more to all the family, I remain. "E"

Written just ten days before Confederate troops attacked Fort Sumter in the harbor of Charleston, South Carolina, this is the last letter in Emma's collection from Cousin Elizabeth. Mail service between North and South was suspended during the Civil War. Elizabeth and Emma apparently never resumed their correspondence.

Part Two

Emma's Country: Irreconcilable Differences

"North and South were equally confident that God was on their side, and appealed incessantly to Him."
— Rebecca Harding Davis

5
(1861)

*W*ar came. The first volunteer company in Massachusetts, and probably the North, had been organized in January by Capt. James P. Richardson of Cambridge. But, North and South, a flurry of enlistments greeted the news of Fort Sumter's thirty-four hour bombardment. Even as young men fought along the banks of rivers they had fished as boys, and died on battlefields that were the farms they formerly had tilled, peace proposals continued to be introduced in Congress until well into summer, to no avail. The young men who had courted Emma in Cambridge and Cousin Elizabeth in Mobile were graduated from high school and went off to court glory on the battlefield.

Emma's World

At first, North and South believed the war was a family spat that would be resolved quickly. They were wrong. The South miscalculated the strength of King Cotton. It counted upon England and the Continent, whose factories required cotton, but a bumper harvest the previous year had left those markets well supplied. When war cut off new shipments of raw materials, the manufacturers benefited from higher prices for their goods. Moreover, Europe suffered crop failures that made it dependent upon wheat from the North. The North also enjoyed the advantages of greater manpower and all of the country's manufacturing centers. To win the war, however, Federal troops had to conquer a territory larger than the combined areas of Austro-Hungary, Germany, France, Italy, Holland, Belgium, and Denmark.

The rift between Americans was personified by their Presidents: Abraham Lincoln and Jefferson Davis were both born in Kentucky, only a year apart. One grew up as the son of a wealthy planter and was graduated from the United States Military Academy; the other was the son of a poor pioneer and had barely a year of formal schooling. Both were students of the Constitution of the United States. Both were men of conscience.

Determined to restore union, Lincoln was an authoritarian President who took charge with folksy good humor, despite his private melancholy. In contrast to Davis's strict devotion to constitutional principles, Lincoln interpreted the President's "war powers" broadly and suspended many Constitutional guarantees, including the writ of habeas corpus. In doing so, he alienated members of his own party, some of whom intrigued against him. But the voters like Emma's father returned him to office in 1864.

The war touched everyone, tarnishing an era formerly glistening with wonder. When Emma and her friends came to maturity, seventeen million Americans—fifty-one percent of the population—were under twenty years of age. Hardly a day passed that they didn't witness some new miracle of progress. The Smithsonian Institution weather services, established in 1854, had, by the eve of the war, five hundred weather stations to collect information for the military. The transatlantic cable, laid in 1858, shuttled news to the United States from England within hours of an event. Indoor running water in 1860 was primarily a luxury for the upper middle-class, but one hundred thirty-six cities had municipal water supplies and ten had sewage disposal systems as well. Also, the streets and a few homes in some large cities were brightened with gaslight provided by a central station. In certain cities, including Emma's Cambridge, tracks were laid and horse-drawn cars initiated local public transportation. While in rural areas mail continued to be delivered to post offices, often lodged in general stores, beginning in 1863 letters were delivered free to houses in cities of 10,000 or more.

The war stoked development. Clothing factories outfitted men with uniforms and, at war's end, re-dressed them for civilian life. In the same way, canned foods fed soldiers in the field, then made the transition into home kitchens. With machines assuming tedious needlework, women's wardrobes flaunted more ostentatious detailing. Products such as chewing gum and razor blades launched national brands. With war alerting everyone to his own vulnerability, the life insurance industry tripled its business between 1860 and 1865. The success of commercial enterprises was reflected in the growing number of wealthy Americans. There were barely a score of millionaires in the whole country when Emma was born; by 1863, there were several hundred in New York City alone. Nevertheless, the first federal income tax, levied in 1862 to help finance the war, was allowed to lapse at the end of the decade because so few people paid it.

Despite the war, America was the meeting place of immigrants seeking to escape food shortages and dangerously unstable political situations in much of Europe. The new arrivals welcomed the opportunity for a fresh start. The United States had no national holiday, no national anthem. The proliferation of a popular press, especially inexpensive magazines, welded a uniformity in taste. And mass marketed manufactured clothes blurred superficial distinctions in appearance between newcomer and oldtimer.

Many immigrants, including women who did not want to work as domestics, found jobs in factories, and cities throbbed with new growth. Men labored on the railroads and in the construction trades. Some became tenant farmers on Western lands. And some took advantage of the government's offer of free land and the opportunity for an education. In 1862, Congress passed both the Homestead Act, giving title to land a settler lived on for five years, and the Morrill Act, establishing land grant colleges. Disregarding the popular belief that rigorous study caused "softening of the brain" in females, some Western colleges were coeducational. In contrast to institutions of higher learning in Europe or the East, they offered such nontraditional subjects as farming in their curriculum.

Whether as diversion from the war or a yearning for their rural roots, Americans turned to sport and recreation. Horse racing was a national passion; baseball was well on its way to becoming a national pastime. Emma and her friends were avid ice skaters and liked to go sleigh riding, two sports introduced in Colonial times by New York's Dutch settlers and very popular in Emma's day. Parties, especially surprise parties, were a welcome counterpoint to war.

Emma's correspondents wrote about their parties as well as how they carried on daily routines and fulfilled patriotic obligations amidst rumors and uncertainties of the war around them. Cousin Mary Sargent, an infrequent letter writer, was a romantic adolescent in Alton, Illinois, approximately 25 miles north of St. Louis on the Illinois-Missouri border.

In the early days of the war, many Confederate sympathizers lived in Southern Illinois, and some of them wished to establish Illinois as a sovereign state. Most of the people, however, favored the Union. In addition to the President, Ulysses S. Grant—regarded as the North's best general—came from Illinois, and, by war's end, more than a quarter of a million soldiers from the state had joined the Union ranks. Mary Sargent liked having soldiers around.

Alton June 14th 1861

Dear Cousin Emma.

You must excuse me for not answering your letters sooner for it has not been because I forgot you, but I have not had a great deal of time to myself. I hope you will excuse it. I was very glad to receive that flower/it was faded a little, but not much I wanted something out of my garden.

You say the girls ask after me. I don't see why, they won't write to me. Mary Willid is the only one who condescends to answer my letters.

We had a letter from Aunt Harriett. don't you tell but I guess I will write to her, and surprise her. When I have time. You say you dislike to recite Physiology to a man. We used to recite with a whole lot of boys that made bad out of everything to a lady teacher. But we made such a fuss that Mr. Newman took the boys and we recite separate.

I never saw such a man as Mr. Newman is when we wanted to recite separate from the boys. He "brought the matter before the school" and said "some folks tried to make bad out of everythin." And we used to play jacks in a window that overlooked the boys—and he said "the girls will please not play jacks in that window, for reason they can find out, if they consider a while" right before all the school. we were so provoked.

We have had a lot of soldiers stationed here but they went

away a few weeks ago but we expect more every day. I do hope they will come Emma, I do wish you would come out here, and make me a visit. We would have such splendid times, if you only would.

Tell the girls I will not write a single word until they answer my letters. Please write soon, and excuse my horrid writing. Mistakes etc. and give my love to all, and accept a large share for yourself, and believe me your aff cousin

Mary

P.S. Tell Alf Father received his letter.

Emma's embarrassment at having to recite physiology to a man, as well as Cousin Mary's discomfort at her teacher's remarks, reflect a marked change in society's attitudes since the Revolution. During the nineteenth century, a double standard of morality developed for men and women. Modesty became the quintessential female virtue.

War news intruded upon good times in the following letter from Julia Battis of Roxbury, the fiancée of Emma's brother William (Bill to his sisters and brothers).

Greenfield June 28, 1861

My Dear Emma—

I believe you had the promise of a letter while I am here and therefore I will try my hand and head at composing a few lines this morning. I don't feel one bit like writing and if I dont succeed you will know the reason.

It is a week I think since you have heard from us but I can give a good reason for William's negligence as he has been very busy in making a new well curb, and he has been so very particular about it that it has taken him much longer than it would a common carpenter. Auntie is delighted with it and says she shall always think of him when she draws a pail of water. He has worked so steady that this morning finds him feeling a little like an old man. He is now tormenting Amelia while she is trying to match a piece into a hole in her dress she just gets it nicely matched and he snatches it away. Monday morning he took a walk down street about half a mile and then turned up the brook road and walked several miles and attempted to come home over the mountains and come out on the west one but he lost his way and came out a mile or so up the brook road above here, he got home about 2 o'clock having walked about 6 miles. he was almost famished when he reached home. Today he proposes to ride to the village in the stage (which is a large open wagon) and walk back with a pail of paint in his hand which he intends to use upon his new well curb & door steps. I wish you could be here now for the strawberries are in their prime and very thick. I went out twice yesterday and picked about 3 quarts in all after they were hulled.

Tuesday night we all went up the west mountain after tea and had a delightful time. We went up the steepest part and as our shoes were very slippery we had some sport trying to climb, we however succeeded in reaching the top with our hands full of strawberries which we sat down and ate viewing the landscape beneath. I shall not attempt to describe the view to you for you know better than I can tell you.

We received a letter from Father last night stating that he would return soon and Mattie and the children with him. I think we shall have a jolly time when we all get here.

We have nice times and are not in the bush exactly for William gets his papers regularly, which gives us information in regard to the war.

I have many more things to say but it is time for me to close. I hope to hear from you the first of next week as we shall be here until after the fourth. William says he thinks perhaps it would be well for you to answer letters you received from Greenfield in the spring. All join with me in love to you and you may extend mine to all the family.

Most kindly and affectionately,
Julia

Apparently, Julia shared the era's enthusiasm for strawberries. The first American species of the plant was cultivated in Cambridge in 1835. Since fresh produce was scarce during the New England winter, the strawberry, which has a short growing season, quickly became popular. By 1857, strawberry parties were held to celebrate the June harvest. The *Boston Sunday Herald* reported in 1863, "Strawberry festivals are the rage here just now."

Even strawberry festivals, however, failed to divert attention from the war for long. "We have nice times," Julia writes, adding "[but we] are not in the bush exactly for William gets his papers regularly, which gives us information in regard to the war." Massachusetts, the most densely populated state in the Union, first received news of the outbreak of hostilities by telegraph on April 12. "Many of our citizens will learn with as much surprise as grief this morning, that the bombardment of Ft. Sumter was commenced yesterday, and civil war inaugurated," announced the *Boston Transcript*. The President issued his first call for troops on April 15 and proclaimed a blockade of the South on April 19.

Busy though he was with chores, William followed newspaper accounts of the Confederate army's early advances. The Union army was ravaged by defections. Approximately one-third of its officers resigned commissions to fight on the side of the Confederacy and, before defecting, soldiers and sailors requisitioned and stored military supplies in the South. John R. Floyd, Secretary of War under President James Buchanan, shipped 115,000 percussion muskets and rifles to five Southern arsenals. On the day South Carolina seceded he gave the order for an additional 124 heavy guns in Pittsburgh to be sent to two forts in the South, but, before the canon could be shipped, he was forced to resign.

William also may have attempted to glean war news from his newspaper's classified advertisements. After May, when federal agents descended on all telegraph offices and confiscated copies of dispatches sent during the past year, secret information often was communicated in classified advertisements with codes and ciphers.

Susan, too, writes to Emma of war news, the death of two men from China, Maine. But the joy of finally moving into her own home is uppermost in her thoughts as she sets up housekeeping in Damariscotta, Maine, a wealthy ship-building settlement near the southern shore of Penobscot Bay. The Reverend Evans is the new minister at the white-spired First Baptist Church in the center of town.

Damariscotta July 31, 1861

Dear Emma

I meant to have written home last night but we were both so tired that we had to give it up—The Gov. (Geo) Davis arrived Monday evening much to our satisfaction and yesterday morning the boxes etc., were safely deposited in our house and unpacked. We found everything safe and in good condition nothing lost, split or broken, except a piece out of an old cup. We were right glad to get them after all our trouble about them.

W.H. unpacked all but the books yesterday and put them up into closets and drawers. He told me at noon that some ladies would be there after dinner to make the carpet—So I took Allie and went up after dinner Clara went with me to take care of him. The new carpet lay upon the sitting room floor rolled up— We were very much pleased indeed with it, both the pattern & the quality—I am glad he did not get a cheaper one. I find my other looks coarse enough by the side of it though I thought that a very good one. We are perfectly satisfied with it—The ladies began to come at two o'clock, and I guess there were about a dosen then some I knew and some I didn't, they were very pleasant. I had to help cut the breadth but we were not very experienced hands and consequently the carpet was cut wrong, or rather one breadth fell short. We measured it before hand, but could not seem to make the figures match any other way. I dont know but if I could have given my whole attention to it I could have managed it somehow, but I had to get the baby to sleep, and let them get on the best way they could. If I had only a half yd. more, I should be all right, as it is we shall have to cover the place (near the door) with a piece of oil cloth or matting. I dont know as I could have helped it if I had been there all the time. The ladies worked fast and soon finished it-Some of them went up stairs with W.H. and put down the study and front chamber carpets. The front chamber carpet falls short a foot on two sides we have a strip from the study carpet which we shall put on one side and cover the other with something or other—My front chamber is exactly like mothers spare room only I have only one closet. We went up to the house again today and have been busy about one thing and another. As our goods havent come from China, we cant tell when we shall get in. WH is going to write again today, we need them very much —(We are going to buy a husk mattress here, so that we have concluded only to have a hair mattress and 2 hair pillows from Boston) Read this to mother. I am afraid we cannot get the trundle bed under our bed it is so low, but we shall manage it somehow—I dont think it will take us very long to get to rights —if our things only come. Everything looks neat and nice, new paper and paint and carpets—we put up our white curtains though they were very dirty—I shall have them washed. I have not got any water hard or soft, but I think our cistern will soon receive water and we shall have plenty—but it will not be very good at first—But I have said quite enough about the house. I

(1861)

havent much to say—I was very glad to get your letter it was very interesting I read a part of it to the girls, and they were pleased I wish I had time to answer it fully but I havent, I wrote this letter to let the folks know I had got my things and I wrote to you because I had written to some of the others before I cant spare time to make my letters interesting as I should like to— The wedding I spoke of came off Monday A.M. I couldnt go as Allie did not wake up till 1/2 past 7, and it was to be at 8. I did not want to go—W.H. went that was enough. It proved to be a ten dollar job—They sent me a huge bundle of wedding cake. It was delicious—two kinds—I wished Bill could have had a taste of it—I never ate any so good before. We expect some more weddings by and by. Allie is not quite so well as usual today. I think he is cutting another tooth. He is very cunning indeed I wish you could see him. He has ever so many pretty little tricks. The folks here are very fond of him. I shall be sorry to leave here still I want to be under my own vine and figtree if possible. We fear that two men from our company have been killed it is so reported. One leaves a family here, and is a member of our church. We feel badly to think Stuart should have fallen so early in the struggle. He will be much mourned in C[hina]. I was in hopes I might have got a letter from home last night. I feel kinder homesick, perhaps I shall get one tonight, but I must say goodby. I forgot to ask for the brown & white dog—all right I hope. Give my love to all the folks. Excuse haste. Sue—what sort of weather do you have up there. It is horrid here, hot and muggy . . . thunder showers and rain and everything else— Will you give this note to Abby Lewis some time or send it no hurry—it is only a letter of sympathy for her loss. How is Maria and how does her father like Washington. Give my love to her. She must be very lonely—I am going to write to Bill & Julia soon give my love to Mary Crosby.

[Enclosed on a separate sheet]

Names of 2 of Jennies pieces The first one is beautiful I think. She has some more very pretty ones—
Suite de Perles Allemandes. 6 Fantasies Elegantes
   sur des air Allemande favors par Theodor Oesten
    No. 2 Schlummulied-Kucken Klange de Liebe
     par T. Oesten (n.) Alperlieder No. 6

Cambridge High School Building

Schoolhouses were so called because
they did, in fact, resemble houses.

Photo Credit: Cambridge Historical Commission

(1861)

As any homemaker moving into a new house, Susan was preoccupied with furnishings. Her hair mattresses and pillows were made of curled horsehair. The inner husks of corn also were saved for stuffing mattresses, and the husking season was considered the time to get the best and most durable underbeds, the mattresses laid over the cords in featherbeds. Corn husks, a versatile material, were used in the South to make horse collars too.

Susan's carpets, purchased by her husband, were sold by the linear yard, probably in twenty-seven inch widths, and cut to fit the room. The patterns—large florals or small geometrics—were nailed or sewn together to match, like wallpaper. To protect the carpets, mats generally were placed in high traffic areas on each side of the threshold and in front of the hearth, where flyaway sparks might cause damage.

The music Susan refers to came from Germany. Between 1841 and 1860, more than four million immigrants, a large number of them German, arrived in the United States. They brought their native music with them. Berlin-born Theodor Oesten (1831–1870), composer and pianist, wrote many pieces for the piano, including nocturnes, tarantellas, marches, waltzes, gallops, and other melodies. Friedrich Wilhelm Kucken (1810–1882) was a conductor and composer who wrote operas and songs, some so popular they were mistaken for folk melodies.

Despite the distances that separated them, Emma's sister and brothers maintained an intimate relationship with one another by writing often. They shared whatever was occuring around them, like the music, as well as their thoughts about each other. Thus, Susan felt "kinder homesick" when she tasted the best wedding cake she had ever had and thought about sharing it with Bill, who apparently had a sweet tooth. Mary Crosby, to whom Susan sent her love, was brother Alfred's sweetheart. Susan also was interested in Emma's friend Maria Morse, who recently had moved to Washington.

When the North set about mobilizing, Washington began to burgeon with unaccustomed activity, attracting new people, among them Maria's father. A few months after his wife's death, Charles H. Morse received an appointment as clerk in the Quartermaster General's Office at an annual salary of $1200. He may have applied for the post in the Capitol in order to start a new life, but Maria and her two sisters, still grieving for their mother, found it difficult to leave friends and all that was familiar in Cambridge. Maria wrote to Emma the adventures of her journey to the capital.

Emma's World

Washington Sept. 19, 1861

Very Dear Emma

I am here as you will perceive from the envelope, but I have had a tedious time of it and ought to be in bed—I suppose you would like a description of my trip, so here it is—we arrived at the depot a little before the cars started; so I took my seat and waited very patiently, soon however a short whistle but sharp enough to take your ears off (almost) sounded and off we went as I expected for good but how I was disappointed We backed in and went out of the depot half a dozen times; just then it began to rain hard, at last we got started and I took my last view of Cambridge (across the river) for one good mile (if you think so). It soon was so dark that we could not see outside but father had several friends on board and it made it very pleasant— There was no such thing as sleep, and yet as soon as the excitement of leaving home was over I was so tired I hardly could sit up. At Framingham & Worcester each we took a regiment on board and it delayed the cars so that we did not arrive at the boat at Allyn's Point until almost 12 o'clock. I could just see the Connecticut Banks & the river and it was beautiful in the dark. We came a long distance on the shores. It was very smooth at the mouth of the river and the point extends out into the sound. The steamboat City of New York is very handsome the stucco work is all gilded around the walls and they have figured plush furniture & large mirrors and chandeliers, plush carpet and elegant staterooms. I went to bed immediately; our stateroom was so small that Hattie F[lorence] and I had hard work to turn around (hoops) and we had considerable sport. . . . The whole bed and all was not so large as our back entry. It rained so hard we could not stay on the open parts of the boat long—the whole country around New York looked dreary enough but I should think it was beautiful in pleasant weather. I lost the sunrise coming up the harbor which I had looked so much upon. We arrived in N.Y. a half hour too late to take cars through to Washington so father took us to Barnum's Museum. I saw a gray and white seal spotted a living hippopotamus and . . . lots of other things (I am so confused tonight I cannot think I forgot one thing) Coming in on the boat—the Chief Marshal Keyes had a real Lisard who was going to make a visit to Fort Lafayette in N.Y. harbor—His name was Sturtevant—brother of Noah S. the great ship builder perhaps your father will know of him—he is

(1861)

a lawyer in N. Orleans—We started out from N.Y. at 10 o'clock A.M. and crossed the Jersey ferry and took the cars in Jersey City—we rode until 4 P.M. Very tedious. When we arrived in Philadelphia a beautiful city everything is neat as it can be we stopped there until 11 in the evening for we arrived just in time to miss the connection train all around—I went to the Independence Hall and took rides through several streets in the Horse Cars—All the buildings nearly have white doorsteps and blinds and everybody was scrubbing the steps mostly marble the sidewalks look very clean and everything is in perfect order—While riding to the depot a daughter of the Regiment was in the car she was dressed in Zouave costume and looked pretty enough—she carried a pistol & I almost envied her she looked very graceful-I would start to draw her picture but I am afraid I should not do her justice. I waited at the depot from 7 until 11½ almost. I took a little nap on the lounge meanwhile but the mosquitoes were so thick I could not sleep long—I made some very pleasant traveling acquaintances a gentleman and his daughter bound for Washington. While riding from Philadelphia to Baltimore some one either intentionally or accidentally discharged a bullet through the car window it was in the other end of the car I was in—it made a round hole in the glass and splintered it all around (some of them went into a gentleman's eye and father took them out) it grazed the man's hair who sat next to the window. . . . I think it must have been accidental as it was dark and if he intended to hit any one he would not be likely to fire into a car in that style—The cars and all went on board of the ferry at Maryland and crossed somewhere. Friday Morning —I was so tired sick last night I could not write any more than I did but I will finish this morning—I feel a little better but am riding in the cars and boat all the time—I am quite sick at my s   h—Hattie vomited last night (I forgot she was quite seasick) the peaches she ate made her sick, they look truly delicious I wish you had one of mine for I have two on my table—a present from a gentleman of father's acquaintance in the cars—If I only had a big cannon I would send one—but I must go on with my journey—I slept by snatches all night in the cars—about two we went on board a ferry, and then took another train—We arrived in Baltimore about 6½ A.M. and I saw where the battle was it looks ugly all around there the irish etc. are truly hideous—but I was quite surprised to find everybody at the window (5 or 6 heads at each sometimes) waving their handkerchiefs furiously—all along the street—every one stopped to look—I suppose it was because there was such a long train I did not count but I should think 20 cars crammed 3 or 4 regiments on board besides the passengers & baggage trains and two cars of horses.

In Baltimore there were so many passengers that they carried them in the steam cars drawn by horses through the city on the horse railroad (so very odd)—it is a common occurrence—the troops all marched. Here father took a carriage and we rode all over the city—I was happily disappointed—it is truly beautiful and neat although not equal to Philadelphia—No picture can describe the house and garden of Ross Wyman Jr., whose father was arrested and is now at Fort McHenry (I have to put in these things for I have such a rush of ideas I shall forget half of it if I don't but I saw the fort and the guns pointed at the city—it looked dangerous—I think it will be dreadful to fire into such a handsome city) the old gentleman's house is very handsome too of dark slate colored stone—I do not know the name—The Washington Monument is magnificient I will write particulars of each some other time—There is quite a firing of cannon this morning I do not know what it is—Now there is a long procession of heavy baggage waggons past my window very handsome and musical—The streets are almost filled with horses being carried to somewhere nothing but horses & baggage ammunition etc. all the time—We started for Washington at 9½ o'clock. There are soldiers encamped all the way. The Relay House is close by the railroad and the troops were drilling as we passed —light artillery—cavalry—and soldiers—there is excellent order there for all the soldiers were away from the depot and on duty—all along the road three or four soldiers were stationed sentinels, you would laugh to see them all grab & rush for the newspapers father bought 10 and distributed them—they will even leave ranks for these and then such a look of thankfulness and a "hurrah"—We got into Washington at 2 o'clock and took a hack and rode Home??? I must try though and make it one—I know I shall be contented in a little while it is very pleasant. Mr. Finney the gentleman we board with is a very fine man and his wife I like—she is quite sick today from excitement—They have only been here a short time and the house is only furnished in the dining room and just enough to sleep and sit down on—when we get settled I will give you a picture of our rooms and the house inside it is very different from those in Cam—or any

(1861)

where else I have been Mr. Finney has a son as tall as Ned but stouter and very awkward (17 years old) but quite social what little I have seen of him. His name is George. And four smaller ones and a little girl two years—Mr. Bean & wife and little boy 5 years board with us they are very pleasant. I forgot to tell you it rained all the way until we arrived in Washington—when it cleared away beautifully. today it is quite warm but not uncomfortable. All our trunks came safe—I suppose you start today for Maine—Oh! how I wish I was there instead of here—I shall direct to Cambridge for you may not go—I must hurry a little as it is almost time for the mail to close I have not seen much of the city and will write next time how I like it etc. —Do write quickly for I shall be lonesome. —Cannonading is stopped I think it is nothing serious—Excuse my interlining this but I thought it would fill the envelope so much I would not take the other half sheet—Give my love to all your family I should be very happy to hear from them—I thank Susan for her present and tell her it is lined up Kiss little Allie for me—There goes a rig with stately tread by the house—I shall write soon as I hear from you nothing preventing—Bid Goodbye to all for me and remember me to them all Alice Ellen Albertine Addie H. and if you see any of my relations—Mrs. Williams Etc. —Goodbye for the present—no one knows what may happen But Emma I hope I shall meet you again sometime. I miss Mother Oh! so much! if she was here I should feel happier for the great care would be taken from me—Pray that I may be preserved if it is God's will. Dear Emma I know you will accept a written kiss—

        Truly your friend and sister,
        H. Maria Morse

Emma was in Damariscotta when she received Maria's letter about the journey to Washington, which included a night aboard the recently commissioned vessel City of New York. Along with its sister ship, City of Boston, it was the premier steamer on Long Island Sound, noted for its speed, size, and excellent appointments. Owned by the Norwich & New York Transportation Company, City of New York weighed 1497 tons and had a wood hull that measured more than three hundred feet in length. A vertical beam engine drove a paddle wheel almost forty-eight feet in diameter. With twin smokestacks, bridge, and flags flying, she was an elegant sight.

On the boat, Maria writes, she saw a "real Lisard," using the slang expression for captured Confederate soldier. The next day she visited one of the most popular attractions in New York City, P.T. Barnum's American Museum of Oddities. Abraham Lincoln, on the way to his inauguration, also had taken his sons to Barnum's museum, which occupied a five-story building across the street from Matthew Brady's photography studio. Afterwards, on a train headed South, Maria encountered Union troops wearing the Turkish-style uniform of the Zouave, an infantry corps in the French army. Accompanying them was the "daughter of the Regiment," a young girl being brought up on an army post, most likely the daughter of one of the officers, treated as a mascot. Later, as Maria peered through a window, she saw the battlefield around Baltimore. Maryland had been a slave state when war broke out; its citizens were divided in their loyalties. When Virginia joined the Confederacy, Union troops rushed into Maryland so that Washington would not be surrounded by unfriendly states. Maryland remained in the Union, but many Marylanders chose to fight with the Confederate army.

Maria heard shelling and saw many regiments because in the fall of 1861, about the time the Morses arrived in the capital, Confederate troops, well-positioned and fortified, guarded all approaches to the city and engaged Federal troops in perfunctory skirmishes. Although the Army of the Confederacy had notched a stunning victory on July 21 at the Battle of Bull Run at Manassas, Virginia—the North suffered 1500 casualties and fled in wild retreat—Southern troops were ordered not to advance even to Alexandria, for the encounter had dispelled the hope of both sides that the war would be over within three months. Instead, the South chose to use its advantage as an opportunity to season and discipline raw recruits.

Both North and South relied on volunteer enlistments and during this time concentrated on conscripting and training troops. Very often friends joined up together and formed a company, electing a popular compatriot to serve as their leader. The practice was criticized by at least one newspaper. Under the headline, "Early Lessons of The War," a Boston journalist wrote of the "folly of giving high command to civilians because they have shown professional, political or other ability," when the times require military acumen.

More citizens, however, were concerned about events in Missouri and Kentucky. Missouri had been torn by the slavery issue since 1857, when the Supreme Court rendered the Dred Scott decision. The Court ruled that Scott, a Missouri slave, who had lived in free states before returning to Missouri, was property and, therefore, had no citizenship rights. Nevertheless, Missourians living near the western border of the state feared that the new Kansas Territory would be admitted as a free state, upsetting the balance between North and South. A border war ensued and continued throughout the Civil War.

Emma was still visiting Susan when her father wrote about Cambridge boys going off to war.

Cambridgeport
October 6th 1861

My dear Emma

Though you have not written to me yet I suppose you will not feel very bad if I sit down and occupy a few moments in writing to you. It is the evening of the Sabbath day and we have had a day of quiet enjoyment the weather has been truly delightful, the sweet balmy south wind has blown around us and it is now so warm that we are writing with open windows, it seems too warm to be seasonable. Mr. Hodges (Arthur's father) preached all day, his sermon this afternoon was truly a gospel sermon descriptive of heaven and the qualities, capacities and methods of enjoyment there, and which seemed so very different from the employments and avocations in which Christians are engaged here on Earth in the Country that the heart said, "would it were so here" but when I thought of the War, & rumors of war in which we shall be engaged tomorrow; even this whole mighty nation I could not help thinking that the Millenium had not yet appeared on Earth. S. Dana Hovey has returned (from Seabury where his regiment is) to recruit and fill up the command. he was in the meeting house with his uniform dress on. Charley Mandell took leave of my Class on Sunday last & supposed that ere this he should be on his way to Washington to join Col Wilsons regiment he was at meeting house today, will probably pass Tuesday. Wm. Dodge has been re-examined and admitted & intends to go as soon as he can, perhaps in a week or two. So you see the young men are going continually. Mr. Mason will not probably be able to preach for sometime to come, although somewhat better, it is thought best for him to absent himself from home and take a journey, which he intends doing. Old Mrs. Hancock is quite sick. Alice tells me she has had a paralytic stroke, slight, but still it is a warning that the system is breaking up and she may be called away at any time, though the first warning is not always evidence of immediate calling away. Alice sends her love to you. Emma Blodget called to see you a few days ago. She did not know you was absent she desired to be remembered to you and hoped you would find enjoyment in your visit. On Friday last was my 50th birthday, only think what an old man your father is. Tomorrow is Ned's birthday and the day of his freedom 21 years old. Alfred has been looking at farms. The Franklin farm seems to be the best one that he has found, and he had concluded to take it, but could not exactly do it as a man has just stepped in and got the refusal of it till Tuesday or Wednesday, when if he does not take it, I suppose Alfred will—if the man takes it Alfred thinks of going perhaps to Derry, N.H. to try there, it is not so easy to get just such a farm as a man wants in these parts. Willie is still at Germantown, he does not seem to recover his health and strength yet, though the sea air is more agreeable to him than to Alfred. I should like to come down to Damariscotta, but I hardly know when I shall be able to come, as the business I expected to have to do cannot be hastened it may not come on till December I expect to have to go to Lowell in about 10 days, and I shall probably stop there or go over to Dracut and spend the time with the Varnums—Mother misses you very much and so do the rest of us, in fact we have been quite lonesome, only two of us in the house, and the other day, I came home at about 3 o'clock and found no one in the house. I opened it with my key and went in & laid down on the Parlor Sofa & read for a long time all alone. What a contrast to the time when we had Sue, W.H., Allie, Bill, Alf, Ned, Hannah and yourself besides Mother and me, so it is, these changes are constantly going on, and soon, they may last long, they must be final. Are we prepared?

I said I miss you, and yet I have you in my Pocket. I showed you to a friend of mine the other day and asked him, as he looked at the countenance, what he supposed the age was, and what think you he said. 40 years old, and when I told him but 17 he could hardly believe me, did you know you looked so anciently. I do really wish I could see that "litle Allie", can he walk yet? how interesting to see and watch the development of his growing mind; I suppose he demands attention and probably gets it. Kiss the little fellow for me and tell him Granpa sent it—The country is full of war alarms, the great interesting fields are now Missouri and Kentucky. in the latter state there is to be a terrible struggle and desolation will doubtless mark the footsteps of the advancing armies towns and cities destroyed, brothers arrayed against brothers and parents against children—and all for the Sin of Slavery. Fremont in Missouri has struck the right keynote, but the government does not openly sustain him, though I have reason to believe that secretly they do, or at least some of the Cabinet do—Mother wants to know if Edwin left a pair of drawers at Damariscotta.

Yours Truly
Father

I suppose you have seen that T. W. Parker Hovey was married a short time ago.

Emma's father supported John Charles Fremont (1813–1890), a Georgia native who, as commander of the Union's Western Army, had issued a proclamation on August 20 taking over the property of rebelling Missouri slave-owners and freeing their slaves. The action aroused public ire and so angered President Lincoln that Fremont—though a popular explorer, soldier, and in 1856 the Republican Party's first Presidential candidate—was relieved of his command and transferred to West Virginia.

When Missouri refused Lincoln's call for troops, Union soldiers marched in and took control in the northern part of the state. The state militia retaliated, inflicting a bloody loss at Wilson's Creek. Subsequently, a state convention in July voted to remove the pro-Confederate leaders. But at the legislature's October meeting, too few members convened to hold a legal session and those who were there voted to secede.

By contrast, Kentucky tried to stay neutral. When Confederate troops invaded the western part of the state during the summer, however, Northern troops pursued them. Attempting to preserve Kentucky's neutrality, the state legislature in September organized a military force to drive the Confederates out. That action placed Kentucky on the Union side, and so divided the state that some families fought each other in battle.

Emma's brother Alfred wrote not about the war, however, but with more personal news.

Cambridgeport Oct. 9, 1861

Dear Sister Emma.

I have not written to you before because I have not had the time. I have been very busy putting through the purchase of a farm, a great many unexpected things have arisen to embarrass me in the matter and have prolonged the time which I ought to have had to work on my place. I think now that we have the thing settled, we have bought the Franklin Farm, and have 20 days to examine title etc. collect our money and settle the Business so that by next week Saturday or before the whole business must be settled, there appears to be no foundation for any mistake now and we are putting things through fast.

Mary has been finishing up her comforters, bought cloth for sheets etc. and will get ready as soon as possible. I think by the first of November, still I cannot say. Mary's Grand father and Grand mother were at her house last night and I spent the Eve with them they are very fine folks, and I like them very much. He wanted very much to marry us and urged Mary to get ready and be married next week, as he is too feeble and old to stay here long, we were very anxious to have him marry us but we could not get ready so soon. he says if he had known it he would have put off his visit here a fortnight. we both of us feel disappointed but I dont see how we can help it now—

I feel very anxious to have things consumated as soon as possible so that I may get at work on my farm.

I will write to you as soon as I know and let you know when we shall be married. I suppose you will come home. I would like to have Sue and Wm. Henry come if they can afford it. I could not afford to pay their fare if I could I would have them come sure.

I cannot give you much news as I have so much to do I leave it for others to write you.

Besides getting ready I have my anniversary Report to read as well as to write, statistics etc. to get.

Mary is pretty well, all the girls are well I believe.

Henry Wilson's regiment went through Tuesday—very fine looking regiment. Chas Mandell remains to join the 23rd Reg. Wm. Dodge cant go he has been examined again and been positively refused admittance Anniversary comes off last Sunday in October on account of Mr. Mason's indisposition etc. .

My love to Sue & Wm. H. I will write you more about the ceremony when I know more about it. Your Bro Alf

Will is better

Alfred and his fiancée, Mary Crosby, were busily preparing for their wedding —he, trying to acquire the farm in Franklin; she, sewing her linen trousseau. An important part of her dowry, it had to contain enough sheets, pillowcases, and comforters so that the bed could be changed regularly in winter, when it was difficult to do laundry. Not only were fabrics hung outdoors apt to be damaged by rough winds and cold, but water was scarce. Wells sometimes froze over so that snow and ice had to be melted even for cooking and drinking water. Soap-making, too, was a foul-smelling chore, better done outdoors in milder weather.

The prevailing image of the ideal wife, held up to Mary and other brides-to-be, embraced more than mastery of the domestic arts. One contemporary writer described the worthy woman as "a soft and tender female, who . . . all weakness and dependence and alive to every trivial roughness while treading the prosperous path of life, suddenly ris[es] in mental force, to be the comforter and supporter of the husband under misfortunes, abiding with unshirking firmness the bitterest blast of adversity."

Robert B. Thomas, in the 1858 *Old Farmer's Almanac,* extolled this remarkable balance of virtues in rhyme in "Recipe For A Wife."

> As much of beauty as preserves affection,
> As much of cheerfulness as spurns detection,
> Of modest deference as claims protection,
> Yet stored with sense, with reason and reflection.
> And every passion held in due subjection,
> Just faults enough to keep her from perfection;
> Find this, my friend, and then make your selection.

Feminist Margaret Fuller viewed the role of wife in the Victorian family quite differently. "Much has been written about woman's keeping within her sphere, which is defined as the domestic sphere," she wrote in *Women in the Nineteenth Century and Kindred Papers Relating to the Sphere, Conditions and Duties of Woman.* "As a little girl, she is to learn the lighter family duties, while she acquires that limited to superintend the instruction of children in their earliest years. It is not generally proposed that she should be sufficiently instructed and developed to understand the pursuits and aims of her future husband; she is not to be a help-meet to him in the way of companionship and counsel, except in the care of his house and children. Her youth is to be passed partly in learning to keep house and the use of the needle, partly in the social circle, where her manners may be formed, ornamental accomplishments perfected and displayed, and the husband found who shall give her the domestic sphere for which she is exclusively prepared."

Almost three years younger than Emma, Cousin Mary Sargent even saw the war in terms of the domestic sphere so she was anxious to learn whether Cousin Elizabeth Horton's father was for the Union.

Alton October 12th/61

My Dear Cousin,

I received your last letter a long time ago & you must excuse me for not answering it sooner but I have had so many things to occupy my mind that I have kept putting it off until it looked so dreadfully that I sat right down & resolved to write now.

I commenced a letter to you in July but I never finished it. How are all the folks ours are well. I suppose you have heard of Uncle William's death before now. We all felt dredfully about it.

Oh Emma I want to see you so much tell Uncle Barbour I think he promised or else pretty near promised to let you come out & see me when you got done going to school. Tell him I want you to come out & stay two or three years with me (that is, of course, if you are not married or going to be) will you I want someone to sleep with so bad except when Eddie sleeps with me I have to sleep alone for Father & Mother sleep down stairs and Eddie's room does not join onto mine. please come.

It was my 15th birthday last August (22nd) I feel quite aged my dresses don't quite touch. Aunt Mary sent me out such a handsome dress & I have had it made gored and open in front & one of these little bits of capes it is real handsome.

Please excuse my horrid writing but I don't feel like writing at all.

Tell Ella & all the girls that they treat me real shabbily. I think don't you Em if Ella becomes any relation to me as perhaps she will I think she might write & keep up our acquaintance at least.

Mother sends love & I suppose the rest do I just hate our school now Our teachers & every thing about them. Our former teacher is down at Cairo I wish I could see him. have you heard whether Uncle Hortons folks are Union or Secession. it makes me so mad to think that any of our folks will be secession there is a celebrated minister (but don't you tell for we are ashamed to own him as relation) in New Orleans (Doctor Palmer) has written a sermon & our minister "said he seldom heard any-

(1861)

thing which made me feel so bad" this man is a cousin of our Mother's isn't it horrid.

 Please answer my letter soon & excuse all mistakes & believe me ever your aff. cousin. Mary Sargent
 Love to all
 Kiss Sues Baby if at your house

Cousin Mary's dismay at the notion of having relatives who were in favor of secession was shared by many, including the President's wife. Mary Todd Lincoln counted among her immediate family relatives on both sides of the conflict. Her eldest brother and one half-sister were for the Union; three half-brothers joined the Confederate army and three half-sisters were married to Confederate officers. Indeed, her sister Emilie's husband, a West Point graduate, was invited to dinner at the White House, where the President personally offered him a promotion to major. Notwithstanding, Ben Hardin Helm chose to fight on the side of the South.

6
(1861)

Father Barbour supported President Lincoln's efforts to restore union, yet he harbored a serious reservation: The North hadn't taken an unequivocal stand against slavery. This disturbed Emma's father and, apparently, he used his influence to dissuade his sons from enlisting. Then he explained to Emma, who was visiting Susan, why he was a peace advocate.

>Cambridgeport
>October 17 (Wednesday) 1861

My dear Emma

Your letter of 10th Postmarked 12th came to hand yesterday. Edwin's from W.H. came 2 days before. Edwin went in search of the Sissie at Lincoln's Wharf where she was said to be, but couldn't find her, he had made arrangement to send the articles. He afterwards learned she was at Wales Wharf, at the South end & on getting there found that "the critter" was going off in less than 10 minutes & so he couldnt get the things on board, but has laid out for the "Davis" and hopes he shall be able to get them on board. Mother wrote the enclosed on Sunday and intended to send it, but found that you would have more than the usual quantity of writing from home & so kept it awhile to make an average. Ellen Hildreth is a little stronger, so that there seems a probability that she may be built up again. Emily is very sick, but not so sick as Ellen has been. Caddie & Edwin are better they have had a terrible time there. Willie has not yet returned from Quincy the last we heard of him, he was going out in a Mackeral fishing expedition, we think he will be home soon. Alfred is in high spirits about his Farm, he thinks it will all be right & though there seem some difficulties about the title that may delay he is driving every thing on to be married and take up "bag & Baggage" for Franklin in a very short period of time I suppose he has given you the story fully in his letter to you I hope & trust he will get through the thing and be in quiet enjoyment of his aspirations, but I have to keep looking ahead as I have forseen the very difficulties (I pointed them out to him) that have arisen, there are so many obstacles, that arise, that we "old fogies" by our sad experience get accustomed to them. I hope the dear boy wont be disappointed it does make me feel kind of sad to have the "loved ones" going off, but it is all right I know—Edwin is suffering very much from the abcess on his hand, he had it lanced by Dr. Chase on Monday, & it is somewhat better, though not yet free from great pain. he may have to have it done again, he is taking medicine for purifying the blood—Sue will I know feel sad to know that Mrs. Curberry's little boy is dead, the little fellow has not been well since she weaned him, but has been declining. Mother went to the funeral yesterday, it was in Prospect Street Meeting House— Mr. Murray conducted the services. there were many of her friends & some neighbors there. Among them Mrs. Ewell who had a dreadful time with Jim who was shot you know in the arm—the limb was filled with grapeshot & so lacerated as to be in a state of almost decomposition, & the efluvia from it very bad & sickening. the Firemen with whom he was connected

Our Minister's Donation Party by Winslow Homer
Photo Credit: Boston Public Library

The Morning Mustering of the 'Contrabands'
Photo Credit: Boston Public Library

have watched constantly with him and have been very kind, but according to her account to mother the sickness and care has been very great & almost overwhelming.

Anna has also been there with her Baby & has also been sick & a great care—they are now getting better. You need not fear that I shall advocate Neds going to the War, but still you know he is beyond my control now & yet I hardly think that any of my children would avow themselves beyond my control, when any question of consequence came to decide upon—they know I think I would look to their highest good, and I think they never had the idea that I depended upon my legal or ordinary tie for that influence that I may have had. Yet you know I do not feel that the War in its present aspect is one on the right principle, though as a principle we should rally around our government to defend it. Yet when our government, acts upon a principle in direct opposition to the law of God and in all its proclamations reiterates the determination needlessly, that it intends still to violate that law—till God by his overwhelming judgments, convinces us that we can do so no longer & then, when he has prostrated us (if he does) we will do right—of course we cannot offer their lives as we should, if duty & conscience and opinion coincided. I have no doubt that God will work out the destruction of slavery, though our Gov't deny their participation, yet I prefer to work with than against God—

Now about coming home. I hardly see that I can come to D. at present I must go to Lowell on Monday next & stay a week and about that time Alfred will probably be married. I suppose you will of course want to be home at the time, and I suppose Sue would like to be here, but I do not know whether she can be or not—I should like to have Wm. Henry & Allie come if they can properly. She will of course be the judge—I will send you money in time to come home—My time is about out and my paper is about used up—I should have been pleased to see little Allie with his mittens—We had letters yesterday in the Journal, giving accurate information of Smarts death I suppose you saw it—there is now no doubt—Dodge was again rejected, disease of the heart, was too apparent & he was decidedly rejected—so he wont try again, this was the 3rd trial—If the Rebels do not retreat from near Washington, there will be a great battle soon. The great expedition from New York, embracing nearly 50,000 tons of shipping & from 25 to 50,000 men, will produce a terrible effect somewhere, tho it is not known where. The only fear now is of a disgraceful compromise—Give my love to Sue & Wm Henry. I am sorry and disappointed that I cannot see them & Allie.

The Sewing Circle meets on Thursday evening at the vestry— We have not yet been called upon to furnish the tea and hope we shall not but, mother will if desired.

Make your own calculations about coming home. Mother can get along without you, though she has much to do for Alfred's coming Wedding.

Following their marriage in Roxbury, Massachusetts, on November 8, 1861, twenty-four-year-old Alfred Loring Barbour and Mary Nichols Crosby, twenty, went to live on the farm in Franklin. Negotiating with his father's brother, who owned the property, the anxious bridegroom had failed to handle affairs in a businesslike way.

"I intended to call and see Uncle James and talk over arrangements as to my carrying on the farm," he wrote to his father, shortly after moving in. "I wanted to see if I could not make some arrangements to have my living (i.e. of the things I raise on the farm) such as potatoes, turnips, Beets &c skim milk) I use about 3 potatoes per day and 2 turnips per week, pint of Sweet milk and once in a while some skim milk. I dont hardly know how to keep account. I wanted to know too how we were to work whether on halves or thirds, perhaps it might be well to have you see him and talk with him. I meant to when I was at home, but I had so much to do that it slipped my mind until it was too late."

Alfred was an inexperienced but hardworking farmer. Soon after his marriage, he wrote to his mother, "Mary and myself both get quite tired and generally go to bed by 7 or ½ past today after getting the chores done, I went to mill (about 2 miles) to have some corn ground. I was some how or other mis directd and went a mile out of my way. found it at last the miller had 3 or 4 grists before me to grind and as he could not get at mine till 3 o' clock it being then ½ past 11 and the mill grinding very slow I concluded as it was rainy and no shed for my horse to stand under I would go home and come tomorrow for my grist. I did not get wet as I took my rubber coat but it was a cold rain. I have been sawing and splitting wood for two or three days past I dont seem to get along very fast as it takes me about 2 hours morning & 2 hours at night to build fires, feed cattle, milk,

(1861)

bring in wood &c then as it is light only from 1/2 6 a.m. to 1/2 past 5 p.m. it is rather a short day."

"Monday Mary washed, helped her all I could Sunday night and Monday it snowed hard so by Monday eve we had 6 to 8 inches of snow but no sleighing, though I got out my ox sled and hauled up a load of wood.

"I keep thinking of things I want, don't like to bother you to much or rob you or your household articles but you know you have got a lot of old saucers up in your closet—now if you could spare two or three or more and an old cup we would like them . . . When anyone comes up let them bring up some fresh fish, say mackerel, cod haddock &c the Butcher has'nt been since we have been here and we dont hardly know what to have for dinner, we have not killed our pig yet so we havent the nice fresh or salt Pork which we shall have soon, they say I must not kill my pig until after the first quarter after the new moon as if I kill before or after that week the Pork will shrink upon boiling.

"I put the entry hall & stair carpets down yesterday the sitting room and dining room are all carpeted & look nicely—Mary is a nice housekeeper good cook, and gives me no chance to find fault—even if I chose to."

In February, when Mary called on family in Cambridge, Alfred informed his mother, "do not judge her extravagant in thus visiting home so often nor by her dress & outfit she has been working on straw and earning something and uses that money to pay her expenses home, she has sewed considerable . . . She has a very nice cloak, this she bought the cloth with money received from her fitch muff—and her mother cut and made it, her sable furs she bought with some money which came from her Grandfathers estate—I am glad she can have these things & coming in this way for if it depended upon me (I know she would not ask) to buy them she could not have them. dont then think that she is extravagant . . . As you will learn by fathers letters I have been sick, caused I suppose by the paint, yet I dont know what is the matter and I have been very much perplexed to find any thing to relieve me. I tried (Humphrey) but could get nothing to relieve me, in fact I could not find anything applicable to me. I tried Lux Vomica which relieved me some. I find Humphrey's not at all like the regular Homeopathic Book I keep having a sort of stitch in my side or in the band around me and where the pain seems to be . . . I do not like to say to Father because I am afraid of wounding his feelings or think I do not appreciate his present of the Humphrey box . . ."

By March the snow was melting and his hens beginning to lay so Alfred was in an expansive mood when he wrote to his mother. "I think myself that I have a very comfortable and cozy home, good scenery and plenty to eat of what is wholesome (though nothing rich) such as good bread and butter, Johnny cake, Ginger bread, salt meat, and semi-occasionally fresh meat, plenty of milk &c . . . Mary says she gets entirely run out for what to have for Breakfast & Dinner though I dont see but what she does as well as any body could she wants to know if you can suggest something we have not, one day Fried Salt Pork and Potatoes, with Squash Pie or Gingerbread—then fried ham with our Eggs, then Egg Omlets or Poached Egg—the Sausage—then boiled dish Sunday Baked Beans. Monday picked up dinner bye and bye, we shall have bread and milk and berries. now I dont know what better she could do, for breakfast we have flap-jacks other things too numerous to mention . . . I think mother she will make one of the best of wives, she is careful prudent and tries to do her part well, she has succeeded, I think far above my expectations—she hates worst of any thing to wash dishes—so occasionally I take hold and help her, she does her washing and ironing and has begun to do some mending—as my clothes wear out some, but you must come and see what a nice little wife I have and what a dear home is mine to welcome you to—I am I think thankful to God for it all and for the blessing of health and I also feel the kindness of those who have helped me in obtaining my treasure."

Emma paid the newlyweds a visit, laden with packages from home, including beef tongue and milk biscuits. Alfred and Mary so enjoyed having her that they invited her to stay the winter and to help Mary sew straw. "She can earn $2 to 3 dollars per week and I tell her I'll give her board . . . ," Alfred wrote home. "But perhaps you would have some thing to say about that." When Emma declined their kind offer because she didn't want to give up glee club and other social activities, Alfred understood. "I thought if I could hold out the inducement of making a little money for keeping us company she might take up with it." In the same letter, he told his mother, "Emma says she would like to have you rip the ribbon off her straw bonnet and have it whitened and pressed at Mrs. Turner's if she don't ask over 45 cts—If she asks over that send it up here there is a band box of ours at father Crosbys you could send it in."

In the meantime, Emma's friends, Ellen and Alice, continued to keep her informed of other romantic interests.

(1861)

Cambridge Port
Oct. 17th, 1861

Ma chere Emma

Your mother said last Sunday night that you wished me to write to you, I have been trying ever since to find time and this is the first chance I have had and yet it is not a chance for I hav'nt opened my books yet and I have barely time to prepare for the Sewing Circle and get supper, but I dont care for the books and much prefer to write to you and try and tell you some news if any are to be told. I believe the girls are all well and most of them intend to go to the Circle to-night which is in the Vestry, is'nt that splendid. I wish you were here to go too, if I had thought I might have telegraphed to you and you might have taken a trip to Boston on a shingle to attend the Circle, but of course you never think of a thing till it is too late. I guess we shall have a nice time, I hope we shall. I hope you will come back soon for I want to see you, so does Alice, isn't she a nice girl, we walk round the square once in a while at recess and discuss passing events. I dont know what I should do if it were not for her, the girls at school are so different and she seems to be the only one left who goes to our church. I suppose you would like to hear about school affairs. We progress in the cause of education about the same as usual, but I guess our class train more than your did, to-day, Abbie has done nothing but train all day. Miss Rockwood, Barry and Wells have assisted her, one of the girls brought a pig to school made out of a lemon with eyes, ears and feet made of matches, the hour before the last Abbie lit one of the matches and such a smell. I should have thought Mr. Williston would have noticed it but I guess he didn't, this is only one instance of their actions but at the close of school Abbie was the only one who had fire, we have dictations as usual. I think they are horrid things, especially when there are capitals. I have done much better this month than last but I have from two to eight every time last month my average was 9.59. In Philosophy I have done miserably, our class is not near as smart as yours, we have just commenced Optics. I like them much better than Mechanics, I had for an average 6.50. and I was number six, wasn't that a splendid average should'nt you be proud of it if you were me, the reason I was so low was because I did'nt study Trigenomentry and Mr. Bradbury always the first of the time called on me when there was any Geometry about the Lecon. In Astronomy I had 8.20 and was number three. I suppose you would like to hear about the meetings, some of them have been very good, the Concert last Sunday evening was splendid, the vestry was crowded and seats were brought in. Last Monday evening the meeting was quite dull, at least the first portion of it. Corey took charge. Messer. Cox, two Hammonds, Monroe, Colber, Hollis made prayers. Mr. Bowker and Hammond spoke, he spoke about falling leaves almost the same that he spoke about last year. A week ago "Lee him" took part I know it is wrong for me to laugh but I cant help it, everytime I see him I think of that Bible Class. Mr. Mason is out of town at present he has been quite sick and has not preached for a good while. I do hope he will get well soon for I want to hear him, we have had several different preachers since he has been sick but none of them were half as good as Mr. Mason. Give my love to Susie and my respects to Mr. Evans and kiss Allie for me. I think I will now stop and finish tomorrow after the Sewing Circle. I had a much better time than I did at Mrs. Goodnough's, they seemed full as social if not more so! The usual ones were there with the exception of . . . . poor fellow I guess he is lonesome dont you? I had a talk with Monroe, and Colver, a speak with Hammond and spoke to quite a number of the old folks. I saw your mother she said that you were coming home in two or three weeks that she missed you and could'nt spare you any longer. I saw Sle. . . . . .s but did not speak to him. I do wish some folks woud'nt tell such stories about me but "what cant be cured must be endured" have I got it right. Charlie Ward was married last evening to Miss Humphrey and Dr. Thayer is going to be next week. I dont think of any more news at present. Please answer if you have the time with my love,

Ellen

Ellen teased Emma, writing that an anonymous beau was lonesome. Another friend, Alice Hancock, suggested that Emma's admirer "had the pip." A disease of chickens, the pip does not afflict humans. The colloquial expression meant that he was annoyed, presumably by Emma's prolonged absence. And, after she and Albertine "seceded" from the other girls, Alice flirtatiously described herself as "dished," that is, ruined or embarrassed, when two young male friends choose to sit beside them at church services.

(1861)

October 19th, 1861

My chere amie Emma

Doubtless you are beginning to think by this time that Alice has forgotten you, or never intends writing to you or something of the sort. But you may depend upon it such is not the case. Many and many a time I've said O dear, I wish Emma was here. You must know I miss you awfully. I suspect I shall want to eat you up, when you come back, so you had better think twice before you conclude to come. Emma, I've got a bad pen, horrid ink, and everything to match, and to crown all, I'm writing in school, so I hope you will excuse all blunders, etc. etc. It is Saturday morning, and I have nothing to do, so the consequence is, I am writing to you. Now, who says I cant write poetry? Mr. Williston is down in Miss Pincis room hearing the first college class, and Miss Willard occupies the seat of honor. I am sitting in the third seat, my seat for this month. Carrie Russell is head, Miss C. Dana next, and I, next. My average this month was 9.82. Perhaps you will ask how my French gets along? Pretty well—"considering circumstances." The next lesson finishes "un intriciur de diligence", but Miss Willard has not decided what we shall take next. I hope it will be an interesting story. We have just finished the orations against Catiline and have begun that for the Manilian law. I did not suppose we were to take any more than the four against Catiline, but it seems that "the powers that be" have decided otherwise in the wise counsels of their own conceit. Ah well! so goes the world. Last Thursday we had Sewing Circle in the vestry. We had a very pleasant meeting, indeed. Ellen, Addie and I went together. We were all sitting on a seat together when your Mother came over and spoke to us, and said she must come and see us for we were Emma's friends. She said you wanted us to write awfully. So the next day (yesterday) Ellen sat down and wrote to you and now I am writing. Your mother wanted us all three to write at once, and send the letters all in a bunch, but we thought we would not do that.

Monday in school 20 min. past 12. Today the first college class got through with Cicero, and at recess they burried their book. It was quite a piece of fun I can assure you. They went over to Slater's house to dress, and get their regimentals etc. etc. Then they marched round the square by Hammond's house you know. Piper came first. He had on an old black beaver with the numbers "62" in large white letters. He had some false mustachios of black wool, and eyeglasses. A white sash round his waist, a large stand up collar, and a great white choker, white streamers on his arms, and altogether he cut quite a comical figure. Then Dodge was dressed to represent President Felton as he dresses at Commencement you know with a long black cambric gown, a large square hat, etc. The others were all dressed in like manner. Then they marched into the schoolyard, and burried the Corpse. It was held in a square black cloth edged with white and was lowered into the grave by four boys. Brinckerhoff was the sexton. At the grave Dodge made quite a speech, consisting of Latin nonsense composed for the occasion. They had a black banner, and another with skull and crossbones on it. I wish you could have seen the whole performance. It was quite "killing" I can tell you. Next Sunday we have our anniversary. Last Saturday night we had a rehearsal at 7 o' clock, but the day was very rainy and but few children were out, so we went up into the gallery, by the organ. Colver played, and Sarah and Georgie Roberts were there. Ellen, Emma Harris, W.[illie] Munroe, G.[eorge] Clapp, & etc. etc. (By the way your "hadorer" was not at Sewing Circle and Ellen and I concluded that it was because "the bright particular star" had hidden its light, away down in a certain town in Maine, which shall be nameless, and would not shine where his eyes might behold its glory.) And when we were about half through rehearsal who should come in, despite the storm, but a certain young man. . .   by name, with his upper story tied up in a small sheet, or certainly something resembling the same. Probably (as I told the girls) he had the pip in consequence of the prolonged absence of his "hadored one": Poor fellow! I hope said disease will not prove fatal in his case, as it does so often among the feathered tribe. But Sunday I observed the Sheet had disappeared. I attributed it to the fact that he might have heard that the sojourn of his "aimarorata" was drawing to a close, and probably his "spirits" had been raised from their depression, and, as you know, the mind has a magnetic influence upon the body. Hence his recovery.

Doubtless many will be glad enough to see you back again. I am sure I shall for one. But one I am sure will be, and that one is—is—ahem!—is—is the—aforesaid—young gentleman! Now dont laugh, for I solemnly aver to you, it is the naked truth. Ask your sister if she dont think so. That is, if you've a mind to.

(1861)

But to return to the subject. I believe, way back in the later part of not the last century—but the last sheet of my letter, I was telling you about the rehearsal. "well, as I was a goin' to say," it was very rainy. or rather foggy misty, and generally disagreeable. When we came down from the S.S. rehearsal to go into the other one, Ellen, Albertine, and I were together. Sarah, Georgie Roberts, and Emma Harris were in one seat, and they wanted us to come and sit with them; But as Sarah and I both stuck to it that we wanted the end of the seat, and neither would give up, Albertine and I seceded and went into the pew opposite, which happened to be Mr. Munroe's. I taking the end of the seat. Just as we had got nicely seated, who should come but George Clapp! Wasn't I "dished" then? Then came Willie Munroe, and finally, to crown the whole Benjamin Colby who passed the other two boys, and came and sat as nice as could be, next me. By this time Albertine and I had got to laughing so hard, that we could scarcely restrain ourselves, when through Munroe's hands came two notes from Ellen and Sarah, triumphing in our misfortunes. Albertine and I laughed and laughed till I certainly thought we never should stop. And I felt so ashamed of myself too! Just before we started out to go home, there came up a violent thunder shower, and we had to wait some time before we could come home. And we young folks, Ellen, Albertine, Sarah, Georgie, Emma Harris, Willie Munroe, Colver Leeds, and myself got into one end of the entry, and enjoyed ourselves immensely, I can assure you. O you cant think how it rained! In a few moments the sidewalks were flooded, and in going home, we got pretty thouroughly wet. Enough of this.

Addie Houghton is going the first of next month. She wants to see you before she goes. You probably know Mr. Mason has gone to Conway. He is to be back next Thursday. Dont you remember Sarah Jane Tandy, who is in Mrs. Clark's class? She is married! She married a Mr. Harris a soldier from Washington. She was married last week in Boston by Mr. Strove. She was at Sunday School and meeting all day yesterday. Did not change her dress in the least. Her husband has rejoined his company I suppose. A week ago last Saturday we had declamation in school. Mary Alden and Carrie Fisher were there. Mary Alden inquired for you. I did not see Carrie to speak with her. I suppose Ellen has told you all the news if there is any. I don't know of any more to tell. I heard Amanda Fellmer and Charlie Titus were engaged, but I can't believe any such story. I should hope Titus was too sensible for that. I have also a wee bit of news for you when you come home. Could not trust it to a letter. . . . Now my dearest friend Good-bye for the present—I hope soon to see you—Then I will throw up my cap for joy—

Your
Alice

Not only Alice, but Emma's parents were impatient for her return to Cambridgeport. Even with Alfred's wedding in the offing, Emma had yet to make arrangements to leave Damariscotta. Her father urged her to hurry home.

Cambridgeport Sat. Evening
October 20, 1861

My Dear Emma

At the close of the Sabbath I sit down to write you a few lines, because I go early tomorrow morning to the principle duties of a juror when I shall be called to pass a week or more amid revelations of crime of all kinds & varieties & shall doubtless find exhibited passions & emotions of a most dreadful nature, & which I must of course be greatly instrumental in punishing. Yet these are the scenes the duties the responsibilities of life from which I must in no wise shrink.

We have had a very interesting Sabbath day. Rev. Mr. Patten late of Jamaica Plain, now of Watertown was our preacher. his Sermon in the morning was upon the text including that exclamation Why has thou forsaken me he was very solemn and very effective, and gave an excellent sermon. In the afternoon, he preached from Deut. 32 11 & 12. As the Eagle stirreth up her nest etc. Bringing up the events and scenes of Bible life as well as that of our own. Mass. Christians seem to have concluded that their nest was comfortable and that they could enjoy worldly life here. God like the Eagle stirs up their nest to show them that they have other duties & other objects. He instanced Job, who had every desireable earthly prosperity when God revealed himself in the scene of discipline so severe and yet so really beneficial. David also, who had much of prosperity & relied so much on the beautiful profile—and Absalom who caused the great rebellion that resulted in his dreadful death and yet how he loved him even in his death and infamy—He

(1861)

brought up the loss of children in families where the Christian made his loveliest nest, and which yet must be disturbed and troubled. This brought out in the evening Mr. Cook with whom Mr. Patten dined and spent time in comparing experiences & also mr. Williams who was very much affected even to tears, and loss of power of speech, so much was he overcome for a moment or so—The effect of the meeting today I cannot but think will be productive of good. It was stated in the Sab. School today that 12 members of our school had already gone to the War not including Mr. Burgess who was not a member of either church or Sabbath school, neither including Horace Blake (brother of Mrs. Ford.)

Albertine Tarbell and Alice Hancock send their love to you— I hope to see you at home quite soon. Alfred wrote to Susan a few days ago, stating that you had probably better come home, this week, by the Carr. except there should be some one coming by the Boat with whom you were acquainted and you should prefer to come that way. in which case you can do as you please about it, you will of course write us at once which way you come, you had better write to Mother, as I shall be away & Alfred may be at Franklin, but I suppose Edwin will be at home so that he can give attention to you. I send you $3 in this which I suppose will be enough with what you have to get you home again. Should there be any reason why you should want any more money, you can get it of Sue & I can send it to her—but I suppose there will be no need or I would enclose more for you. Mr. Evans called here a few days ago & said Mary would be ready to go in two or three weeks. She would like to have Mr. Henry come up and spend some time & take Mary home with him. Ellen Hildreth is getting somewhat better though she is very very weak. Emily is also getting up a little. Caddie is quite recovered & about the house. Edwin is recovering. Flora Burt is there taking the place of one of the nurses that has left they have had a severe time but are now hoping to have rest. Willie has returned from his visit to Quincy, he sent home the day before he came, some birds that he shot & we had a bird dinner. Edwin has had an abcess on his hand & also very sore finger of long standing. I hope now that he has had it lanced, it will get well. Give love to Susan, for me & tell her I shall write her when I can, there is no reason why I have not except occupation so that I did not have time to write all & I have written you you know —— Goodbye my dear Child God bless and return you to us in good health etc.

Father

Flora Burt, a neighbor, helped out as a nurse. Nursing was regarded as an appropriate way for women to express their nurturing instinct and their duties were seen as an extension of the unpaid services of housewives. Although the Civil War opened some opportunities for women (at least three hundred women, masquerading as men, joined the army), male physicians warned that the female brain and nervous system could not withstand the intellectual effort required by the professions of law and medicine.

Meanwhile, sixty-year-old Dorothea Dix, appointed superintendent of army nurses, worked throughout the war without taking a day off. She also recruited many women volunteers, stipulating only that they be over thirty and plain looking, dress in brown or black, and wear no bows, jewelry or other adornments. The writer Louisa May Alcott was among the volunteers stationed in Washington, D.C. where, for the first time, women staffed army hospitals. They were paid forty cents a day; experience was not necessary.

Florence Nightingale had established a school of nursing in London in 1860 and some of the nurses she trained came to the United States to teach nursing. Not until 1873, however, were the first nursing schools in the United States opened at the Massachusetts General Hospital, Boston; Bellevue Hospital, New York City; and New Haven Hospital, Connecticut.

At eighteen and unmarried, Emma's war effort was probably limited to sewing and knitting for the soldiers. Her social life continued almost as before. Since she had a pleasant singing voice, dressed fashionably, and was pious, Emma had much to recommend her as a houseguest. She was also better educated than most young women of her generation and could converse on a range of subjects. Small wonder she was in demand. Shortly after her return from Maine, she received an invitation to visit Cousin Mary Sargent. (Mary Evans, who planned to take Emma's place in Damariscotta, was Susan's sister-in-law.)

(1861)

Alton
December 3rd, 1861

Dear Cousin Emma.

I received your last letter, at the same time, that I wrote to Sue, and I have delayed, answering it, for one reason, and another, until I have brought it, to this late time. Mother said, if I would write you, a letter, she would do, my sewing, for me, and as I would rather write, than sew, I availed myself, of the opportunity. I wish you would come out, here, and see me, but perhaps you would not enjoy yourself as much, as you do on east, you will try, and come as soon, as you can, won't you? I should be delighted, to see you.

How is little Alfred Henry? how I wish I could see, him. I am not going to have any new dresses this winter. I have got one, made over out of Mother's, you have seen it, it is red, and green.

Tell me all about your dresses, when you write. How is your best bonnet trimmed? or do you wear your pink one? I wish you could see mine, I think it is a perfect beauty. It is not good skating, it has been first rate. I have got a real nice pair of boy's skates, iron. Father bought them, for me, they cost $1.25, the girls here, with the exception of two, or three, have boy's skates.

Tell Ella, I think she is real mean, not to write, to me. I owe Gusie Ricker, and Mary (Willard), both letters. How are all the folks. I should like to see them, all. I am glad you have got, such a nice fellow, for a beau, Emma. I hope you will marry him, and then Ella, will be a kind of cousin, that will be splendid.

I think Susie Haswell might, write, to me. I don't think the girls act, quite right, they ought to write more.

We heard from Uncle William, through the paper, he was at Valparaiso, Chile.

I am getting along first rate, at school. I don't always get 10 though by any means. I always get 9 in writing. I study Robinson's Arithmetic, it is a very hard one. Frost's United States History, Towen's speller, Weld's Grammar, the same almost exactly like the one, I studied on east, but the Grammar is not at all like it. I read out of Sargent's Reader.

Are you going to have a festival, Christmas, at your Sabbath School. We are at ours. We are going to have trees, for every class, but ours, our teacher says it is all folly, and we can't have one. I think it is too bad. They wanted brother Eddie, to speak a piece, with a little girl, but Mother says she shan't let him because he is too small. He goes to the Grammar School. He has just commenced Grammar, we have got a splendid teacher, in his school, better I think than in the high school. Eddie is the youngest one, in the school. But I must close give my love to all, and especially that dear little baby. Mother sends love. Goodbye from

              Cousin.
              Mary

From Mary's letter, it seems that the report of Uncle William's death (October 12/61) was greatly exaggerated.

Her disappointment about not having a new dress may have been the result of shortages during the economy's transition from peace to wartime. Soon, however, factories and farms in the North, adopting techniques of mass production, fueled an economic boom. The South, on the contrary, lacked manufacturing industries and quickly depleted its limited resources. Then clothing was made of carpets and draperies, newspapers printed on the back of wallpaper. At the height of inflation in the Confederacy, flour fetched $300 a barrel.

On the eve of the war's first New Year, Maria met her stepmother. Apparently, Mr. Morse married a woman from Cambridge, someone Emma knew.

              Washington
              Dec. 31st, 1861

Dear Sister Emma,

I can almost hear you say—well she has written at last, but not when she appointed. But my dear don't get impatient for I have one of the best reasons. I have not been able to use my right hand for nearly a week especially in writing matters, because of my thumb. I thought I should have a felon but it has <u>very</u> wisely concluded not to be one. Today the sore came to a <u>head</u> and I opened it, it is so much better that I can manage to write you a few lines. Your last letter was gladly received but under very peculiar circumstances. Mrs. Kirshner was in the room making a call upon your friend, and father had another young man at the table transacting business—Minna brought it in—I did want to peep into it and under <u>any</u> other circumstances it would have been quite a trial to my patience to be detained so long—Need I say, I had patience? You may possibly understand me—But enough of this.

I am sorry to hear of your sickness. I wish I could see you—it is a great denial not to go north with father, but Florence cannot be left alone—she has not sit up, off the bed, until today and then only a few minutes. I can hardly imagine you to be sick who are usually so well and did you take the diptheria or is it prevalent?

And Miss Willard is to be married—how much she will be missed—that was a handsome present. I heard about the circle from Aunt Josie—she said Mr. Cummings was the hero of the evening—is it so? I was in hopes you went and would tell me about it—

I remember Mrs. Swissidon well and am not surprised at events. I begin to take everything as a matter of course. Emma, I did think I should have a visit this winter from you but I despair now as we are about to have an addition. We will go to housekeeping in early spring I expect and then I may hope—I rather think it will not be long before I shall come north but as I said I cannot hope for anything and am not surprised at any event. That is rather unfortunate about Mrs. Houghton and Addie—Thanks to Mary Alden and I wish to be remembered to her whenever you see her—How aggravating you are not to tell who is coming—"I would like to see him or her" (definite) well! what of it? I hope they will come after all my guessing etc. Now are you under oath not to tell? if not do relieve me—You need not trouble yourself about my not puzzling your letter out—I don't trouble myself in that respect at all if I have a sore thumb (oh! how it aches) but never mind it is in a good cause. Since I last wrote I have received a call from the Russian (that de arnand) that I spoke to you about in my last (I believe it was but I told so many different ones that I hardly know what I have said and what I haven't to each) He stopped about an hour and invited me to go to ride with him some day when we could both agree— Did you ever hear of such presumption? I had only seen him once before. I shall go when I agree to it. Oh! dear! how lonesome I am for Minna has gone. I attended the lectures here last Friday I went with Mr. McFadden, a gentleman from Maine who boards here. He has only been married a year and has been through college—He is not sober by any means but real good hearted (handsome) I never had a better escourt—he was head and shoulders taller than I—I felt quite proud of him (am I not

The Old Bull Dog On The Right Track
Photo Credit: Boston Public Library

wicked?) Well! What a looking sheet such an one never went out of my hands before—Everything is lively here. I have valuable additions to my experience every day. I see so much art and cunning that I suspect almost everyone until I know better. — The young people (mankind particularly) are so different from those I have been accustomed to meet. I have to keep my eyes open I assure you. —I shall have to close now with much love to you and a kiss—Remember me to all—I shall expect a letter Thursday—if you haven't a sore finger.

Your sister,
H.M. ———m

I would like to have Mary Alden write in my album she told me she would—Do you think of any other one I would like. Has Willie Munroe written? I would like his if not—I would like to have you give it to Minna or Remmie if you see them after those I mentioned—You can leave it at Breea Brook's in the brick block or Austin Libby Mr. Ware's church when they have written and she will give it to Minna—

Thursday Evening

Dear as ever—

Here is my little epistle not sent yet. I did not have any envelopes and had not time to go out to get one. Since I wrote the above my thumb has nearly recovered and my new mother has arrived. I am very much pleased with her. She is social and agreeable—We are expecting great times here soon in about four weeks so says my Russan friend who called on me Tuesday evening again—He is going home at that time and invited me to go with him urging very much. Is it not funny? I have not decided yet. What think you about it—would you go? He is wealthy, talented and handsome—I shall await the advice of my sister before I fully make up my mind—He will take a pleasure trip all over Europe occupying about a year—What ! a chance—Write soon—I had some very handsome new years gifts. A silver napkin ring a set of collar & undersleeves (nice muslin) a silver dollar, and a fan, blue & spangled with tassels—What did you have? A happy New year! it is not too late although I intended this as a new years present—It is the custom here for gentlemen to call on all their lady friends on N. Years and I received two calls. Mr. Kirshner &

Appleby—Emma what do you think of me? I do run on so about the gentlemen but so! have a little charity for you would do the same were you here I am confident—How sober you will look when you get through. But cheer up I have good news for you next time guess——

Your Sister
Maria

WHO IS COMING?

Perhaps Emma tried to prepare her friend for the arrival of a stepmother by writing Maria to expect someone special. Maria, however, had not figured out the significance of Emma's hint. It seems she was more interested in the gentlemen who called on New Year's Day.

George Washington adopted the practice of paying New Year's calls from the Dutch in New York, and, while he was President, each January hosted an open house. The custom spread throughout the country until it became so popular that newspapers began listing the names of people who would be "at home" and their calling hours. With newspaper lists in hand, strangers sometimes visited house after house, helping themselves to food and drink at each stop. Because of such abuses, public announcements were discontinued.

7
(1862)

In the nineteenth-century, middle-class Americans developed social consciousness and a sense of propriety. Concern for appearances especially was important. Indeed, the quintessential voice of the day, Ralph Waldo Emerson wrote, "The keeping of the proprieties is as indispensable as clean linen." No wonder then that Susan responded indignantly to Emma's news of Mr. Morse's remarriage.

Damariscotta Jan. 5, 1862

Dear Emma

I really dont know which of us is in debt to the other, but I thought I would write you anyway. I was very sorry that you had been sick, it must be something new to you to be obliged to stay indoors anytime. I couldnt help thinking how fortunate it was that it didnt happen while you were going to school for then you would have had to be absent. I am glad you are getting better but you must be very careful and not get cold. I hope you didn't at singing school, or tire your throat singing. I havent heard of much sickness round here lately. Tell father I received his letter last night and am very very much obliged and will answer it soon. It was just what I wanted. He didn't tell me whether mother's cough was any better I hope it is, we find Phosporus a very valuable remedy in case of cough. W.H. had quite a severe cold on the chest and throat last week he used it with success. Little Allie has a slight cold in his head. I think caused by going into a cold room and staying too long. He has only had one cold before this winter, and I take him out a good deal, and carry him all over the house. But the past week it has been very cold and windy and we have kept in pretty snug—we keep very comfortable down stairs. The water in our bedroom frose night before last, also in our sitting room closet, though we have a fire all night. Last winter when Mary was visiting in Maine she frose her feet, and this week they troubled her much with swelling and aching. I rubbed them with brandy & salt which cured them right up—I enjoy myself very much with Mary, she is real kindhearted & good with Allie, and a good deal of company for me, though not of course half as good as you would be. Now that Louisa is gone, we have more to do but we get a long very well, we find a very perceptible difference in the way wood and provisions last. I have had enough to do to clean out the dirty places she left. Oh dear I wish it took as long to make dirt as to clean it up—But I am very much afraid Mary will not stay with us as I think she wants more young & lively company. she is not much acquainted down here. We are going to have her go to singing school. But there is another thing in the way. There is a young man who has been waiting for her for a year or two, who is away from Boston now, but is coming next month, he has written to her to be sure & be home when he comes as she hasn't seen him since July (and seems to be quite attached to him) I very much fear she will not be contented after he comes to Boston, and I dont of course blame her. I should feel so myself—by what she says I cant tell she jokes so about everything—Now you mustnt say anything out of the

(1862)

house about this for perhaps she wouldn't like to have it freely spoken of. I wish I could find somebody that would stay with me, that I liked and could depend upon. It seems these hard times as if somebody would be glad of a home that needed one. Did you ever find out who Sarah's beau was? His name is Ian Lippincott. he is not as old as Sarah. M. says he is a nice fellow—

This week we didn't do any washing, but have been doing little old jobs. New Years Day Eve we made some lasses candy and popped Alfs corn. In the A.M. we had roast goose, stuffed with onions etc. In the P.M. we put a comforter into the frames and tacked it before night. I think we shall quilt this week. Thursday Mr. Sargent came to dinner & passed the night—he is preaching for W.H. this P.M. and will stop over tonight. We find enough to keep ones fingers busy these short days.

I have lost nearly all my milk now, and do not nurse Allie at all in the day time, he drags on me badly nights, though I have but little for him. He wont let anybody but his father get him to sleep except in the night he wont go to him then at all. He is real cunning—he calls "Mary" & Clara he says "baby"—and if you say Wheres Allie he says "here he is"—he points to his "bread basket" & stomach he shows a great deal of will, but we try and make him mind easy—I wish the folks could see him. I think every day he seems more cunning—

Do you hear from Maria often now. I should think she would feel dreadfully to have her father marry again so soon. I should, if he got the best woman in the world. But then I am not surprised I expected it all along, though not so soon. I thought he would wait a year at least, it is just like him. But perhaps Maria would feel relieved to have the care taken off her. I should hate to leave off my mourning if I were her. When you write give my best love to her. I have lost my gold pen it seemed like an old friend. I cant write decent with this steel one, but you must take it as it is—

I have written all I can spare time for now and must close. I think you will find this rather a dry letter, but I will try and make the next one a better one. You must give my love to all the folks and my friends generally. How does Mary Callender do. give my love to her if you ever happen to see her and Abby lewis & many more. I dont forget them though I have little time to write. Goodby—Yours very affectionately Sue

I forgot to tell you that little Allie manifests an extravagant fondness for salt cod! He is very much pleased if you give him a piece. He eats very heartily indeed of most everything, we dont give him any meat.

Susan's home remedies—thick syrupy phosphorus to treat a sore throat, brandy and salt rubdown for frostbite—were selected from an inventory of domestic health care practices available to enterprising housewives. Do-it-yourself medicine was popular not only because many communities had no physician, but also because the medical practices of professionals, which included bleeding and the use of leeches, were often frightening and unsuccessful.

Women who administered domestic medicine, sometimes known as kitchen medicine or folklore medicine, passed on their knowledge from generation to generation, from friend to neighbor. In addition, they acquired information from medicine shows, lectures, testimonials, almanacs, newspapers, and books. Self-help medical manuals, such as John Gunn's *Domestic Medicine: Poor Man's Friend*, often became best sellers. One book even explained how to amputate a limb and ventured that anyone who could not follow the easy directions was a fool.

But home remedies were not intended to take the place of a physician's expertise, only to supplement it. Susan's Humphrey Box, a "domestic kit," contained numbered medicines and a guide on how to use them. Medicine by the numbers, as it were, was central to homeopathy, a system of treating disease with minute quantities of drugs which would, if given in larger doses to a healthy person, produce symptoms similar to those of the disease. A professor at Homeopathic Medical College in Pennsylvania, Frederick Humphrey broke with prevailing practice by prescribing more than one medication at a time. He was one of more than 2500 homeopathic physicians in the United States at the outbreak of the Civil War.

When Emma suffered a cold, Susan cautioned her to take good care of herself, lest the symptoms trouble her for a long while. Then, she offered some sisterly advice of a more personal nature.

Damariscotta March 30th 1862

Dear Emma

The contents of your last letter were extremely acceptable, as is usually the case. I am sorry however that you have taken a cold because I am afraid it will hang on and trouble you. Still it may be that with care you will get wholly over it. This season is very bad for getting colds and few can escape them. (we have all got them here) I wish I did have time to write more letters to my friends—I often think of Freddie and Abby but my writing opportunities are extremely limited and I must confess that I have little disposition to write out of the home circle, because it seems a greater effort than formerly to write properly—If I should write to any one else, it would not be like yours, because I should not feel to use that freedom which I do towards our family—it would not sound as if I were talking—But I can & I am thankful, express myself to some unfettered by any restraint I regard it as a great privilege . . . I am glad that Bill has had a pleasant visit at Alfred's and that mother too had a short visit in Boston I couldn't help laughing to hear you say, it was fortunate for you that he didn't come home while mother was gone, though according to your account she only staid one night. it would seem as though he were a very formidable person to provide for. I should think now that mother might go away and stay several days as well as not. I hope you will get so smart soon that she will feel easy to but I dont suppose she would if you were ever so smart, it is very natural for a mother to assume all the care & responsibility, still if you should watch constantly, and have confidence in your own powers, you might relieve her of much of it. I wish I had done so, it would have been better for her & me too. But I was disposed even to the last, to let her decide and plan for me, I dare say I should be now if I were there, and she is still less fitted for it than formerly, for she has borne so much care both for herself and others. But there! I suppose you will think I am always a preaching, and I didn't really mean to, but sometimes things strike me so forceibly, that I think a word or so may help others over the places where I myself stumbled. I will refrain I was quite interested in your account of the visit to the Evans House. I have read about it somewhat in the papers but not so particularly. There are some elements of romance even in this war, aren't there. Still the cost of such romance is too dreadful. I wish aunt Harriet's venture might result in her getting a good partner, who knows what may happen. I dont feel much like joking about so serious a matter however—I had a couple of pamphlets from the Sanitary Commission last week soliciting funds from the Ladies of D we have about $10 on hand which we have been reserving for a fitting occasion, we shall probably send to that object this week. I hope Gus Smart will find Williams body though of course it would be little comfort except to know that he was buried at home. How dreadful such a search must be.

I am very much obliged to you for the information you gave me about the parties I enquired for. I try to keep track of the Cambridge folks all I can. Your opinion of George Clapp is certainly very flattering. How is the brown & white dog? I haven't heard much of him lately—If you should get a beau, I never should know it in the world unless you told me, and I am afraid you wouldn't. I shouldn't wonder if Mary's lover should come here before long. He is visiting in this state and may take it on his way home. I should like to have him very well because then he might be content to let her stay here, and he is all the time at her now to come home, but she says she shant do any such thing. She means to stay all summer but sometimes I am afraid he will prevail upon her to leave. It would be better for her and her folks, and me, for her to stay and she knows it. W.H. wants her to stay here till she gets married he says he will do well by her. She is improving wonderfully. She can get any meal alone, and this week she made cookies and biscuits for me, and washed the floor with a mop twice. But I have to watch or she will do too much and make herself sick. She is not very strong but is better than when she came. A young friend of Nelly Philbrick invited her and Mary out to sleigh ride this week, but the going was so bad the stable keeper would not let his horse go out, so they had to give it up. Last Tuesday we all went down to Alfred Jones Father's farm. His brother Daniel Jones has charge of it we had a nice time. Mary and Allie went to the barn to see the "lammies". There was a turkey there and Allie was dreadfully scared at it. Mrs. Daniel Jones has a dear little baby 3 months old. The old gentleman is quite intelligent. He served in the 1812 War. He is over 80 years old. He has a great many valuable geological specimens. I forgot to say that Alfred has come back again. He is going to open a store in Mystic, Conn, in about a month. I had half a mind to tell him to call on you, but thought it might look too much like fishing. We all took an awful cold coming home (except Allie his was slight) Mary and I have had grand snuffing sneesing and barking matches ever since, but I think we are better today. W.H. was so hoarse he

(1862)

could hardly preach but he had to all day. He exchanged with the Methodist minister this P.M. Allie's "comforter" troubled him again this week, another large swelling appeared, which had some communication with the first one, which again gathered and broke, making him suffer considerably, one or two days we had to hold him most of the time. It is still open, but the worst is about over. he has had a slight bowel complaint today I think he ate something that hurt him. He has cut both stomach teeth through. He has got 16 teeth now. I think he has got along nicely. Little Allie is very cunning indeed. He says Cock a doodle doo very plain and cut cut da cut. If you ask him where he got his teeth he will say papa, or mama gave them to him. he says "yes mama" when I ask if he is my good little boy. Mary and I went down street shopping yesterday. We bought Allie two little every day dresses. I will send you a piece of each, the blue was 20, the other 12½. I got him a grey flannel skirt besides, also some curtains for the windows white cotton ⅞. 10 cts y/d. I guess you will think that I was flush, but I got a wedding fee this week 3.00, I hoped for 5 but they are not very well off, and I suppose t'was all they could afford. The fellow was about 20 & the girl 18. He is going to California soon. W.H. was quite amused at the wedding. I did not have any invitation. The bride wore a blue thibet with brown spots, drapery sleeves and puff lace undersleeves (tremendous ones he said) hair curled with no ornament, white gloves etc. After the ceremony, the cake was passed round without any plates. She went to work very deliberately pulled off her gloves in the most unconcerned manner. W.H. said she seemed to regard it as quite an every day affair, in other words "took it easy". She has no mother, brother or sister and has kept house for her father about a year. Now she has taken in a husband—I believe however she is a good hearted girl if not quite so refined. —She is a member of this church I believe. She didnt send any cake, I doubt if she knew the custom—Today she appeared out in her usual rig, except white gloves and a lemon colored silk bonnet with yellow & white roses outside and white strings. W.H. says it was the worst bonnet he ever saw, so you can judge for he hardly ever notices anything. I forgot to ask if the loss of your cat had been made up yet. I did not feel as much sympathy in your bereavement as I ought, I suppose. They are poisoning cats this way. I wish they would try a few of the dogs. there are about six in this street that ought to die—I liked mothers dress very much indeed but forgot to mention it before. I send a dollar bill in this (I only spent 2 yesterday) and I would like some time when convenient to have mother get for me a couple of pretty good bosoms (such as used to be a shilling I suppose they are more now) at Kinniworths. Then I want her to take out what she paid for your white stockings that I brought here by mistake. I have needed and worn them this winter, if any money is left, I would like a handkerchief for W.H. small size, not extra nice he is all out, his are either worn out or lost. That pretty one that mother gave him has disappeared in some mysterious manner. I dont know where. I shall send more money as soon as W.H. gets any, which I dont know when will be. I want some things which I cannot well get here. Mary will send for her things by & bye, but tell mother not to trouble herself, get them when it comes in her way—I cut an advertisement from the paper which I thought might suit pa, but I dare say it wouldnt do any good. You might give it to mother, and let her give it to him if she thinks proper. But I must close for it is tea time. give my love to all and excuse this miserable apology for a letter. Yours very affectionately Sue.

Susan expected the ten dollars saved by the women of her church would be contributed to the Sanitary Commission. When President Lincoln issued his first call for troops in April 1861, the women of Bridgeport, Connecticut, wishing to be of service, organized a society that evolved into the United States Sanitary Commission. This government agency, unique in United States history, was entirely under the auspices of civilians. By war's end, there would be about 7000 local groups like Susan's in Damariscotta, making bandages, raising funds, sewing and knitting, preparing and packing food, training army cooks, visiting military hospitals, sending Bibles to the battlefields, and writing letters to the wounded.

Cambridge women—sometimes using their own clothing for fabric—made a total of 17,248 articles for the troops, including 1882 pocket handkerchiefs, 3664 pairs of drawers, 22 jars of pickles, and 1091 pairs of slippers.

Nevertheless, when the war was over, the Commission's final report noted that the associations had been formed "to systemize impulsive, disorderly, and uninformed sympathies and efforts of the women."

(1862)

At first, President Lincoln had been skeptical that women could substantially contribute to the war effort. After the peace, however, he said, "I have never studied the art of paying compliments to women. But I must say that, if all that had been said by orators and poets since the creation of the world in praise of women was applied to the women of America, it would not do them justice for their conduct during the war."

When Cousin Mary Sargent wrote again in the fall of 1862 though, a Northern victory seemed far from assured. Although General Ulysses S. Grant took Fort Henry and Fort Donelson, toppling the Confederate advantage in Kentucky and western Tennessee, General George B. McClellan had botched the Virginia Peninsula campaign and by the end of August, at the Second Battle of Bull Run, the South had regained almost all of Virginia.

Still, Mary's question for news about the 38th Massachusetts Regiment may not have been a request for information about the war so much as a fishing expedition for word about Emma's boyfriend, Sergeant William Henry Whitney, the man she would marry. (Sgt. Whitney was promoted to second lieutenant March 4, 1863 and, in 1865, mustered out as a captain.) It is possible, however, that at this time Emma had another beau, since the 38th, organized in the summer of '62, included three companies from Cambridge and Emma knew many of the soldiers. There were no barracks in Cambridge so, during training, the men were furloughed every evening and reported for duty every morning. When the regiment left for war, the city provided horse cars for the recruits, but, flushed with military fervor, the soldiers preferred to march.

South Western Female College
Evanstown, Ill. Sept. 6th, 62

Dear Cousin Emma

I guess you think I have forgotten you but you are mistaken. I thought as long as you were in no hurry to answer my letters I wouldn't hurry to answer yours. Here I am at boarding school at a place I expect which is too small to be put down on the map but a place which is quite famous for its schools & colleges. 1st is Garrett Biblical Institute, 2nd A Young Mans University, 3rd our <u>famous</u> college and besides these there are the public schools.

Sept. 8

I was obliged to leave my letter until today. I am writing in Study hours but I have almost learned my lessons (there's the bell) I am feeling better every day and think I would be perfectly contented if I could only hear from Alton. I have not heard from there since I left which was a week ago today. I expect Mother up in about two or three weeks. I think she will stay in chicago for the present. I do not think I shall stay here over a year for next year if I live I expect to go to Mount Holyoke with my most intimate friend Miss Lucy Blair she is so sweet I felt dreadfully to leave her. What has become of Ella Whitney why doesnt she write to me. Mary Willard is the only girl that writes to me I think she is a real nice girl she sent me her photograph about a year ago. I have never had mine taken and I guess she thinks I never am going to.

Evanstown is a very pretty place it is right on the lake shore. We go down to the lake every day pretty nearly for our walk.

Give my love to all your folks. I wish you would send me your photograph. I would like Ned's and Will's also if they are willing to send them. I expect to have some taken when I go into Chicago and then if you truly want one you shall have one. When you write to Maria tell her to tell Hattie to write to me and tell her my direction. Please write soon. Give my love to your mother and to all the rest of your family. Tell Aunt Harriet I will write her as soon as I hear from Father.

Please excuse poor writing and mistakes and believe me as

> your loving
> Cousin
> Mary
>
> Direct to
> South Western Female College
> Evanstown
> Ill.

Write me all the News and when you heard last from the 38th Mass. Regiment.

Cousin Mary's homesickness did not diminish her pride in being at a place famous for its schools. A college, like a hotel, was the mark of a community's importance. And one of the ways in which religious denominations competed was in their eagerness to found schools. As a result, the number of colleges in the country increased rapidly during this period, especially in the midwest. By 1870, Illinois had no fewer than twenty-one institutions of higher learning.

Learning was not limited to schools, however. Lectures were very popular, too. Cambridge established the Dowse lecture series, which continues to this day to present distinguished speakers. The best—like Henry David Thoreau and Samuel Clemens—enjoyed international reputations and drew huge crowds wherever they performed.

In an age of orators, Senator Charles Sumner of Boston, one of the most powerful men in the Senate, stood out for his rhetoric on peace and abolition issues. In 1856, after a Senate speech in which he uttered pejorative remarks about a colleague, South Carolina Senator Andrew P. Butler, Sumner was caned unconscious and suffered permanent injury at the hands of Butler's nephew, Representative Preston S. Brooks. On stationery with John Barbour's business letterhead, Emma's mother began a letter, which Father completed, describing the throngs at one of Sumner's lectures.

Barbour & Son
Commission Merchants and Brokers
In India merchandise
No. 1 Central Wharf

We tender our services for the purchase, sale and shipment of Linseed, Saltpeter, Gunny cloth, Gunny bags and other India produce, and assure you that all orders shall have the most prompt and careful attention. We have great facilities for the shipment of bulky articles at the very lowest rates of freight. We solicit your favors and are confident that we shall render satisfaction to those who may entrust business to our care.

Respectfully,
BARBOUR & SON

Refer to
  Lee Claflin, Esq. President Hide and Leather Bank, Boston
  Messers. Glidden & Williams, Boston
      French, Wells & Co.
      Twombly & Lamson
      Henry N. Hooper & Co.
      Webster & Co.
William Claflin, Esq.

William Hurter, Esq., Mobile
A.J. Cameron, Esq. New York

Cambridgeport Nov. 2, 1862

Dear Emma

I said I should not write you this evening, but as I finished the letter to Elizabeth sooner than I expected, I thought I would write a little, and I can't tell you how I long to know how you got there, and how the family all are, but I must wait, only think you went off without eating anything, and didnt go after all till 7 o' clock and perhaps later, after you left about 5 o' clock Julia came back, she asked if Will had been down, I told her no, after asking if she might, she went up to his room, and he was fast asleep, had slept all the afternoon, he said he thought I would call him before you left, he came down, and they both went off to R to tea, then I was alone, a few minutes after that little girl of W. Callenders came after the black kitten, you ought to have seen her, and me, get her into the basket, she struggled a little if not more, however, we got her in and I hope she has a nice home, it was quite a relief to me to get her such a good place, after that I was alone again. I went and set the table for supper, and got things ready, thinking Father would be home a little after six. I took my knitting and sat down to the window, for it was moonlight, and watched, till I was ready to give up. I almost thought he had stayed talking so long, that the boat had started with him in it, but about 7 he came, and gave the reason for the delay, so you lost the opportunity of sailing down the harbour before dark, but what fine weather you had if it was not too warm yesterday. I thought the ride would be fine, I kept myself very busy yesterday, cleaning. I cleaned all the windows in the two front chambers, and entry, inside and out, it was very warm. I made three pies, and made some hash for dinner. I took up the Chronicle and saw the (6th) company, Capt. Tylers, was to visit Cambridge, and march through the streets, where the boys lived, as many as they could, and repair to the City Hall, and partake of a collation prepared by the ladies but there was a misunderstanding and they did not get here as early as they expected, so they marched up to the hall and had there Collation, and then marched around the city Mrs. Munroe Aunt Julia Addy and myself started to see them, but we were too late to see them come out of the hall, we went home again, when we

(1862)

heard them, soon we heard them and we went to Mrs. Rollins, because they would pass by there, they did pass by but went through Pearl to Franklin, and up Franklin, to Magazine to pass by patch, we felt quite vexed that we went away, and they went right past the house. Addy wished you was here to rush around with her today I have been to meeting all day. Will preached it was cloudy in the morning at noon it was clear and warm but this afternoon the wind has got east and a fog has come up, it is dreary and cool with every appearance of a storm. I wonder if you carried your key off with you I was sorry I did not think to ask for it. Father says it seems as if I forgot most everything, the rubber boots and shoes, the supper, chamifor and I dont know what else but I think if he had seen all that was in your trunk he would not have thought I forgot most everything, but goodbye Father will finish.

Mother has no right to tell, how I scolded her about forgetting things, but as I never forget any thing myself, perhaps I have a right to scold—The members of the Dowse Lectures were not drawn and the lectures are postponed—we send you the paper of Saturday, in it you will see Oliver Webbers Marriage—This is to be a "Tin Wedding" at Di Webbers on Monday Evening at which we all are invited to bring in our "tin" but as the article has risen in consequence of the War and I have no money to spare to buy any I think I shall stay away, you know I dont very much fancy tin & wooden weddings—When a Couple live long to count half a century of wedded life, and the 50th year finds them still living upon Earth, then the Golden Wedding that brings with it loving hearts that have come into existence since the day that made them one—it may be well and is interesting—We shall expect to hear from you on Tuesday morning, the day of the Election, when we are intending to beat the traitors north, and show them that the advancing sense of propriety and intelligence will not tolerate treason here though under the mark of patriotism, at least I hope so—Sumner delivered his Speech at City Hall on Saturday Evening, the Hall was crowded at ½ past 6, an hour before commencement. Willie and Ned went. Will staid an hour, but couldn't stand it longer. Ned stuck through till half past 10 & came home highly pleased though awfully tired of standing in the crowded room, tho he was more than 3 hours in the delivery the room was as crowded at the close as in the commencement—I do not know of anything of importance to write you. Sab School was pretty well filled today. Mr. Williams enquired if I met Capt. Barstow aboard the boat. We had quite an interesting Missionary Meeting tonight. Mr. Mason called on Willie Munroe to engage in prayer. I suppose his anxious mother trembled—but he made a beautiful prayer—Mr. Williams. Farnsworth Bap. Albert Ford, Charley Nelson & others took part—I send you a Chronicle, you will see my advertisement in it. There is a chapter of Chronicles I also enclose taken from a Campaign Paper left in our yard called the Patriot.

Yours truly,
Father

In addition to the items she neglected to take to Damariscotta, Emma apparently forgot to leave her house key at home. Mother's chatty letter, crammed with news of Cambridge doings and folks, advised against mailing the key. She also attempted to smooth over the differences between Susan and W.H.

Cambridgeport Nov. 16, 1862

My dear Emma

I received your letter, with Sue's to Father, Tuesday morn. I need not say I was pleased to hear from you, and to hear that you were well, and getting along so well in the housekeeping line, I am very glad you could do so much, as to help your neighbors as well as yourselves, when they were in trouble. I am glad to hear that the sickness has abated. I hope it will become healthy there again. Martha Hancock told me today, that Miss McDonald was dead. I saw Martha the Sunday after you left, and told her that I had a few grapes, she could have for her, but she said her brother who lived out of town, was going to send for her and she thought she would be gone, but she did not go, and Martha felt bad when she heard of her death, fearing that she might have felt neglected, as she did not visit her, supposing she had gone, she is to be buried tomorrow, I think Tuesday the day I received your letter, it was so pleasant, and Will was not coming home to dinner I thought I would leave ironing, and go to Boston so I cooked some sweet potatoes, and left a stake for Father to cook, when he came home as he thought I better not stop to cook it. I went, but when he came home, he was in a hurry and did not stop to cook, but ate his potates and

(1862)

a piece of pie, and went to attend some business he was not expecting that afternoon. I spent a very pleasant day at grandmothers. Aunt Mary ann was there, and Eliza and Sarah Eliza called in, they had been shopping. Eliza bought her a thibet dress, brown, at one dollar yard, it was very nice, Aunt M. told me that Henrietta was going to board at home until spring, she did not know when she would be married, his boys are to board in the country till spring, then he intends to go to housekeeping, she said he had an elegant piannafort sent there that day. H put hers into the little room at the side of the parlor, he wanted her to use his because it injured it to lay unused, he had a man come to tune it, it has several more notes than Henrietta's. Harriet talks pretty hard about him, she says though he is a good "bread and butter sort of man" Aunt Abby thinks she is stronger, but she cant go to meeting, or any where else alone, she will work round, she says, she shall lose the use of her limbs if she dont, they had a letter from Margaret. W.H. had just got home from Fortress Munroe, where he was sick, he hopes to stay at home till after Thanksgiving, she told them some funny things about the woman that lives in the house with her, said she got mad, because her husband wouldnt give her but 25 dolls to get her a dress, and went to bed sick, and ever so much more, I couldnt help laughing Aunt Rebecca has not heard from E for a long time she feels anxious. Ellen has not heard from her husband for a long time. Aunt R. sometimes fears he has deserted her, though I would not speak of it out of the family. I hope it is not so, how many troubles there are in this life. Aunt Hildreth came down to see me yesterday afternoon, but she said uncle said it was going to snow, so she thought she would come if she could not stay long, it is very cloudy and cold, and appears as if it might snow very soon. we have been out all day, and Father has gone to the Mission school this evening. I sent your class book and the pencil I did not send any word about the collections I thought you attended to that. I should have been very lonesome last week if Father had not have been home to dinner, for Will was not home one day, he is working on the road in Boston, and part of the time in Roxbury. Father dont get home till near half past one, and sometimes near two, do you see I have long mornings, but short afternoons I have cleaned your room, and Ned's this week. I had your quilt washed, and put on, and I put the new delain quilt on Ned's bed, now I have only Wills room to clean upstairs. I go slow but I shall get through by and by, I have not done much sewing that will show, all the new work I have done is to finish that grey skrt, I told you I was going to make. I cleaned your closet, and washed three white waists, and two underwaists, and a flannel skirt, that wanted a new waist binding. I have been mending my old winter dresses, and other odd jobs. Thursday eve we went to the reunion of the high school Mrs. Munroe came over and went with me, Addie did not get a ticket, and she could not have gone if she had, for she had a dreadful sore thumb, we feared it was a fellon it pined her so, Mrs. M. advised her to go to the Doctors, and see but she said she wouldn't, yesterday I heard it was better. George W's oration was very fine it was on the times he came out very bold against the peoples party Mayor Russel sat right down front of him, he is one of that party, he was over an hour, a little, in delivering it. Miss Winnets poem was very good; it was all through about half past nine, after the people left, the association went into the small hall, to have a social chat, and transact business. Ned came home by half past ten, I asked him what kind of a time he had, he said, A terrible stupid, he didn't enjoy it much but I will try to send you the Chronicle, the report is to be in next weeks. I dont see what become of the one pa sent I hope you have got it. You ask who Oliver W. married I dont recollect the name, it was a girl in Boston, we did not know her, it was in the Chronicle we sent you, he was married at the Doctor's and now they have both gone to the war. What an awful time our Cambridge boys had, in the vessel, down the harbour in that storm wasn't it too bad, the friends have felt very bad. Mr. Rollins, and Mr Patch, went down. Mr. R. borrowed a frock and went as a butcher, as they could not admit him unless he came to bring something, like stores. I do not know how Mr. P. got in, but they are gone now. Ned says the Lady Webber married was a nurse in the Hospital, her name was Lee. Ned says tell Emma that several girls enquired after her and E. Taylor very particularly, and wished you was here.

    About your key, no I do not think it best to send it by mail. I shall get along without it. I think you accomplished a good deal last week. Sue must not worrie so much if she can help it. W.H. tries the old method of getting the baby to sleep, he thinks it the best of course, it must have seemed strange for you to stay at home all day Sunday, it was very bad here. I saw Mrs. Dr. Morse to meeting today. I didn't get opportunity to speak to her. I forgot whether I told you that Miss Abigail Hovey had a shock

(1862)

of Palsey, she has not spoken yet, more than half her person is useless, they do not expect she will live, the poor old lady takes on bitterly about it, she does not know what she shall do without her Abigail, how much it has made me think of My Mother and Aunt Abby.

Ned says to tell E. we went to Mr. Roberts Friday to sing, there was not so many there as the time before Ellen and yourself away, and W.M. Monroe was engaged to take tea and pass the evening at the house of his teacher in Chemistry, Proffeser I should say, so he was not there, they expect to meet at Colvers next time. Mrs. Crosby went up to see Mary last Thursday, I went up to carry the Almanac for her to take to Alf, she told me, that Mary had sent an invitation to her, and the family to come up and spend thanksgiving with them she said W.C. said he could not it was so much trouble to get so many of them there and then he said it would cost so much he could not afford it she was much obliged to them, but she said if they would go, they wanted our family to come too, but Father says we could not go, he could not leave, but I am at the bottom of the sheet and must close, the clock has struck ten. Goodnight dear E, tell Sue I shall write to her next. I hope to get a long letter or two this week much love to all from your loving Mother,

S.
S.
B.

With two pianofortes, Aunt Henrietta's house was somewhat unusual, but there was no denying the popularity of this instrument that was advertised as providing an orchestra in the home. After 1830, the number of European imports declined and by the mid-1850s Chickering pianos, manufactured in Boston, were the piano of choice in concert halls as well as homes. American fascination with gadgetry and tinkering produced innovations—the one-piece frame, stringing and scaling changes—that contributed to the American-made product winning gold medals in international competitions. By 1860, factories in the United States manufactured 21,000 pianos annually, enough for seventy Americans to buy one every working day.

Her mother complimented Emma for keeping busy and being helpful while at Susan's. Except for letters home, however, Emma may not have been keeping up with her correspondence for Maria had not heard from her. In this letter, dated on Emma's nineteenth birthday, Maria was dramatically aware of time passing.

Washington Nov. 20th 1862

My dear Sister—

I have quite given up ever hearing (until it comes) so I will write again. I know you have some good reason which will appear in due time. This is number three, possibly my others may not have reached you. It is now six weeks since I arrived home, I can scarcely realize it we have been so busy. Yesterday and today are the first days we have felt settled. Our house is in order and our carpets down except the dining room. I am a regular schoolmarm. School commences every day at nine o' clock when they write a half hour and the lessons follow. I wish I had a few more to make it more interesting to the children as well as myself. They feel rather lonesome—they have few mates in Wash. Most of the little girls are rude, running in the streets. I wrote in my last that I expected to visit Baltimore and would see the Cambridge volunteers but I was unable to go until it was too late. Mother wished to go with us and as we had no girl it was rather hard to get away. I was sadly disappointed, but such is life.

The celebrated "Monitor" has been here for repairs and I must tell you about it all. We knew nothing about a public exhibition and Gilbert Towles happened up at father's office and father asked him to call at the door and inform us, instead he invited us to accompany him. I was out at the time in the hospital and did not return until just before the time appointed. Mother went with Aunt Josie before the appointed time so I just decided to keep a previous engagement and deprive myself the great pleasure of seeing the "Monitor". It has happened that the gent feels any such "cut" and has discontinued his calls. I am very sorry to have offended him as I did not think of such a thing. Oh! If I only had a brother it would relieve me of a "peck" of trouble. What will I do? can you help me out or give me a little advice? Don't think I am seriously affected about the call for I am not. Emma since I last wrote I have entered the "twenties". Oh! how auld I dew feel! Today or tomorrow is your birthday. I know one is yours and the other Nellie Raymonds'. I cannot tell which. Accept the congratulations of your sister. May the new year be a garden spot in your life with those following none the less pleasant. How I would like to pat you nineteen times and give as many kisses. Have any presents been received? None in this direction. I had hoped I would receive a photograph Album but it is not for this time. I wonder if you are in Maine now. You know you spoke of it when I spent the night with you. How is Susie, and the little ones? I was sorry not to see them. I just missed it. I heard from Aunt Josie tonight she says nothing new in Cambridge. You have had an anniversary recently. Have you not? What did you do?

Grandfather and Carrie have been quite sick which called Uncle Emry home.

Emma it is rather hard to write with nothing to start upon—no news—and I hope you will excuse this apology—I wanted to write you something if it wasn't so smart. My throat feels so badly I shall have to stop. It is nothing serious I think.

Tell your father that we have been made acquainted with Hon. H.K. Whittaker we like him very much. He calls frequently. Mr. and Mrs. Paine are here now.

My love to all.

Your loving sister
Maria

I have not written half I suppose which I wished to say but next time. Thursday eve. As it has rained very hard all day I could not get your letter to the office. I received your splendid letter and I felt a hundred times happier for I was a little anxious. What a jolly time you had going down Would I like to have been with you. I will write more soon. Please send a piece of your dress material.

[On the envelope flap] Kiss the baby for me: write oftener to Maria. Glad the other man isn't in office he discredits it.

Like Emma, Maria was a Sunday School teacher, but she also took on the duties of schoolteacher. Her life was indeed hectic, especially since at this time the Morse family was busy moving into a new home. For the next several years, Maria, her two sisters, her stepmother and father resided at 350 New York Avenue, Washington, D.C.

Maria's experiences, with Gilbert Towles and as a schoolmarm, point out just how separate men's and women's spheres were in mid-nineteenth century America. Since colonial times, some widows had operated dame schools in their homes, but not until Americans began to settle the West and the Civil War created teacher shortages was public school teaching an acceptable occupation for single women. Then, because men were not available, attitudes changed. Teaching, like nursing, came to be considered an extension of woman's instinct to nurture, and single women were hired at 30 to 50 percent of the salary of men teachers. Within a few decades, an educational heirarchy developed. Men filled most administrative posts; women taught in most classrooms. Once the public perceived teaching as a woman's job, moreover, the profession suffered a loss in status. Men who chose careers in education, therefore, sometimes resented women teachers.

As schoolmarm, Maria was responsible for teaching her students proper standards of behavior, which perpetuated society's segregation by sex. In the preceding letter, she commented that little girls who ran in the street were rude. Little girls were expected to be little ladies. In contrast to mill girls and new immigrants, a middle-class lady was the era's ideal of femininity—woman as status symbol. She pursued handicrafts and cultural activities, spent substantial leisure time shopping, and observed a strict code of etiquette.

Maria feared she had breached the code of etiquette when she refused an invitation to visit the Monitor, the North's first ironclad warship. On its maiden voyage in March, 1862, the Monitor accredited itself in combat by defeating the South's ironclad, Merrimac. The confrontation between iron battleships, both steam-powered, revolutionized naval warfare. Afterwards, rather than risk its falling into Union hands the Confederacy sank the Merrimac. The Monitor continued to perform heroically. By providing cover during the spring and summer for General George McClellan on the Virginia peninsula, it saved the Army of the Potomac. When the Monitor came into port for repairs, the public was invited to visit the celebrated naval wonder.

Maria wanted to go, and Gilbert Towles, a Washington patent agent and draftsman, offered to escort her. But she had a previous engagement. Misinterpreting her refusal, he was offended. Maria lamented ever being able to understand men without the guidance of a brother and asked Emma for the benefit of her experience. Emma complied, apparently sharing her own disillusionment, too.

(1862)

Washington
Dec. 8th, 1862

Dear Sister Emma

    I received your long and welcome letter but have not had time to answer it until now—I am afraid this will not compare in length with its companions but I know you will excuse all when I tell you the "whys" & "wherefores" What a glorious letter yours was and how much news it contained! Your accounts were exceedingly interesting. I would like to have been with you several times. thanks for your thoughts and feelings I can sympathize with you; how well I remember our talk about three o'clock in the attic on Auburn street. I would enjoy giving Alice a good shaking. I have altered my feelings toward her—and do not ever care to receive a letter from such a girl—I think her very mean and sincerely hope she in turn may lose the day <u>if</u> she has gained it, which I very much doubt—I rather <u>guess</u> someone is trying your jealousy? Let me encourage you and beg of you not to <u>pine</u> under such misfortunes. I have been through similar scenes and have learned to give and bear it with all patience scrapeable—Now I am afraid you will say, "I never will tell Maria another thing for she does not feel for me but jokes?—I have been treated just the same way and know its beneficial affects—I am hard hearted now and have come to the wise conclusion that young men are a perfect nuisance sometimes and torment the lives of poor girls almost out of them—I don't know but that it is wrong but I have made up my mind to return <u>tit</u> for <u>tat</u>—That Alfred Jones must have been very interesting <u>but</u> I hope you did not lose your heart for when you come to Washington you may wish you had it again—There are <u>lots</u> of the same kind only a little <u>kinder</u>

    You must excuse me also as your subjects were so promiscuous that mine cannot be otherwise if I answer and remark as I read along in your letter. I remember well Ellen H. particularly the day the Prince was in C. I was quite interested in her—It must have been a great loss for she was old enough to be appreciated by her older sisters, you will understand what I mean—Remember me kindly to Caddy and Emily—I have sad news also which has occupied my time so much. Florence has the Typhoid fever also & although not very badly as yet—but—she is very sick—I do not feel as if I could leave her any length of time, if she should be taken I should indeed feel <u>lonely</u>—She

Emma's World

wants me to do everything for her—May she be spared yet God knows best. I think she is not dangerously ill at present—but the least thing may prove fatal—

Alfred & Mary next present themselves—Fortune seems to have emptied the "horn of plenty" at their doors—I know they are happy and would wish them everything pleasant—Mr. Kunard has just called and I must stop a few minutes—he has gone and Minna has snatched my letter for fun (as you will perceive by the finger marks) and tried to bother me by making believe read—I think your present was beautiful and very appropriate—How the presents showered—I shall be very much obliged for that cake, I am afraid I shall rob you. Your speaking of washing day recalls my many disagreeable experiences in bygone days. I do not have any such days now. I do like boarding and intend if ever I ——————— to always board unless to alter my mind—"High School Reunion" I almost cried when I saw this I had not thought of it before but how I wish I could have been there. You know the resolution passed by our class—By the way I have five prospects of a visit North next summer or before if possible—Harrah!! Poor Annie. I pity her it will disfigure her face but this is nothing if she does not care—I am glad you received attention you are selfish a little and want all, is it not so? I do not blame you a bit for staying I should have been just so wicked (that is if it is so) I am glad my friends have not forgotten me at C. —My love to all feminine & respects to such masc. as you think proper—

The knitting Bees—I know that Cummings co[mpany] have been introduced—Ellen had something for you—a new idea—Willie feels bashful and doesnt want to be bothered about you so he turns his attention for relief to another—Don't 'spair—Thank Mary Alden if you see her and tell her I intended to call did you? I am glad it so happened that we took a class together —I think of you every Sunday—My scholars are about 12 & 14 —Who are in your class—Mine Elizer Herd, Anne Walker, Elizer Shake, Susan Harmon, Addie Burke, Lizzie Tealman—So Lizzie called did you give her my directions Cor. H. 9th St. north. I should not for fun object to seeing old friends I have not seen him yet. I am sorry about Ned—He wrote father a week or two ago that he had decided to stay at home this winter so I suppose he had some prospects of business You must feel anxious about him—But breath spent in prayer is not wasted. There is a young married man here (Mr. Butts) that reminds me

(1862)

of Ned very much in every way. He is a very nice man. Mrs. B. is Florence S.S. teacher—Oh! that Alice! I dont know what to think of her—I have just read the account again—Do not fear to write me anything as no one sees them but myself.

I have been nowhere since I last wrote and have seen nothing new. Mr. Hammond just called. He looked very natural—Remember me to Ned, Alf, Will, & Sue. Write soon for I am anxious to hear—I want a continuation of our chats. Do you understand—Is Miss W—who is you know as attractive as ever? I want all the news—Hadyn McLellan sent father an orange fresh from Port Royal, it looks delicious—Min[na]. and I have great fun about George Appleby, he told George Finney that he should not dare to walk with Miss S. and I again without taking his dogs to protect him, we stuck so close that our hoops were in the way (he only said it for fun!) so M & I ask him if he ever takes fid[o] & tig[er] to walk with him—He understands the joke but says nothing—he does not know that we know. I have deferred my visit to Baltimore on account of Florence—We have received two journals from Boston—You cant know how homelike they look to us—I came pretty near going into Boston to see that Painting at Williams & Everetts when I saw the advertisement—Write all the news and changes—I do wish I could spend a night with you soon—I wonder what you all are doing —Minna & Hattie have gone to bed—father to the meeting & I writing to you—Is this letter not a puzzle—I rather think you will get some news.

Give my love to your father & mother. Ask Mr. Barbour if such a person as I can write anything to interest him—He did not ask any questions so I cannot have anything as a base—does he wish a letter?

That was a funny party—I should have thought you would have felt awkward—I thought of you on your birthday and wished I could only get at your shoulders, cheeks or ears—I dont care which—You think yourself old What think you of me? An old maid I suppose—I can sympathize with you in flesh now —I have grown out of all my dresses.

I am almost ashamed to send this but for want of time am compelled to—I know that this will be accepted however—

Your Affec. Sister—
Maria—

Maria's intention to "always board" was not unusual. Household help was expensive and people moved around a great deal during this era, so many middle-class American families preferred to live in hotels or boarding houses. Footloose fortune seekers ready to follow beckoning opportunity also found it more convenient to be unencumbered by furniture. For newlyweds, boarding provided a comfortable home without the expense of setting up housekeeping. Mary and Abraham Lincoln boarded until the birth of their first baby. Although this arrangement wasn't as popular among farmers in the South as it was in the Northeast and West, boarding contributed to the egalitarian spirit of the times by encouraging intimacy among strangers who shared meals at the same table. After a while, "American plan" came to mean hotel accommodations with meals.

Maria was sympathetic to Emma's romantic predicament, and outraged at Alice, who presumably stole Emma's boyfriend. But another friend, Albertine, joshed Emma about losing a gentleman's company.

Cambridgeport Dec. 14/62

Dearest Emma

I have just returned home from the Sabbath School Concert it was a very interesting one. Mr. Charles Nelson was there and gave an account of his trip to Fortress Monroe to see his father. He is in the same regt. that Albert is in he only saw his father about fifteen minutes he also saw Albert said he was in fine spirits and was looking nicely. He visited Hampton [Roads, Virginia] while there and he said that there was scarcely anything left but ruins.

I suppose you little expected that I would write last Sunday. I judge so by you saying in your letter that I should get it just in time to write then but I did not get it till Tuesday. I was very glad to hear from you. You seem to be enjoying your self finely. If there is not any young man in this place there seems to be I should think a plenty of unmarried ministers. I am very sorry on your account that you are to be deprived of that gentleman's company that started for England a short time since. If he is thirty three or four he isn't too old for you. I think you ought to have given me his name. I wonder if he ever expects to find his better half. Have you had a letter from Ellen Ricker since she has been gone?

Mrs. Emory Morse is going back to the hospital some time

(1862)

this week she is very much interested there. I think she must be an excellent one among the sick soldiers, she seems so pleasant and has such an easy way about her.

I went to the Singing Club last Thursday evening had a very pleasant time indeed. I think it was the best one I have attended; at least, I enjoyed myself better there was quite a number there which had not been there before. I had the pleasure of a little conversation during the evening with Mr. Palmer. I had the same invitation to meet next time at Mr. Goodwin's don't know as I shall dare venture there it is rather far to go alone though I want to go very much.

Last Monday, Freddy Lewis and Mr. Cummings came in and spent the evening.

You wished to know how Hattie Wright is I guess she is doing well. I saw her Thursday evening she doesn't seem to be as intimate with Miss Palmer as she used to be. Have you attended Church today? Have they a very large Sunday School? Is Mr. Evans connected with it in any way? We commenced today on the 24 Chapter of Acts

I suppose your folks will tell you about the sermon today, for I saw Ned. this afternoon and he said he thought some of them would write. I would like to see Allie and Eddie very much. I have never seen Eddie but once and have never seen Allie.

Martha Burrage sends her love to you. Give mine to Suse. Kiss the children from me. I have not heard from Albert for over a week and don't know anything where they are. We begin to feel a little worried. Excuse all the mistakes and write again soon. Hoping I shall soon see you home and with lots of love I remain your

true friend
"Albertine"

Albertine enclosed a small, pressed green leaf for Emma in this letter, which voiced her concern about Albert. In her next letter, she mentioned two Cambridge youths who died in battle, possibly at Marye's Heights outside of Fredericksburg, where an estimated 11,000 Northern soldiers were killed or wounded on December 13.

Boston Dec. 21st, 1862

My very dear Friend,

I received your letter Saturday morning, was very glad indeed as usual to hear from you. You will notice by this heading of this letter I am away from home. I came over here after the afternoon services to attend a Sabbath School Concert to the Baldwin Place Church cousin Annie wished me to come very much. It has been a bitter cold day, though I think I have been paid for coming over. They had a very interesting concert indeed they are much better carried on than ours; the children take part, there was eight little girls that spoke and they done well I assure you. Mr. Dexter of Boston also addressed the school. The Pastor made some remarks, closing with some also from the superintendant. The singing is not I think quite equal to our school though very good.

At home Mr. Mason preached for us in the morning from 2 Chronicles P2.5 In the afternoon a stranger, I think his name was Mr. Howes preached for us from Psalms 37-3 it was a very good sermon indeed. This afternoon was the anniversary of the Mission School on Harvard Street.

I think you must have enjoyed your sleigh ride very much wish I was lucky enough to get one. I dont understand what you mean about my speaking in a very formal way in regard to Mr. Cumming's explain yourself. He was to meeting all day with Abby to day he hasn't been here to meeting in the day times before for a long time.

I am glad you thought so much of that Geranium leaf—perhaps you would like to know where I got it in the first place. The day the 38th left Boston (which day I trust I never shall forget) while Mary and I were talking with Albert in the street in front of the depot—A soldier which was near by had a boquet it had begun to wither so he threw it to Mary I believe and when we got home I found this Geranium plant in it so I took it & planted it and it is going nicely. I think a good deal of it. I suppose you would like to know what kind of a time I had at Mr. Goodwin's last Thursday. I had a very pleasant time indeed. I went down in company with Miss Palmer and her Brother (Ham) not caring to go down alone, besides I did not know where they lived, but I did not come home with them I suppose you can guess who it was—if you can't I shant tell you. Alice Hancock was there with a young gent which seemed to be quite attentive to her. He was a stranger to me. Mr. G. nor Ellen does not attend them, we merely had an invitation there. We are to meet next time at Mr. Noye's.

Give lots of love to Sue. I would like to come and see her very much also you dear Emma I dont think I can get a vacation so as to come this week.

Belcher Hancock also Mrs. Hawkes has had a son killed in this last battle. We have not heard anything from Albert yet. You must excuse the writing of this for I have had to write as fast as I could in order to get through before Annie for she is doing the same as I am (the rest of the folks are to bed) for she is a much faster writer than I am, she has just finished hers. I shall expect an answer Saturday, with much love and wishing you a Merry Christmas I remain your true friend Albertine.

P.S. I am half dead with a cold which I have had ever since Thanksgiving. I had lots more to write but have not time now. A.T. [Albertine Tarbel]

Geranium plants, such as the one the soldier tossed, had long been popular in America. Originally from Holland, the cultivated species was known in England as early as 1690, and it is likely an early colonist carried the first plant with her to the New World. By the time Emma was born, hundreds of varieties were grown in the United States, most, if not all, imported from Europe. Sometimes called a cranesbill (geranos is the Greek word for crane) after the seedpods which resemble the beak of that bird, geraniums thrive well in ordinary garden soil and were cultivated not only for the flower, but for the root which was used as an astringent.

In passing, Albertine informed Emma that she saw Alice Hancock with an attentive young man. Emma may have wondered whether Alice's beau was Alfred Jones or the bashful Willie in the romantic triangle Maria outlined. Once, in a teasing mood, Alice had warned Emma in Damariscotta not to stay away too long because her "hadorer" suffered from her "prolonged absence."

As 1862 came to a close, many Northerners shared Albertine's concern about the war. After General McClellan's aborted effort during the spring and summer to take Richmond in the Peninsular Campaign, Union forces were defeated again in August at the Second Battle of Bull Run. In September, the Union Army had prevailed at the Battle of Antietam, but at exorbitant cost—11,500 killed or wounded Northerners; 9,000 killed or wounded Southerners. Still, on September 22 President Lincoln had used the victory to issue the preliminary Emancipation Proclamation, warning Southern states that if they did not put down their arms and rejoin the Union, he'd declare their slaves "forever free."

The North was unable to sustain its gains. Even after the President appointed General Ambrose E. Burnside as commander of the Army of the Potomac to replace General McClellan, whose forces had suffered from his excessive caution, the North continued to lose. Following Burnside's retreat December 13 at Fredricksburg, Virginia,—more than 12,000 Union soldiers were killed or wounded—the General by his own request was removed from command.

The loss of the "Monitor" on New Year's Eve capped a devastating year. On Christmas Eve the recently repaired ship was ordered to leave Hampton Roads, where it has been assigned to blockade duty. On its way to North Carolina, the first of the North's three ironclads was battered in a storm off Cape Hatteras. Around midnight on New Year's Eve, it went down with four officers and twelve men aboard.

Albertine was a keen observer and the next letter suggests that she enjoyed a little gossip. Since she may be "judging them wrongly," however, she asks Emma not to repeat the tales. Finally, she clarified the confusion over Alice's companion.

Cambridgeport Dec. 27th, 1862

Dearest Emma,

I had given up the idea once of writing you today but have since thought better of it, seeing that you was so good not to disappoint me Saturday I will not disappoint you, for I know how good it is when away to receive letters from friends at home. I think you had better be still telling that my letters are to short think yourself lucky to get as long ones as you do, for I never write very long letters without it is to Albert and then not always (I aint <u>mad</u>)

I am glad to hear that you got a letter from Maria last week if you have not answered it when you write give my love to her, tell her I have not forgotten her if she has me.

Have you attended Church today? I have been all day and intend to go out this evening. Mr. Mason preached for us in the morning. He finished the last of his resurrection sermons he was very good. This afternoon we had Rev. Mr. Childs from Boston he was begging in behalf of the American Tract Society to help send off more tracts and books to the army. He told several instances of how much good they had done among the soldiers. He was very interesting indeed.

Mr. and Mrs. Hastings (formerly Carrie Rice) was to our Church this morning they are on here making a visit. I think things look strange for Mrs. Rice told me a short time since they were intending to spend the winter at Ohio. I also understood that he had sold his house in Boston. I dont know but I am judging them wrongly dont say anything about it from me. Going to meeting now—Here tis ten o'clock and I have just commenced writing again. I have had company and they have just gone so that is the reason I was hindered. I heard that it was a cousin that was with Alice the other night. I did not attend the last Sing for it was a very unpleasant evening & dreadful muddy and having a severe cold thought upon the whole I had better stay at home. Thought they might possibly get along one night without my assistance. I heard that there was only a very few there. It is to meet New Year's night at Mr. Robert's hope after that one I shall see you to the next. I am glad Emma to see by your last letter some signs of your coming home. I think you have made a good long visit. When you get home I hope I can have the pleasure of your company to the Sings then I shall not have to go with Mr. and Miss P. (They are very agreeable) You dont know how you offended me. I went over to Freddie's a few minutes today she sent her love to you, said she thought of you Friday afternoon; also said she hoped you would get lots of presents New Year's I do the same if you get so many that you dont know what to do with them you may will them to me. Tell Sue Abby said she had not forgotten her Prentice was to meeting this evening. We had a very interesting meeting this evening more so than we have had for some time. I did ride on the horse car last Sunday. It was to cold to walk it isn't the first time that I have done such a thing and perhaps it will not be the last. I did not have a pile of presents Christmas all I had was simply a bottle of hair oils which stuff I believe you do not use, but to me it was very acceptable I read to a piece in last night's paper about Bank's expedition Albert's Steamer headed the list of the steamers that was with him so it is the first time we have felt sure they were with Bank's though we supposed they were. The paper states that they are bound for Ship island I dont doubt but what you are interested in that regt. I believe there is an Orderly Sargeant in it so of course there is a great attraction there. Remember me to Mr. Evans & Sue. It is getting late & I must close (write soon). Wishing all a Happy New Year.

Albertine

(Excuse all mistakes)

For almost a month, soldiers of the 38th Regiment remained aboard the *Baltic* at Hampton Roads, Virginia, going on shore only occasionally to drill and to practice target-shooting. The ship was so crowded that one passenger later recalled, "It required skill in gymnastics to go from the bunk to the deck without coming in contact with some animate or inanimate body."

All the same, horses were brought aboard, adding to the confusion and precipitating rumors about where the steamship might be bound. The *Cambridge Chronicle* reported that the expedition, led by Major-General Nathaniel P. Banks, was headed towards South Carolina, the heart of the rebellion. But on December 4, the *Baltic* joined a flotilla steaming out of the harbour and, although it headed South, New Orleans was the destination. The *Baltic* drew too much water to cross the sand bar off the mouth of the Mississippi River, however, and had to stop at Ships Island in the Gulf of Mexico, "much to the disgust of the regiment who had conceived a strong dislike against the place," according to Corporal George Powers.

Powers, who wrote a history of the regiment, wistfully described Christmas on the island, which was "dotted with canvas villages." He remembered, "Santa Claus did not make his appearance. The jolly old saint, in his fur cap, would have been sadly out of place in that sunny clime. One poor fellow, in a fit of absent-mindedness, hung up his stocking in his tent, but indignantly rejected the idea that the army pastry found there was from the old friend of his boyhood."

The Mississippi River was a crucial military objective. With Naval support, Grant had attempted several direct assaults on Vicksburg, a key city, at one point even trying to dig a canal to divert the Father of Waters, before the city fell. The Louisiana campaign, in which many Cambridge men were wounded and died, secured the river and split the territory of the Confederacy in two. Major-General Banks was honored by a grateful Congress for the "skill, courage, and endurance which compelled the surrender of Port Hudson, Louisiana, and thus removed the last obstruction for the North to the free navigation of the Mississippi River."

8
(1863)

*T*he Mississippi River victory buoyed Northern spirits and, as planned, on New Year's Day, 1863, the President, using wartime authority granted to the commander-in-chief of the army and navy of the United States, issued the Emancipation Proclamation.

Emma's father recognized a similarity between the end of slavery in the South and the deliverance of the Jews in the Persian Empire after Haman, the chief minister of King Ahasvirus, tried to annihilate them. The biblical story, however, appears to be fiction. Scholars have been unable to document that a king named Ahasvirus ever lived.

Long active in abolitionist causes, John Barbour had been one of twenty-three charter members who signed the preamble of Cambridge's Anti-Slavery Society in 1834. The Society lasted only one year, but he continued to be an active abolitionist. His home may have been a station in the underground railroad and, possibly, "the man waiting to be put through" in his next letter was an escaped slave.

Cambridgeport Jan 2, '63

Dear Emma

I have intended to write you before this time, but when I say to you that on the night of the 31st I wrote till very late and last night I was working to put through public documents to go to Washington, and did not get home till nearly two o' clock in the morning, and that I have been every moment engaged since the morning, and that a man is now waiting in my office to be <u>put through</u> and cannot do it without my assistance and that I <u>have to steal</u> a few moments "at home" after dinner while he is waiting. You will I know (as well as Sue) excuse me for the present —I have no complaint to make about work I am able to do it and do not feel that I work any beyond my capacity or desire, but sometimes it comes thicker and thicker than I want at the moment. I intend to write Sue and am sorry that she should have thought I could have been offended at what she said in her letter—there could have been no such thing—I wrote to her a free and unbending letter and she in reply one full of sympathy just such an one as I should expect from her warm true generous womanly sympathies. I valued it & I always shall value the emotions that prompt such thoughtful and noble sympathies that bind genial and congenial hearts together. Tho distance may continue to separate the body but I must close by saying God help Abraham Lincoln for the Proclamation of Freedom to the millions & more of slaves no longer such by law, but free to do as the Jews did in the day of Ahasvirus but I hope there will not be the need of such work though I might <u>consent</u> that certain rebels might hang on an institution as <u>high as Haman</u> did— I send you $5.00. We think you <u>had better come home</u> sometime next week, if you are ready and it is convenient to Susan to have you come. She has had you some time and has so enjoyed your company that Mother does not like to sever the connexion, but I think she now needs your assistance. She has had much to do in your absence and misses you dearly. She is quite lonesome being alone nearly all the day. I am not able to be at home so much as I expected to be. Write to me to let me know what day you will come and the Road on which. I suppose the Boston & Maine as usual but state if it is so and the day in season so that I or some one may meet you at the depot. Should you remain longer you need not consider this an imperative order, but use that judgement for which you are accountable remembering that there may be others in Cambridge besides Mrs. Mason who would be pleased to see the <u>pleasant sun light</u> of your countenance.

If I recollect a right you owe me a long letter. What do you think of it.

yours truly,
Father

Apparently, John Barbour's post as deputy collector for the Internal Revenue Service in the fourth district was a demanding one and he worked late. Also, his stationery now reads: Henry M. Wiswall, successor to A.I. Barbour & Co, 491 & 493 Main Street. Choice Groceries. Through the influence of his friends Charles Sumner and Henry Wilson, who cited his business ability, honesty and integrity, Mr. Barbour was subsequently appointed superintendent of the Internal Revenue at Boston and then supervisor for the District of Massachusetts, Rhode Island and Connecticut.

Contrary to the authoritarian, emotionally reserved, and rigid stereotype of fathers of this period, John Barbour enjoyed an affectionate and relaxed relationship with his children. He was accessible and supportive when Alfred purchased the farm and he was not offended by Susan's candor. Neither did he insist that Emma come home from Maine before she was ready.

Emma prepared to return to Cambridgeport, however, much to the delight of her family and friends. Addie Cox, a neighbor, particularly looked forward to seeing her.

Cambridgeport, Jan 6th, 1863

Dear Emma: I suppose you have got nearly tired waiting for a letter from me but I have not written to anyone for so long that I hate to commence. I thought I must try tonight if at all for I hear that you are coming back next Wednesday. <u>Wont I be glad to see you?</u> I believe I have looked out of the window most every morning when I am making the beds, and could see nothing but a closed window and curtains down too. Carrie is back so I have had her for company some of the time. She has not been here for four days.

You wanted I should write all the news. There is not much as I see except war news. Wm. Utwill has got his discharge and has arrived at his home. They did not know he was coming. Mr. Fowle has also got back. He says they will have to offer a pretty large bounty to get him to enlist again. To-day Aunt Julia & Uncle Thomas have been getting some things ready to send to Newbern to Uncle W.—

My thumb is not very strong yet so it is pretty hard work to write. It has not been quite so bad as a felon for it did not affect the bone. I do not want another like it though. Aunt J. laughed at me because I said "I would not have one ever again. There was no need of it."

You must take care of Charlie and not let him drive that fast horse so as to upset the sleigh. I wish I had a Charlie or somebody to take me to sleigh-ride. I have not had one yet but "never despair." I suppose will be a good motto as there has been no very alarming snow storm yet.

One thing more and then I guess I must bid you goodnight for I ought to write a few words to Mother and my hand is getting tired. About the kitty for we have only one and she he is nearly as large as his her mother. It is fun to see them playing together. The kitten is so fat and lazy. When she gets to playing if she jumps at the old cat she can't stand it and so gives a jump and goes over the kitten in a hurry. She is so spry and jumps up so high that it is quite laughable. I saw your puss this morning (I believe it was) on the trellis waiting for the window to be opened and wondering where Emma was gone to I expect.

Give my love to all and wish them a "Happy New Year" for me. I must now wish you the same, although the day is past, and
    remain as ever your friend,

Addie

(pray there wasnt any mistakes)

Writing the war news, Emma's friend reported that a neighbor has completed his tour of duty in the army and that it would take a "pretty large bounty" to get him to re-enlist, which reflects a changing attitude about the war. At first, the Union and Confederacy depended upon a volunteer army raised by the states. As the fighting

(1863)

continued, however, enlistments lagged. A bounty system in the North, under which men were paid for volunteering, was supposed to be an incentive to enlistments, but it led to abuses. Some soldiers deserted as soon as they received the bounty money; bounty jumpers enlisted again and again in different places under different names.

Eventually, North and South were compelled to institute a draft. In April 1862, the South had begun conscripting men between the ages of twenty and forty-five. Later, when that failed to raise the necessary troops, the range was extended to males between the ages of seventeen and fifty. Beginning in March 1863, the North drafted men between the ages of twenty and forty-five.

Both sides permitted a draftee to hire a substitute; the North also exempted a draftee on payment to the government of $300. People protested that it was "a rich man's war and a poor man's fight."

Once a sleepy country town, Washington now played host to some of the nation's most powerful, wealthy, and talented people. War policies and politics dominated many a gathering, but the capital was also a magnet for artists and writers as well as politicians, spys, and businessmen. Social gatherings brought together people of disparate backgrounds and ideas. For a well-connected young woman like Maria, it was a heady time and place. She received many exciting invitations, among them one to a novelist's salon. She accepted with trepidation.

Washington Jan. 20, 1863

My dear Emma,

I began a letter to you Jan. 9th but was able only to write by piece so I have decided not to send it but give you a whole new letter—School! School!—is the cry, my daily life may almost be embraced in the following programme; rise at seven, breakfast at half past, practise a little my singing lesson and ready to start for school at half past eight. Direct the youths how to behave and hear the lessons until twelve, then from twenty minutes to half an hour, hear missed lessons and eat lunch, chat with the boys until one o cl, then proceed as before until three; prepare for dinner and sometimes attend receptions or receive company in the evening. I have made several new friends and acquaintances this winter and am enjoying myself quite well most of the time. I do get very low spirited often on account of my poor health have a good cry and feel more resigned. If it is the means of leading me to have more faith and trust in God, I ought to be happy, but I am deprived of many privileges; going to church troubles me more than any thing else. When I see all starting for the evening meeting I cannot but feel badly still I am so much better off than many around me I will not murmur. I sometimes wish I had remained North under that Dr's care even against Uncle's advice. I believe he could have helped me—I am not as well as I was there. I am thinking strongly of consulting a physician here, have not as yet but have tried water treatment at home. —Sometimes I am afraid I must give up my school, but am waiting to get the advice of the Dr. But enough of this. I knew you would be anxious to know or I should have said nothing.

I have not attended any of the public receptions yet but went once to Mrs. Southworth's the writer, who has a lovely little cottage in Georgetown—she spends her time from Monday morning until Friday eve in writing and upon that eve receives all her friends who feel inclined to visit her. Mr. and Mrs. Delano friends of ours are very intimately acquainted with her and invited us to go with them. She has a fine library and a nice collection of engravings—I was happily disappointed in her personal appearance. she is very modest and unassuming we were highly favored in hearing her read a piece, it was called "The Maniac" I believe, and one would have thought there was the reality before him had he not known to the contrary—she recites beautifully. I hesitated attending the soiries of a novelist but she seems so pure and simple, I am not sorry now. She was very cordial & invited us to come again—We were going this evening but our friends were unwell & unable to go. Twice a week Ronie Hattie and I take a singing lesson of Mr. Townsend who used to live in Cambridge or Boston. My voice is quite weak but he says I can sing sufficiently loud for the parlor. I have taken so that I may know how to use my throat in teaching the boys—I found I made my throat sore trying to lead them and find it very beneficial both in talking and singing. Mr. Pierpont is a most interesting member of our family, he is constantly amusing and instructing us—he is very aged his eightieth birthday being next March—but still he retains all his faculties. Oh! What a list of things I have to tell you of! I will begin at the beginning. Thanksgiving was not celebrated here as in old Mass—the walk was so long to our church that I went with Mrs. Pierpont to the Episcopal, it was so new to me to see the services. I did not receive much benefit but have learned

(1863)

one lesson, not to go again. In the evening we all gathered in the Parlor and I will introduce you to the company—Channing Whitaker, Miss Barbour. He (private) is the son of Hon E.R. and one of the most consciencious and pure minded young men I ever met, he is twenty-one and rather young appearing, having been in the army about two years and not having seen much of the world or rather society—None better, however, and time will prove it—Mr. Nichols—a widower of (58) very delicate in health, dyspeptic, but very intelligent he is so quiet and unobtrusive that you will hardly know he is in the room usually—Mrs. Pierpont, whom you already know, aunt Josie, Cousin Ronie, Mr. Fletcher, a young man from Boston who knows every body—he was one of the librarians in the Athenaeum Boston—a great talker by the way very off-hand in his remarks—You have the company now. We played several games & among them "Simon says up, down," with forfeits—I do not remember playing the last named since I was at your party—do you remember? Great fun we had just like little children, it was rather a young amusement but Mrs. P. made everything so comical & we were all home folks so we enjoyed it, the kissing was not practised, except 1 or 2 but all the other little forfeits—Christmas we spent quietly—until evening. Mr. Whitaker has always spoken whenever a present was given, of a sugar whistle—he seems to have always wanted one from a youth and never was fortunate enough to receive it—We all determined he should have his wishes gratified once and Mother and Ronie went out to find some they could scarcely pucker their mouths to ask but when the question was put a broad grin followed from behind the counter—they could find them in only one place and eight were bought in the evening and a procession formed and we marched in tooting and presenting the whistles—He seemed perfectly overcome and was unable to respond to the call—We had a pleasant time but the company separated early on account of Mrs. Whitaker. She will not live probably until Spring—she has consumption and is entirely diseased. She does not think she is dangerously sick but is planning for years and expects when spring opens she shall be strong again. It is very sad to be with her—My vacation passed away almost before I had fully realized it had begun I had made plans for sewing finished and letters sent off in many directions but one solitary article received its finishing touch—I was not well and idled away my times—

Emma's World

New Years! the day of all the year for the young ladies generally. I dreaded it considerably but passed a very pleasant day—had quite a number of callers—furnished cakes lemonade etc. In the evening Mr. P. invited us to his room and he read his poem on "Fashion" to me—it occupied over an hour excellent of course—Then all went to the Fair held by our church in Odd Fellows Hall. In connection with this five or six Tableaux were given every other evening the first week and every evening the second. Hattie took part in many and I in one—. Faith Hope & Charity—I was Faith dressed in white with a large silvered cross in my hand resting on the floor and my eyes trying to look the gaslight out of countenance—The Tableaux are to be repeated in March—Our church realized a little over a thousand dollars.

The walls of the new church are about one third raised it will be the finest in the city.

Several evenings we have spent with the Delanos and enjoyed them very much—the two sisters are fine singers—

Emma, I do wish you would write me oftener you must have time—I am thirsting for a letter or do you go upon this principle "every line of mine is worth one of yours?" Father has had two business letters from Willie Whitney he does not get strong as fast as he could desire—You have seen him undoubtedly—Tell me all about him and remember me to him.

I wish you could see Hattie now she has grown and improved so much—Florence had a photograph which is quite good—private she has a beau I don't like the word gent. don't I feel old—time I was hurrying up by the way I have been having two quite solemn times lately—one of my friends whom I respect very highly has gone a little farther and I have disappointed him—I feel so strangely yet I cannot engage myself in my state of health and will not until I am well, unless I can't help it—I have told no one except Mother, there will be no harm in telling you if you keep quiet. I don't like to have everything of this kind known except to Emma and she is part of me and I believe there was a covenant between us—Here it is half past ten and I must be off to my room—I retire at nine usually but this is a special occasion. You must write me soon—With much love always your friend

Maria

I have waited sometime before writing you in hopes I should have some decent photographs—but they are too ridiculous. I

(1863)

see Frank Gardner every Sunday he calls quite often—We have good times talking over school days—Do you know Miss Rice's address—I promised to write but am not quite sure where to direct. Give my love to your Father and Mother, my reg. to all the others. I am waiting for that promised photograph.

Although poor health was considered ladylike, Maria hoped that her health would improve with "water treatment." Hydrotherapy, as set forth in *Letters to Women on Anatomy and Physiology for Women,* written in 1845 by Mary Sargent Nichols Gove, held "there is an electricity or force in water which unites with the heat of the human system . . . and that all curable diseases may be cured with water." Mrs. Gove wrote, "God is in the water."

She advised against many routine practices: "purgatives to stimulate the bilary secretions and disgorge the liver; leeches to the anus to load the nescenteris veins; moxas and issues to the right side of the abdomen to displace the irritation; venesection to lower the inflammatory state, and many similar agents: as well as the excessive use of butter, fat and oil." She was against bloodletting, too, because all blood in a sick person's body was bad and, since not all the blood can be removed, she said it made no sense to bleed the patient.

Mrs. Gove attributed disease to "the artificial and enervating habits of society, the dissipation of fashionable life, and the destroying labor of the industrious portion of the community, [which] have brought many difficulties upon women which are comprehended under the term 'female weaknesses.'" The once sickly author credited her improved health to water treatment and wrote, "Let the sick, then, look over the catalogue of their sins; for every violation of the laws of health is sin, and comes back upon us with its penalty of pain."

She continued. The remedial treatment, by means of water, should be "first a thorough cleansing of the external surface . . . cold water should always be poured over the whole surface, or the cold sponge or plunge bath used directly on coming out of the vapor bath . . . followed by vaginal syringe to be used with as much friction as possible and at least a pint of cold water, as often as three times a day, more if any uneasy sensation is felt in affected parts . . . sitz baths three times a day," 20 or 30 minutes or longer each time. "A lady can sew or read in the sitz bath and thus lose no time." In addition, she recommended wet sheets, plunge baths and douche for painful menstruation, and wet bandages about the abdomen for white people with "bound boweles." Water therapy was so popular that some women frequented "water-cure houses" for treatment.

Apparently, Maria was well enough to socialize, enjoying her visit to the salon of writer Emma Dorothy Eliza Nevitte Southworth (1810–1890), better known as E.D.E.N. Southworth. Although Mrs. Southworth did not belong to any feminist group, she introduced into literature the democratic ideal of the unprotected woman, who with no guardian, father, or husband to care for her, successfully rescues herself from difficult circumstances. The most popular and some say the best writer among America's mid-nineteenth-century sentimental women novelists—Hawthorne's "scribbling women"—she influenced literary men, most notably Henry James.

Like Maria, Mrs. Southworth had been a schoolteacher. In 1850, a year after her marriage, she and her husband went west to Prairie du Chien, Wisconsin, where she taught school until the birth of their son. Four years later, when she was pregnant with their second child, her husband deserted her. She returned to Washington, D.C., where she had been born, and resumed teaching in the public schools. A close friend of Harriet Beecher Stowe, Mrs. Southworth turned to writing when her schoolteacher's salary, $250 a year, proved inadequate to support herself and her children. She published her first story in 1846 and the first of more than thirty novels in 1849. All of her novels sold at least one hundred thousand copies and four sold more than a million. Eventually, her earnings soared to $10,000 a year and, in 1859, she purchased the house in Georgetown. She never remarried.

Mr. Pierpont, whose poetry Maria admired, was an ordained minister with many talents. An enthusiastic traveler, he had toured throughout Europe and the Middle East. When he died at age 91, he held a clerkship in the treasury department. His obituary in the *New York Times* noted that "Mr. Pierpont was a thorough scholar, a graceful and facile speaker, a poet of rare power and pathos, . . . advocate of the temperance and anti-slavery movements and a man whose convictions, purposes and impulses were all upon the side of truth and progress. His strong desire for securing advancement and reform may have led him sometimes into injudicious steps, and diminished his influence for the causes he sought to advance, but the heart was always right and temperance, freedom and Christianity had no firmer and more consistent friend or advocate. He leaves an enviable reputation as a poet and his pathetic "Passing Away" will live as long as our language is spoken or written." He is buried in

(1863)

Mount Auburn Cemetery, Cambridge, where an impressive marble monument is etched with a roster of his achievements.

Maria's busy social life left little time for letter writing. Her next note to Emma was a running commentary, compiled over almost a month.

Washington Feb. 5th, 1863

Very dear Sister—

I received your letter tonight and it did my heart good—You would feel pleased to have seen me when Father called "Miss H.M. Morse"—I knew whence it was and such a long, finely written, "Newsy" letter thanks. I have been thinking that I would write you again without waiting for an answer, but yours came before I had time. You are having a pleasant time this winter—I judge from what you write, but rather lonesome without those dear friends who are away in Rebeldom. (I dont know when I shall get time to finish this, what I have written is in a room with a dozen persons laughing and talking) Goodnight Ma Chere) February 18th—What a long interval but no time until now—We have been busy making a carpet and have had company most every evening—I feel so out of sorts tonight that I rather question whether it is best to proceed or not. I know though that converse with you will soon cheer me—You are there at home and had a pleasant visit at Susie's—how grand you must feel with two little nephews—Ahem! I would like to see them—I never heard of a "donation party" before your description was quite interesting—Your journey home was not as interesting as to Maine? if I remember correctly—Albertine you said was at your house to welcome you home—I remember well something you told me when I spent those nights with you— Has this anything to do with it???? Well I did think the pole seemed a little stiff—perhaps when I lived there the fault rested in myself—I used to be quite bashful you know (but all say now that I am recovered I dont believe they would say so if they could see within) The people here are certainly very cordial— Last night for the first time since I came from the North I went to a party. I really felt awkward. I have kept at home so much of late and only associated with those so much older than myself— I was quite surprised to find how old maidish I had become. Now dont laugh but I have certain thoughts upon this subject— Dont say one word—Those "sings" must be pleasant I would

Emma's World

like very much to form one of the company now and then. — Your present was much like mine—It is this form. Oh dear I cant do anything the clasps extend nearly to the back of the book with a buckle on the front—it contains fifty. I have it nearly filled—I will give the names of each—Mr. Whitaker—Brig. Gen Mays (Father's department at the head) Emma's Ellie Appleby—George Appleby—George Ellis (Mother's cousin & my new one) Hattie Allen—Uncle Emery and Aunt Josie—Charlie Ellis (Brother to George) Mrs. Rutman (of Worcester [Massachusetts]) N(don't tell) Sammie Allen—Clarke Wilson (of Boston) who died bout three weeks ago) William Barbour—Lucretia and Henry Carlton (Concord, N.H.) Col. Sibly—Aunt Harriette—Mr. Henry Barnes (formerly of Wash. now at Detroit)—Cousin Frank & Ellen—Mrs. Bankard & sister of Baltimore—Cousin Ranie & George Hobbs of Weston—several more promised—I should think you would like Az's—Oh if I could only peep at those letters ———

Tuesday

One more trial and I believe I shall finish this letter I am ashamed to send it, but have not time to rewrite it. I have been very unwell for a fortnight past yesterday and today I have been abed. (a dysentery but I have taken something which I feel will check it if it has not) The weather is so rainy and the mud so thick that I believe it was caused by this. We have had company besides our boarders and tonight three from Boston are coming to spend a week so I shall have not time (only to read letters) I am the only one in the house except the girl—It is the last day of Congress and all have gone— . . . ? I couldn't When they started it was very pleasant now it snows, rains and hails—I imagine them getting a good drenching unless it stops before three o'clock—I have heard T. Mason Jones in "Garibaldi" and "Curran and his Canteen friends'"

I was never so well pleased with any speaker he is an orator —Have you heard him? He has been to Cambridge I assume. Mr. Whittaker [undecipherable] says standing bear it [undecipherable]ish any company—He is very kind—Tonight there is to be a sewing circle in our society for the first time. I am appointed one of the managers. (I think it will be mismanaged —I shall try though and learn how) If it is possible I shall go as it is only four doors from our house and let sickness go if my Pa

(1863)

will allow, which is rather doubtful. We all like the new minister very much. He is just the right one we think. I want to attend all the meetings and do what I can toward building up the Sabbath School. Last Sunday evening we had a S.S. concert—Mr. Howlett preached a little sermon to them. Mr. and Mrs. Williams are here, now—I only have seen Mr. W. I can get out so little that I fear I couldnt see his wife—

The gentleman (Mr. Conant) who boards with us gave Hattie, Florence, and I questions to solve according to our different capacity—Today mine is "if there was a corresponding river in Africa in the same latitude to that of the Amazon in S. America which would be the warmest" I have not decided yet—Is it not a puzzler and to give the reasons why? Our evenings are very profitably spent usually. all the ladies folks sewing and the gentlemen & all carrying on the conversations—I am reviewing my French & Latin and trying hard to read what little I can. Such a host of sewing I have on hand—Two dresses which almost set me crazy every time I think of them. I have stolen this time from them—Hattie & I study every day—I wish you could see us —now she grows very pretty—Her hair coils lightly all over her head—she is much taller than when North and is together changed—quite companionable but I must begin to look out for myself I shall begin to dance in the brass hotel . . .

They are breaking up the church hospital here now—Mother has a cousin here sick and he does not know where he will be sent next. It is a most doleful feeling—How thankful I am that I have your photograph it is a great blessing—I look at it almost if not quite every day. Father and Mother are going to have one, have theirs taken very soon. I have had no new ones but am looking forward to the time when I am to stand before the camera's mouth with such a sweet expression as if I wasn't afraid— it snows very fast and each flake is as large as quarters used to be so near as I can recollect. I believe they increase—I would send you one but am afraid the mail would not carry it. (It just lightened and thundered who ever heard of such a thing, when it snowed.) The Divere girls from Baltimore are here now making a visit—it seems very much like old times—Last night the President and Mrs. Lincoln held a levee. I could not go but have heard that there was a great crowd, and much dress and show. How foolish and wicked in these times! I am ashamed of our American women. Mother and I have received a call from Mrs. Geo. Bontwell and daughter—they are very nice people—not such as I have mentioned but good & sensible—I do wish you could be here again I would enjoy myself so much better—You would laugh if you could put an ear in the door—ever since I have been writing this page Mrs. Conant (who is an endless talker) has been giving me an account of her trip—I never saw her equal every little fancy & thought that passes through her mind finds vent. she is one of the best of ladies though.

 Still later   When I finished this last I took a notion to go down stairs to get rid of what I mentioned and then found something which must be attended to. Our company have come —five—and we are very busy—They are gone to Fort Albany today to see a brother whose little girl they brought on for a surprise—He has not seen her for a year and a half—I only wish I could see the meeting—Here I am determined to finish now— my room is waiting to be swept—my broom beside me etc. —I expect if Mother should come up the stairs she would give me some advice about doing my work first but never mind for this time. Yesterday we went all over to the Capitol from top to bottom with Mr. Curtis as our guide. I saw many new things—Mrs. Bottomworth brought us some very handsome presents. Mother an elegant bronze inkstand—Father a rosewood writing desk— green velvet lining Florence a workbox black walnut with crimson lining Me a willow work basket varnished & lined with red kid and all furnished with whatever I might want.

 I must close now as I hear someone coming and will try and write again soon from, Your loving sister—Maria Do write as soon as you can. I am ashamed of my waiting so long but it could not well be helped—busy. Give my love to all who may enquire—Tell me about all the girls I know. Where are Annie & Lizzie. Carrie & Sarah Fisher—Sarah Pearson & Connie N. — Have you seen Miss Rice? Whose photographs have you? How is Orlando? Salubrious? Will you write soon? Do you feel very old? Almost twenty one Oh . . . . .

While Emma was in Maine, she apparently wrote to Maria about the Reverend Evans being feted at a donation party. Maria may have been unfamiliar with the expression, since these social gatherings, also called giving parties, were rarely held in cities. Parishioners of a country clergyman brought presents of clothing or food to the party to augment his small salary.

 Writing of parties reminded Maria of her shyness. In a self-

(1863)

deprecatory aside, she threatened to dance at the brass hotel, become more forward or brazen.

At the time this letter was written, few 1823 quarters were in circulation for Maria to compare with the large snowflakes. The coin had been reduced from 27 mm. to 24 mm. in circumference.

Her tour director around Congress was probably Samuel Ryan Curtis (1795–1866), a member of the House of Representatives from Iowa in the 35th–36th Congresses.

While Maria relished the pleasures of city life, Albertine, in Concord, Massachusetts, sampled rural pastimes and revealed an interest in Emma's brother Ned.

Concord Feb. 12th 1863

Dearest Emma:

I had really begun to think that I was not a going to have a letter from you while I was here, but it has come at last and better <u>late</u> than never.

It is snowing quite fast this morning and looks as if we were going to have a regular snow storm. If we do I hope I shall have a sleigh ride.

I am having a <u>tiptop</u> time don't I wish you was here with me wouldn't we have a nice time. Has there been any skating in Cambridge since I have been away! I have not been but once and then I didn't skate more than fifteen minutes it was not very good. I was in hopes that there would have been some skating today if there had been any there was quite a number of us going together. I have had one sleigh ride since I have been away. I guess we went about six miles there were five others besides myself. Don't you think, Emma I am in a straights to ride? I guess you will say yes when I tell you I rode down town with a <u>dead hog</u> last Tuesday! that was the day I received your welcome letter. Perhaps you wouldn't ride in that style but you see I don't care. My Uncle was going down it so I thought I would improve the chance of riding.

I know a little now what a comfort it is to have little children around you. I don't know what I should do if had more than one here, though I can't say much for the little one that is here is the greater part of the time as good as a kitten, but you know they have their cross days as well as anybody else. But today Nellie is not very well and therefore kind of cross. Since I have begun I have had to leave off and hold her for she came and looked up into my face as much as to say hold Nellie a little while so I couldn't refuse her. Then I had to leave it again a few minutes and when I came back what did I see but the ink all out in the chair that I had been sitting in and Nellie playing with the pen and bottle wasn't that interesting?

I received a letter from Mother last night she said she was in (too) Mr. Jewell's house when he was brought home. I should have thought it would have been a very sad sight. I was very much surprised to hear of his death for I did not know that he was troubled with that complaint even if I had known it it would have [seemed] sudden I dare say of a death is generally sudden at last.

I hope it will have a good impression upon Lottie and Henry. Mother also wrote me about the death of another friend in Watertown who was killed in one of the battles it was Harrison Craig. I don't know but you know him.

Death is all around us there was a death in the family that live in the next house to where I am staying it was an old gentleman 70 years old he has been sick and almost helpless for a long time. I have known him ever since I can remember.

Last evening my cousin and my self went out and spent the evening into one of the neighbors whose son, a young gent is a student at Harvard College but that don't make him any better for that. They played cards, that is about the only thing they play here. Don't say any thing about it. I have got about tired of the sight of cards; all I have to do is to sit and look on.

I am going out again to morrow evening and I think very likely I shall have the pleasure of seeing them play them again; I don't wish you to think I help them play for I do not.

Ain't I a naughty girl I have not been to meeting since I left home it isn't because I didn't wish to but the folks that I was going with were not very well but hope I shall have a chance to go next Sabbath we have to ride when we go. I shall I suppose go the Sabbath after for I intend now to be at home by that time. I think Emma that is pretty well. I didn't think that of you. I didn't suppose I should hear of you going any where again with Oxxxxxx P.xxxxx. You need not fool me any longer. I am very sorry that you had an engagement the next time. I don't doubt but what you felt verry sorry. I'll bet folks will talk now. I'm sure they will have reason enough of as is. Where was Miss

(1863)

Pxxxxx all the time perhaps you exchanged brothers. Perhaps it will be one of these days Mrs. Bxxxxxxx and Mrs. Pxxxxx stranger things than that happen. What say you to that? I am glad you enjoyed yourself so well to the sewing circle.

I am also glad you had such a full house the time the "Club" met at your house. I would like to have been there very much. Tell Ned as long as there were so many at his house I guess he didn't miss me much. I hope it didn't trouble him so that he could not sleep any that night for if that was the case I should feel very sorry. But you tell him I don't think much of that for as soon as he found out that I was going away he had it to his house very good excuse. But never mind. I am going to Sing tonight at least I am going to spend the afternoon and in the evening they are there is some more coming in and then they are going to have a sing.

I suppose the Sing meets tonight hope you will have a pleasant time. Remember me to your Mother and Father. Give my "specks" to Ned. I suppose he will say he can't see any better for them. I should like to hear from you again but do as you think best. I intend to come home the last of next week if nothing happens.

Albertine

P.S. Don't for pity sake let anyone see this excuse all mistakes.

Albertine M. Tarbell

Will you please hand this to mother and I will be very obliged to you

Albertine

"I'll bet folks will talk now," Albertine pretended to scold Emma, highlighting the era's concern with appearances and what other people thought. This characteristic sensitivity to propriety was a hallmark of the Victorians, not only in the United States but in England, too.

Albertine's enthusiasm for sleighing also was typical. In March 1863, the *Boston Post* reported "sleighing is capital in the city and suburbs. It was profanely improved yesterday. Brighton, Cambridge, Lexington, and other resorts were thronged with the wicked lovers of the sport."

Ice skating had just as many enthusiasts. Susan wrote to Emma of neighbors who left their sleeping youngsters at home, unattended, while they skated.

Damariscotta, Feb. 13, 1863

Dear Emma

    As we are to have a minister here tomorrow night I thought I might not have a chance to write then and perhaps not Sunday so I thought I would make a beginning tonight. I dont feel much like writing so you neednt expect much in the way of a letter. In the first place I can hardly see, for the "Club" is upstairs and I have to have the Parlor lamp, which burns dreadful dim, and Eddie is sitting in a chair by my side and is inclined to be fussy, and then I am tired and sleepy for the children or rather E. kept me awake a good part of the night. Allie keeps calling Papa from the bedroom, and Sarah has gone out——
    The scene has suddenly changed—The lamp burns brightly now, all quiet in the bedroom. Eddie asleep in the carriage, and the singers in full blast up stairs. I can hardly write for listening to their sweet strains. They have learnt some new pieces, and have a fifth singer. they make a good quintette and sing finely I dont feel much more inclined to write than before for I still feel tired and sleepy—I dont know what has got into Eddie this week he has been quite fussy particularly nights, much to the discomfiture of his father he has in several cases, beat a retreat. I wish he could get used to it. I rather think E. is teething by his actions I do not find it difficult however to get along with him. Tonight I ventured for the first time to give him a little soothing syrup. W.H. has urged me to for several days but I hated to. I hope it will make him more quiet. The little dear is real cunning. I dont know as he can do anything more than when I wrote last, he sits in his carriage and chair a good deal of the time, he would play on the floor, but I dare not let him for fear of Allie. All the other babies seem to be performing tricks but him. Sunies can fix her hands together when you tell her to & say papa (or what they call so) and Katy Shepard can pat-a-cake, and shake goodbye, and ever so many cunning things. I was there yesterday, and she was actually dancing in Lissies lap —Allie has not been very well for a day or two, nothing particular the matter with him, only he is cross, and I suppose he dont feel very comfortable. I suspect that eruption on his legs is caused by those flannel drawers I have taken measures to pre-

(1863)

vent it. He is getting to be real neat and clean, and is not so pole-y as he used to be. I asked him tonight who he was going kiss, and he said "aunt Emma", but he never will admit that he wants you to come back, he always says "no-no". He is real cunning, he and Eddie play real prettily together, but some days he bothers me most out of my senses. Sarah is a good deal better than she was last week, the work goes on in fine style, no dirty dishes or broken ones, none set on the table slanting, no dirty looking individuals about except me of course. But I miss some one to catch up Eddie, and amuse Allie. She has tended the children more this week than last and she has been sewing for me, she offered to, and I thought I would let her, but, I dont think she is fit to do hard work yet. On the whole I prefer Mary. She stays at home more. I suppose she will be back next week. Mrs. Withaw wants Sarah to come there, she needs her as much as I did last summer, but Sarah thinks she cant take so much care. I am going to have Mrs. Wales & Hutchins to tea soon, and afterwards Hammond & wife. I set out to call there this week but one thing and another prevented me. I suppose I might if I had had resolution enough. But I haven't done much of anything this week. Monday I spent in binding the delaine quilt. I have them both done now. Tuesday I cut out two shirts for W.H. and Wednes. I went over to Col. Chapmans to spend the P.M. We had a fine time, and a very pleasant company. I carried the baby. Sunie and her baby were there, Mrs. Mark Hall, Mr. and Mrs. Austin Hall, Mr. & Mrs. Stetson & Mr Bulfinch, Mrs. Avery and her children, a Mrs. Chapman widow of the Col.'s brother and a Miss Rafter. We had a real social time. After supper all the men went down street to see Capt. James Hall who came home on furlough, in the stage. He you know was honorably engaged in the Fredricksburg affair, it was to relieve his battery that Gen. Bayard lost his life. The citizens determined to make some demonstration accordingly he was removed from the stage at Edwin Flye's House, and placed on horseback, and a cavalcade of about thirty escourted him into the village. Last night there was a splendid supper given him at the Hotel. W.H. and Bulfinch were both invited but neither went, though assured that nothing objectionable would be admitted. He felt that as it was at the Hotel, that some of his pious members might feel grieved or that he might lose influence with the less scrupulous. He wishes to be very careful now, as there have been all along slight indications of seriousness in the community, he would wish to be the last one to dissipate them by his conduct. I cannot but respect his course. (The singers have adjourned to Fannie Flyes and I am solus, there is a great tramping and shouting on Back St. I dont know what it means I feel kind of skeert as the wind blows, and latches rattling all over the house gates and blinds banging, while Eddie now and then gives an uneasy hitch in the cradle. I expect he will wake up every minute.) By the way Fannie Flye is going to Boston soon to make a visit I dont know where. The skating mania is at its height here, crowds of married and single go out. Mr. and Mrs. Borland were there and every little while he would take his sleigh and drive home to see if the babies were all right then return and go at it again. Mr. Bullfinch was out on the ice all the P.M. He inquired very particularly for you. Poor W.H. is too busy to go skating. Fannie Chapman has gone to Medway to sew on stars. I am going to write to Alf to hunt her up. She is a real nice girl. We had a turkey for dinner to day and an apple dumpling. I thought of Bill and wished he was here, or you. By the way we had a new barrel of flour this week, but Sarah has not quite got the hang of making yeast bread yet, we have splendid yeast now it would do you good to hear it pop. I bought a skein of yarn (2 cts.) and some shirt buttons 5 cts. a dosen, and a sheet of wadding 10 cts. and I got 5 cts worth of cotton 2 fer a cent at Husseys. The reason he sold it so cheap was because they were undesireable colors, blue red and green. The same day a peddler came here & I sold him a few of the newspapers I had been saving. There were 5½ lbs. He gave me 17 cents, I bought a little tin pan and a jumble cutter.

I have written an awful long letter "but I believe" I have got to the end at last. I hope you will have patience to wade through it. I havent heard anything from the floss cloth yet. Love to all Goodbye
　　　Sister Sue
　　You see I tell you all my troubles just as they come.

Saturday (Private)

I thought I shouldn't fill more than a sheet and a half, but I have not said all I want to yet. Seems to me your boots were dear what kind were they? We get good Balmorals here for 1.50. I might have had them but I liked mine better they were stouter. Bills undershirts too. I dont know what they could have been so

(1863)

high, I never paid over a dollar. I guess Boston prices are worse than D.- prices. I think your calico was cheap. like the plaited trimming you know there is some here for 18cts but it is poor enough. I went into Mrs. Potters the other day. Lissie sent her love to you, she wondered you had not written. They told me that Callie was engaged, but I was in a hurry and did not inquire into particulars. I told Lis' she must write to you. Katy S. was as cunning as could be Sunie dont seem to be very fond of her baby, she is always talking how cross it is, and how it drags on her, but I presume she loves it some of course. Her husband is expected home today, he is to stay several months. Have you been to call on Henrietta yet. I wish now I had sent her the vases. I dont know as I can ever get anything better give my love to her when you see her. Have you done anything yet about the slippers? I am always on hand for them you know. Tell Pa I am much obliged for his long letter. I will answer soon as I get time, this is written by bits. Eddie kept me awake most all night. W.H. slept sweetly upstairs. I feel pretty slim today. I dont want anyone but you & mother to read this page. I have something that troubles me. Ever since the first donation night and I dont know how long before W.H. has missed his gold pin. I thought may be I had tucked it away, though I had no recollection of doing so, but I have searched every crack and corner in vain, we fear it must have been stolen. Should you think M. . . . could have taken it. When I was fixing the little room I saw an old pinholder in the drawer it had a steel pin in it, and was broken at the end. Now W.H.'s was split on the end and tied together with a piece of thread. it might have been broken off and the pin changed. I have nt had a chance to look since Sarah came, if I could I would look over her things. She always seemed perfectly honest, but since my experience with Louisa I have learned the lesson to keep my eyes open & not trust too much. Dont say anything about it will you only to mother. The other day Allie did a n. . . . thing, and I slapped him pretty soon, he got his rocking chair and knelt down and said, "God, Allie do N. . . . thing in his drawers Allie naughty boy: Pretty soon after he said, "Allie no do n . . . thing anymore" Where do you suppose he learnt it. That old agent did another in his room. Mary was dreadful tickled about it. Allie can say the first verse of Bo Peep all through He can say another melody of the same style, I think I had better teach him some hymns but he dont take to them as much as he does to nonsense. I tried to. I will send home your stone if I think of it. Sarah is going a skating this P.M. Now you must be sure and keep this page private wont you. Think of me for a day or two to come, overwhelmed with ministers, and babies. Eddie seems better today I hope he will be good tonight.

I haven't told you all the news yet. There is to be a wedding here Saturday night at six o' clock. I am not acquainted with the parties. As W.H. expected to go away, he wanted the man to set some other time, but he would'nt. So W.H. is to start after they are gone, he will probably go as far as Waldoboro tomorrow night, and the rest of the way Sunday morning. I hate to have him ride in the evening—Mr. Leland will be here, and Mrs. Austin Hall declared she was bound to come to the wedding—so we shall have a lively time. I've another extra piece of news. I've got a new black silk dress. I am going to send you a piece of it, if I dont forget it. The way I happened to get it was this. I was down to Hussey's and saw the piece and liked it. I went home and told W.H. and he said perhaps he never could afford to get me better than now, and I had better have it. So he went right down and got it. It was a dollar a yard, just 15 yds in the pattern and it is an inch wider than my other black silk. I like it because it is so much like mothers. I wanted a plain one, but he had none that I like less than 1.33 and I thought this would wear best. I thought I would "strike while the iron was hot". but I got worked in a curious and provoking way about my other dress. You know I wrote home that Mrs. Hutchins and I went down and looked all over the dress goods and couldnt find a thing. Yesterday I went down and I saw on the counter a pile of real pretty mohair plaids just what I wanted. I asked the price he said a shilling. I said where were these when I was down here the other day? Oh said he, "they were in the store all the time" I thought it strange because he said then he had nothing less than a quarter, but I told Mrs. H. and she said he had probably had them stowed away in some drawer and just brought them out. Sarah went right down and bought her one, green and white, and today it is all gone, snapped right up and he says the next he takes out will be 20 cts. I felt real disappointed to think I had sent for one, and put mother to all that trouble, when I might have been suited here, and have to pay so much more besides, but I couldnt help it. You see, there are tricks in trade here as well as everywhere else. However, if she has not got one yet she need not for I guess I can get one if I look sharp. She or you

(1863)

misunderstood me however in my letter, perhaps I was not explicit enough. I did not want a delaine, but mohair or mixed goods of some kind. I said if she could not find anything, I would get a delaine down here, (as that was all I could get) I am afraid she will make an exertion to get a delaine Kenworth and Hovey usually have those goods close by the door, and I thought she could examine them with very little trouble. If I had known certain that she had not got one, I would have bought the green one yesterday, but as it is I am in a pussle all round, but it is no fault of mine I am sure. The express came in today but brought nothing. The reason I sent home to have mother get one was that goods are going up so fast, but I am real sorry to be cosin so much trouble, especially to mother. Are you quite sure you read the letter carefully. But I shall let it all rest and it will come right in the end I dare say. I bought me a moreau skirt real good piece for 25 cts because it was a remnant I paid 30 cts for silesia to top it with. I bought some linen for 50 cts. yd. 1 half for 12 cts. and 3 cheap ones 3 for 25 cts not all linen.

Susan's letter showed very well how ladies passed their time in entertaining, visiting, and shopping. Her comment that "the goods are going up so fast" indicates how the loss of cotton from the South affected prices of fabric. Thus, buying a silk dress did not seem as extravagant as it might have when cotton was more plentiful.

Susan's anxiety about Eddie's teething was more than concern over his discomfort. Parents and physicians believed that teething was a leading cause of infant death, perhaps because it often coincided with weaning from the breast. Babies brought up "by hand," bottle fed, also had a higher mortality rate. They were susceptible to infections which sometimes led to the potentially fatal "congestion of the brain."

Although Susan's father was a temperance advocate, she used "soothing syrup" to medicate her teething child. One recipe for the palliative included cherry brandy and rum. It is likely that the concoction put an irritable toddler to sleep, thus soothing the parents.

Susan purchased a jumble cutter to bake for her children the soft cookies, jumbles, that were popular at this time.

In writing to others, Emma most likely passed on some of the amusing anecdotes her sister shared about Allie and Eddie, for Maria mentioned them in her letter, which painstakingly recounted the details of a tragic death.

Emma's World

Washington March 28th/ '63

Very dear Sister

I have just received your letter and sit down <u>immediately</u> to answer and hope I shall be able to finish it at one sitting—Your letter was splendid only the beginning made me feel a little badly I suppose you will say I deserve the same, but this is what makes me feel thus. I was cross and sick and had lots of company to entertain and I could not compose my mind enough to write <u>anything</u>—I think you must have perceived it in the undertone of my letter. Next time If ever that time comes when you have occasion to admonish your sister (please put the beginning at the end)—I forget though this a rather a poor beginning for me—Our company, five from Mass. have all gone (last Thursday) We went to the depot with them and father met Mr. Garrett the president of the railroad who was going in the same train and he gave father, mother, Mr. Whittaker & myself a pass to Baltimore and take the return train home that night. This was a great surprise to us and we enjoyed it much—We had the end of one car to ourselves and we had a jolly time. I expect the rest of the people thought we were some wild beings—never mind though it was dark and we could not be seen or see the others. We did not get as far as Baltimore though, for about (18) miles this side the train stopped and the conductor said they did not stop any nearer. B. and we would arrive ten minutes too late for the return train, so out we got and stopped at a telegraph station until another train should come. They were sending messages from "out west" to Washington—I thought I would like to understand those secrets, but nay The operator telegraphed to Washington and enquired what time the train started—it said "five minutes later than usual" All this in a minute or two—is it not wonderful?

You speak of the good sleighing—We have had a very wet, rainy winter. I have been out very little except on business or to show my friends the sights—I have been to quite a number of lectures I believe I wrote you before I have <u>no</u> beaux now. All have gone since Mr. Yedro—I can't imagine <u>what</u> is the trouble unless it is because I would not go to a lecture with one and to see the Minister with the other. I do not care much only I do not wish them to be offended or think ill of me—I forgot one who seems to be "edging around" he is a captain on Gen. Hamilton's staff—his name is Herbst (don't say anything for he is in Boston

(1863)

now I expect). He is the one who so gallantly saw us to N. York last summer. I told you about him. He has called three times in two weeks but will soon go to New Orleans—He is very smart but it is great "ego" and I do not like that at all. He urged me very hard to go North with him and make my visit now so as to attend that great dinner in Boston given to Gens. Butler and Hamilton but I was not inclined (my fare would have been paid and all but it would have been great encouragement and I do not mean to give any—but oh! what a temptation (not to the dinner for I should not care to go where wines will be used so freely) to go to Mass again and see you oh! how I wish it—and a few others. I must tell you Mr. H. is strictly temperate—only imbibing cold water, no tea or coffee. All I care for him is to talk, he is an excellent lawyer and has the gift of 'gab' fully developed—If you should happen to meet him give him my regards—Has this not been a long story—I often think what would young ladies do if it were not for the beaux—I suppose remain old maids—I should think your ride was rather a cold pleasure under difficulties. You said nothing about the cold weather. Then George Clapp was the favored one it seems to me he gets favored often—You mention Georgie Roberts—she must be quite a large girl by this time—is she pretty—Is Willie Russell waiting upon her and Willie Munroe upon her sister Tell me all about Annie Whitney, Lizzie and our classmates and who are waited upon and by whom—Where is Sarah Pearson? You do nobly about this same only it seems as if the girls all ought to be going after two years nearly—Who will be married next now Louise Arnold is off the dockets—She has created quite a sensation—I heard she went to church in Cambridge—By the way can't you give me extract from a certain letter. I am afraid I am too curious but I am very much interested in my dear sister—Again I was showing my album to Mr. H—and he looked it over and over and opening at yours without my saying a word said (to be continued) well yes now what do you guess, are you at all curious? Well I won't tell you now but by and by—Well here is a great bundle from Maria from Mr. Whitaker. I wonder what it is a piece of hoarhound candy almost as large as my head and molasses. I will enclose a piece it will be a great pleasure to know that you can have a bit from the same. I told Mr. W. tonight that I had a sore throat and was quite hoarse and this is the result—he is very kind, always caring for all. He knows about you and says he feels quite acquainted through your father and myself. You will have no trouble should you happen to want a few bibs, skirts etc. to know how to make them. I can't help laughing when I think of my experience. I have scarcely seen a baby for three or four years much less seen such articles —I was thinking yesterday and wondering if I could make a shirt without looking at a pattern. I shan't trouble myself at present though until there is some prospect. Dear E—you are not the only one that does and says things which they wish they had not—here is another speciman who sometimes wishes she could take her head off if it would be practicable or at least hide it in some dark corner—you say you are going to have some more taken of your photographs if they are better or vignettes may I have one—I am going to have some more taken too and I will do the same. What a pity you lost all those that fell to the lot of Ned when you were away—I feel quite greedy or selfish for mine and tease all I can get (when I know they would like to have me possess one)—What a pity you could not exchange. I know Liz is crazy almost for one of yours—How nice it will be if he gets a commission but I fear they will have a hard time there his time is almost up though and he will soon be home. I wish I too could talk with you doesn't this seem stupid compared. If father and mother have any left after those promised I will certainly look out for you—Did I ever speak to you about Mr. Norton, my S. School teacher when I first came here. He is a young man married and until within a few days had two beautiful little boys—He and his wife are particular friends of ours—They have been exchanging boarding places lately and had emptied an old secretary full of old papers and private documents into a drawer and the remainder they put in a basket—Their little Charlie (3 ½ years old) a most interesting little fellow had been playing with those in the basket running from one room to the other and he tossed them upon the sofa and some fell back of it upon the window seat—This was in the afternoon —soon the little boy came to his mother bringing a paper and asked what it was—she shuddered hardly knowing why she opened it and found it poison, she asked if he had touched it and he ran laughing into a corner and she placed it away securely. He had not eaten any this all seemed to be a kind of providence—The next morning he woke and peeping over his crib asked if he could come and "seep side of mama." She smiled and said baby brother is here and there is no room, soon the maid came and took the baby and then Charlie felt privi-

(1863)

leged and crept softly in. He nestled close to her and she asked if it did not seem good to be in bed side of mamma. he laughed and kissed her saying Mamma, Charlie hungry. The girl prepared a cracker with jelly upon it and he took it into the sitting room to be dressed—waiting for the girl at the window—Just then the blind blew to and she opened the window and Charlie cried, "Stop you brush away my sugar. she said, "No, that is not sugar and called Mr. Norton—She almost tore into the room thinking he had taken a pinch and put it upon his bread and eaten it. He commenced vomiting immediately and she found that her paper was safe and that in throwing it around it had sifted out on the windowsill—She called a doctor immediately and all the antidotes were given and he seemed much better at eleven o' clock after that he grew drowsy and at two they could not possibly keep him awake. The doctor came every hour and they called at three just before he came. Mrs. N. took him in her arms and found his forehead covered with sweat The doctor entered and it flashed at that instant across her mind that he was dying. She enquired and the doctor said Yes Charlie threw his head back and breathed twice. This was all the warning she had never dreaming but that he would get over it—They feel very much afflicted—It is truly a sad case—Mother and I called yesterday. She feels that it is all right but so very hard to bear—This will make you sad but I know you will feel interested.

Well as you want to know so much but I was going to tell you. It was this: that my Emma had the most character of any and he liked hers the best.

It is getting to be quite warm weather here. When the sun ventures out we have had several thunder storms when it hails and [undecipherable]. Did you ever hear such a thing?

Write soon. I have set an excellent example. You cannot imagine what a proud feeling came over me when I read that my photograph occupied such a prominent place in your book. I know it does not deserve such but this was not the idea either. That it was there at all expresses it exactly. Give my best respects to all. I suppose your pa and ma are well as you said nothing to the contrary.

I have finished this at one sitting wonder of wonders and must bid you goodnight as they are waiting for me to play beanbag with them downstairs. We have all kinds of Gymnastics here. Mr. and Mrs. Conant are greatly in favor of such exercise—Mrs. Conant is very much like Mr. M . . . . . . only better if anything—I feel greatly privileged in living in the same house. His conversation is rich.

I do not know whether I shall go North this summer or not—time will tell—Father says No now but he may alter his mind—I wish he might get away he is tired.

Where shall I put in my name. I almost forgot to sign it. Wouldn't it have been a pity you might not have known who it came from.

Your loving sister,
Maria

The grieving woman in Maria's story probably had to cope with guilty feelings about her son's death, too. Mothers at this time often were preoccupied with their children's health; children under the age of five accounted for half of all deaths. Also, as the nature of earning a living changed, men were gone from home during the day, leaving women with the responsibility for child care. Physicians, novelists, and other social commentators responded with an avalanche of material on child-rearing that, for the first time, promoted motherhood as a woman's most central and important role. To improve a baby's chance for survival, experts recommended vigilance that came of good mothering. In effect, during this period, a child's welfare passed from God's to mother's hands.

Susan, a devoted mother and an educated woman who enjoyed reading, must have been familiar with some of the latest theories, such as the therapeutic benefits of fresh air. The health of her children was critically important to her and, as in this letter, she frequently discussed their illnesses with Emma.

Damariscotta April 24th, 1863

Dear Emma

I desire a few moments this evening to commence an answer to your last favor, but how long I shall write is uncertain. it will be as long as the baby will let me. he is asleep now but is quite restless and I expect every minute he will wake up. I am looking for a watchful night with him. He had a very sore arm, and has worried considerably today his vaccination commenced to take about Wednesday, and has gone on very slowly since then. I think that it will reach its hight by tomorrow or next day. He has not made any fuss or seemed sick at all till today but it has

(1863)

seemed to pain him a good deal today & he seems slightly feverish. I am in hopes it will soon be over. The Dr. was in yesterday and said it looked well. The weather has been very fine this week and we have improved it. I have taken the children out every day and they have enjoyed it so that they cry when I bring them in. Eddie rides in the carriage and Allie takes his cart that Uncle William made and drags his "dollie baby" in it. If he sees any children coming he says "See my pretty car, Uncle William made it." Oftentimes the other children in the street come out— the Flyes, Erskines, Clapps, Willie Wales, Hutchins girls, Brights and Mary Harrington. Sometimes they are most all out at once and they make quite a group. When I take the baby in, they beg the privilege of riding Allie. yesterday the wind got out East and Allie got a slight cold in his head. I find it takes a good deal of my time, but it does them a great deal of good I think. Allie has taken a wonderful liking to his rag baby of late he talks to it and goes through all the manoevers that I do, and he wont go to bed without it when he wakes up the first question is "where's my dollie baby?" He was dreadful pleased with his dog. I gave it to him the first thing when he waked up, he never said a word but smiled, and then bit its head off. Little Eddie ate all his too before we were up. I thought they were very cunning little dogs. I think your new dress was real pretty. I have seen something similar here. Ellen Philbrick has one with black instead of white plaid, but yours is prettier Mrs. Hutchins bought her a purple & black (half mourning) mohair, she paid 40 cts. it was a beauty. Mr. Hutchins went to Portland yesterday she feels very lonely without him, he expects to make a visit home the 4th of July. I have not done much this week in the way of sewing we have had rather a broken week and I have given more time than usual to the children. I have been into the neighbors with them 2 afternoons. Mary has been cleaning house this week, and has all the front part of the house done but the study. today we cleaned my bedroom and a dirty job we had. the carpet has not been up since we came the other part of the house was but little dirty. I have been making a little Garibaldi for Allie but I have not finished it yet quite. Fannie Flye got home this week. she has made a long visit I have not yet seen her. Mrs. Flye is going up the first of May. I would like to go as company with her, but think I cannot make it convenient before the last of the month. The ship building goes on briskly here, and every day the Methodist bell rings at 7, 12, and 6 o'clock to call and dismiss the

Emma's World

laborers. Mrs. Clapp opposite boards 4 men, one of them was brought home today badly cut in the knee. I ran right over, and carried linen to, but the doctor had it all dressed, it was not so bad as they feared at first, he was a green hand. We have had a dreadful accident here this week which has cast a gloom over the whole place. Perhaps you remember Mrs. Mc'Lean who came in here one stormy day with Mrs. Hutchins. she wore a pink cloud. Her husband was proprietor of a steam saw mill 3 or 4 miles below here. Last Thursday P.M. by some unknown cause, he became entangled in the belting and machinery, while at work, and was whirled on a sudden and frightful manner among the bands and was mangled by the circular saws. As soon as possible the mill was stopped but of course not in time to save him. —He lived half an hour after he was first drawn in —but it took till nearly night to extricate him and get him fixed decently to carry home. his head was struck by a rock and it is probable that he was insensible, though he spoke twice & asked for water, and to rub him. he was crushed and torn in a shocking way, and could not be laid out, but was buried just as he was dressed, almost all his bones were broken. If I were with you I could tell you more particulars though they are very painful. Private. His wife was hourly expecting to be confined and they fear it will have a bad effect upon her. Of course she was dreadfully agitated, but her mother is with her and will leave nothing undone to save her if possible. she thinks she shall not live and dont wish to. They have a little boy the age of Allie—and he had an aged mother and a <u>foolish</u> brother living with him—They were worth considerable property when they came here but they embarked it all in that mill, which has been a losing business from beginning to end and proved to be his coffin at last. It is feared that after his business is settled there will be nothing left for his family. her parents will probably provide for her if she lives—but the old lady & her son are badly off—WH attended the funeral on Thursday. he said it was a heart rending spectacle. What a dreadful load his poor wife has suddenly thrown upon her I pity her from my heart. They were said to be very happy together—unusually so—Saturday. I left off writing last night because W.H. wanted me to talk about some plans for next month about going home to. We were busily talking, when we heard Allie coughing in the bedroom, and feared the croup had fastened upon him. We gave him goose oil and rubbed him,

(1863)

and one of us awake with him all night. I had a nap the first & W.H. the last part of the night. He got easier about 3 o' clock I was very much frightened. he has not had so bad a spell before he did not have the least sine of hoarsenss when he went to bed he seems better today though he has a heavy cold upon him. I dread to have the night come. he has acted like the very old Harry today so witching & mischievous. Eddie was quite rotten last night and is rather troublesome today, but I think his arm is beginning to get better. I think he has got along uncommonly well with it—W.H. was in a draft at the funeral and he got another cold, he added to it last night being up so much, and today he is as fussy as can be. he has got an awful cold he can hardly see out of his eyes, and his limbs ache. I tell him if anything ails the children, he is sure to give out too. It makes it hard for me. Of course I am tired sleepy, and would like to be fussy if I dared, but it wont do for me. I must keep the rest up— WH is running all down. The doctor says his blood is very low, he needs rest very much he has had so much care, so much sickness & death it wears upon his sadly. I am afraid he will be down sick so you see what you will come to if you get married. If I had known all beforehand I should have thought I couldnt live through it, but I did, you see and manage to be pretty comfortable part of the time. It was Will I didn't know. But perhaps your children wont be croupy, nor your W.H. fussy. but Eddie is crying for me and I must leave off—Sunday. —Both the children are better. Had a good nights rest. Allie's cold has gone into his lungs, it is much looser and better. He rested pretty well last night. WH is exchanging with Mr. Gould of Alna today—He came last night in the stage. We did not expect him till this morning but he could not get a team to come. I must own I felt sorry to have him come I felt so tired and anxious about Allie but I soon got over it. He made himself very agreeable. He told me to soak Allie's feet & it would help him I did so and I think it did help him. Mr. Gould & his wife are going up to Boston about the time I am. Maybe we shall come in company.

 Mr. Hammond left here last week. he is going to labor among the contrabands. I guess he did not carry out his intentions of clearing out this vile place. it was too much for him it would be a herculean task for any human being—the temperance Society stumped though (there wasnt public spirit enough to sustain it.) Hammond said it was the worst place he ever got into and I agree with him but I must close this affair. I dont know as you can pussle it out.

> Goodbye
> Sue
> Love to all

Do you hear from Alf—I wrote him a month ago but have had no answer. Friday was his birthday.

[Enclosure] W.H. started off this morning for Alna. he is a good deal better of his cold I guess it was only being kept awake that made him feel so badly yesterday. It is awful windy and I am afraid he will get more cold. Eddie's arm is getting better, Tell mother than I am much obliged for the half sheet she sent me, also to pa for his scrap. It had just the effect they intended for I should not have been satisfied with yours alone it was not very long but as long as you were not very well, I will excuse you cheerfully—I am never troubled with your difficulty—not knowing what to write about, on the contrary I could make my letters 3 times as long if I could only get the time to say all I wanted to. My trouble is how to condense, but you are not so wordy an individual as myself, but I suppose what you do say is more valuable. I am sorry however that you experience that difficulty in writing to R.W.B. —you must profit by that advice in the paper I sent. If you are ever at a loss what to write to me, you must take my last, and answer in detail, thats the way mother does—I dont mean to dictate of course, only throw it out as a suggestion.

(Allie & Eddie are playing on the floor Allie is making a house for Eddie to knock over) So you have had a visit from Mr. Wheeler. We supposed he would go to Skowhegan, did he say he met W.H. at Hallowell? I suppose now he will soon be getting married and settling down. By the way did you know he was an old admirer of yours you had better look out for him. Mr. Sargent intimated to me that he would have tried me if he thought it would be of any use, but I was too far gone. Perhaps he wanted you because he thought the goodness ran in the family. I shouldn't have quarrelled with you but as mother says one poor minister is enough in a family. You will doubtless do better, and I am well satisfied with my W.H. he is a dear man anyhow. But what nonsense I am writing. I must sometimes write nonsense to keep off the blues. and then O.P. again he is determined to haunt you, but I would not go with him one more

(1863)

time. Wouldn't sister Georgie give it to me if she saw my kind advice to you. I was very much astonished to hear that Bill had left Mason. I hope he will do well. I should think you were highly honored to be elected a Life Member. I presume you were sensible of it. That must be a heathen set in the Hidden house. I have read Agnes of Sorrento in the Atlantic I dont think much of it. I long to get where I can see some Harper or Atlantic again. I never see any more. Mr. Harris the preceptor lent me some bound Atlantics before he went away. It was before Eddie was born and I had more time to read. I dont read anything but the papers I feel like an ignoramus. I would like to borrow books if I could but this is not a reading public. I have a good many odd minutes I cant do anything else in. Mr. Edwin Flye is expected back again. he was appointed paymaster but did not go on where he was summoned, consequently some one else stepped in. I guess he didn't care much. He had two or three more chances offered to him but would not take them. I have heard from Mobile but I dont see how we can get an answer to reach them. Of course I would not encourage blockade running. Perhaps if we sent to N. Orleans they might get it. Everett Stetson has a cupola built upon his house.

The plight of the Widow Mclean, whose husband died suddenly, was one with which other women easily identified. Unless she was able to slip back into the home circle, a widow's lot was difficult. In addition to husband, she usually lost her home, status, and income. Widows of Civil War veterans were the first to benefit from pensions.

Although she was pleased to hear from family in Mobile, Susan "would not encourage blockade running." (Wilmington, Charleston, and Mobile were the last Southern ports to remain open.) Profiteering attracted some daring Yankees as well as Southerners and fortunes were founded on blockade running. By 1863, Confederate ships—many of the most successful of which were owned by the government and commanded by its naval officers—plied regular trade routes with the mainland by way of Bermuda and Nassau. According to Union records, more than 1400 blockade-running vessels, many of them custom built for the purpose, were captured or destroyed.

The "contraband" Susan mentioned referred to black soldiers. General Butler had refused to return runaway slaves, calling them contraband of war, and the Emancipation permitted them to join in the struggle against the Confederacy. Approximately 180,000 black soldiers fought in the war and 38,000 were killed, an estimated mortality rate more than 40 percent higher than that for white soldiers.

Despite her generally blue mood, Susan, ever interested in fashion, identified a neighbor as the one wearing a "pink cloud," a light, loosely stitched, knitted scarf.

9
(1863)

*A*lthough Susan complained of not receiving mail from Alfred, he kept in touch with Emma. Understandably, their brother had little time for letter-writing. His farm kept him busy, and to make ends meet he took on another job, as a clerk. Perhaps he only managed to jot a few lines when business was slow; Emma's letter is on half a sheet of store ledger paper.

Franklin April 26, 1863

Dear Sister Emma,

I think I owe you a letter, if so I wont owe you any more, how cold it has been today—so unlike the past week, the grass is however green and every thing begins to look pleasant. Mary is still at work sewing straw, as fascinated as ever by the work. I have not left the shop yet I meant to this week, but Greene is busy and drove and dont want to spare me I work early and late in order to get my farming a head, I hope however soon to get through, have you a new hat this spring—the new style is the Garibaldi Mary will describe it to you when she comes down perhaps show you one she thinks of making for Gracie, tan colored is all the go for hats or bonnets, the black hats are as well as the tan—

My hens are doing pretty well this spring—they have been laying well, sometimes we get 10 or 12 eggs per day I have four hens sitting on 51 eggs 2 more want to set and I shall probably gratify their desires this week. I expect to have 2 bossies this week then look out for the nice milk.

Topsy has three pretty little kittys 1 black and 2 malta—they are real cunning. Mary is intending to come down on Fast day and stay a few days. I would like to come with her but it is impossible for me to do so, perhaps it will be so bye and bye that I can come. Do you keep up the sings as yet? I almost wished I were at home and able to meet with you, though since I've been married Mary thinks my voice is not good or I cant sing well.

Did you see Mrs. Wheaton Daniels (Mrs. Kings daughter) when you were here, she sat in our pew in church, she has got a fine little boy. Mary and I went over to see it the other day.

Mary had a letter from Grace yesterday in which she said that Ned was coming up last night, we looked for him but he did not seem to come, we shall be very happy to see him and have you accompany him up here when you can. If he will write me the day or two before he intends to come I will drive or have my boy drive over to Medway for you both, as the roads are pretty good now. I would like to have the pair of Plaster hounds on the Parlor what-not (the ones chained together) sent up by Mary—if she can carry them without breaking—you can remind her of them, the statues I had up here I had varnished with a preparation which we varnish bonnets with, and it made them look nice. Mary and I were out to walk this P.M., we came across a large black snake 3½feet long it was however dead, last Sunday we saw 2 large ones alive, dont you wish you'd been there. Good bye love to all from

Alf

Send the Chronicle, Harper or something (yourself) from home by Mary.

(1863)

"Don't you wish you'd been there?" Alfred joked about his finding a snake. Much as Emma missed her brother and enjoyed the country, given a choice, she might have opted to spend some time with Maria in Washington.

Washington, May 2nd, 1863

My dear Sister—

I have passed through so much since I received your last letter that I have had no opportunity to answer before. Yours was a <u>treat</u> and what remark do you suppose mother made? It was <u>this</u>—"I had rather see any letter come into the house than that" —now you are surprised but I will tell you <u>why</u>. I admit I have been very selfish with them not reading <u>or showing</u> them to anyone but telling the general news. I said I was more rejoiced at yours than anyone's and <u>read</u> a great portion out aloud to her. Mother says— "Now that <u>is</u> something like generosity" and enjoyed it very much—I imagine she will rejoice with me next time. I had not thought that she would be interested in hearing it as she was so little acquainted but all the while she was wondering why I kept your letters so private. She said I never gave any account of myself or letter I became so absorbed. Now this must not make you feel unpleasantly for it is intended for the reverse—But you will wonder what has happened within the last fortnight.

Mollie Appleby—Ellie's sister was taken about two weeks ago with inflamation of the bowels—her life was despaired of for several days but-at-length she seemed a little better. I have watched with her over night several days. She did not continue thus long. Pneumonia and inflamatory rheumatism followed and after a most <u>agonizing</u> sickness of two weeks died on Tuesday eve at nine o'<u>clock</u>. She was the most patient sufferer I ever saw—never complaining and "oh! how kind you all are to me?" was her thanks for every little attention. She is Ellie's only sister the youngest in the family and a great pet (10½ years old). They are feeling very sad but almost relieved that she has not lingered on in sufferinng. Mother watched with her two nights. Last Thursday on Fast day she was buried at the Congressional burial ground.

This was quite an eventful day here—Dr. Sunderland the Presbyterian minister—(where mother has united) gave a tremendous sermon in the evening on the affairs of the nation. His congregation is very much divided in sentiment and it will tear his church asunder but—he says "it is my duty to my God and my people". It is the talk of the city at present. —the sermon is the first of the kind delivered in Washington and will be printed in pamphlet form and sold. The house was crowded full two to three thousand persons were present—A glorious time in store for this our Capitol—

Tonight I am about sick with a cold, sore throat and coughing every minute—I feel about tired out—I have been making my spring bonnet today the same that I had last winter (drab rept. silk) drawn upon canes plain on the outside—blue and white flowers inside and drab strings. I have just finished a morning dress calico and have flounced (Two) my black figured silk and made a new waist. I shall next take my old green silk and see what I can do with it. Mr. Conant and Mr. Whitaker have a blackboard made to order and given to us three children (I) for school purposes—It is very useful and he has drawn a head with throat and mouth etc. giving us a lesson tonight on physiology. You know I never studied this at school. He is very kind—better than Mr. Williston I believe. He would open a school here in Washington if his lungs were strong and can you believe it—choose me for his assistant—His breath is very short and he has a cough I fear he is not to be here very long. Thursday eve—I could not finish before—so I will try again—What glorious news we are having—our city is in great excitement—fifteen hundred prisoners came up yesterday with many officers—they were insolent enough making their boasts of how many Union troops they had killed. Many feared a mob or lynch law would be taken up. A large force however kept the spirit under—It has rained very hard yesterday and today. and I do not know what the army will do. It was a solemn fast day and it does seem as if the cry of the country had been heeded by the Almighty Ruler. A little thing though will change the cry of triumph to that of mourning. The wounded are expected daily.

But to change the subject—I shall hardly recognize your house if I come North which is very doubtful this summer—I am wondering how you succeeded in your debut at the Glee Club. you must have been very nervous and fearful although I have no doubt but that you did do admirably I would like to have been there. Your refusal of OR. . . . .'s invitation must have been very trying—I am glad you did it though for my sake —if I should visit my Emma at the home of O———

(1863)

Oh. . . . . did you ever? I hope not. —I almost envy your having so many opportunities to attend those concerts. I have not heard a decent concert since I have been here. Last winter in Baltimore I heard Gottschalk that was very good. What startling news from Hattie Allen. I was very much surprised that such an occurence should take place so soon. I think she is running entirely ahead of me. The gentleman though is one of the best. He is a true man judging from what I have seen. I am glad Hattie has fallen into such hands.

By the way have you heard from New Orleans? I am expecting another engagement ere long. And then when the three years is finished a trip to the capitol. Washington. Is this probable? I am greatly obliged for all that information about our schoolmates. I look through my album with great pleasure and can see each as I read their name. Emma you will sympathise with me this week for I go if pleasant tomorrow to the dentist the siege will soon commence and I cannot say when It will end. I am afraid it will be a long one. I have waited already too long and am fully resolved to be foolish no longer. Do your teeth remain sound and no toothache? Dr. Loomis formerly of Cam[bridge] is one of the principal dentists here I am not wholly [decided] which I shall call upon him or Dr. Noble. I expect to become old and hollow cheeked immediately. A friend of mine here has just had a gold plate fitted she begins to seem old.

Father has been very fortunate and we are all delighted he has been promoted again to a ($1600) clerkship third class—he can only go one higher unless he has charge of a Department and he has a better prospect of the 4th class than any other in the office.

Truly we should be very thankful in these hard times—provisions are enormously high and every thing is dear, I hardly know what we should do without a kind father in Heaven.

The remark was made in my hearing— "What is the worth of an aimless life." It impressed me very much and I began to think what my aim had been. I hardly had any definite object in view I found upon searching but I trust I have something now however humble it may be. Dear E—I know how you feel upon this subject but we very seldom exchange thoughts. Do you not think we could be mutually profited by thus doing?

Tonight there is a Sewing Circle at Mrs. Amos Kendall's of Kendall Green but as it rained so hard I was too late for the omnibus and am not at all sorry I stayed at home for we have had an excellent treat from Mr. Conant and I can finish this letter. I fear I have waited so long that you will feel badly again but I have had no time and am so tired that I am truly ashamed of this horridly written and composed scribble—But you know your sister's imperfections and failings and also her deep love for her dear sister Emma. Remember me to all—and receive a hearty kiss from,

Sister,
Maria

Maria accurately evaluated the impact of Dr. Byron Sunderland's sermon on "The Affairs of the Nation." Published as a pamphlet, it sold out several editions. In addition to his post as pastor of the First Presbyterian Church for thirty-nine years, Dr. Sunderland was chaplain of the United States Senate and the American Chapel, where in 1866 Frederick Douglas delivered a lecture for the benefit of the National Home Association of Colored Orphans on "The Assassination and its Lesson." The subject so offended Chief Justice Salmon P. Chase, a Lincoln appointee and a member of the church, that he protested the use of the church for that purpose and publicly criticized Dr. Sunderland for permitting it.

In addition to other duties, Dr. Sunderland sat on the board of the Columbian Institution for the Deaf & Dumb at Kendall Green, the 100-acre estate of Mr. and Mrs. Amos Kendall in northeastern Washington. Amos Kendall, a Kentucky native, was postmaster general from 1835–40 and a chief figure in President Andrew Jackson's Kitchen Cabinet. A philanthropist and humanitarian, he made his fortune setting up telegraph companies as business agent for Samuel B. Morse. He also founded the institution located on his land.

Mr. Kendall vested the title to his entire estate in the United States Government, and the Secretary of the Interior was authorized to pay for the maintenance and tuition of "deaf mute children", male or female, from Washington, D.C. as well as army and navy families, who wished to attend. In 1864, by an act of Congress, a collegiate department was founded and named the National Deaf-Mute College.

The concert Maria attended was a performance by the well-regarded American pianist and composer, Louis Moreau Gottschalk (1829–1869). A front page story in the *Boston Post* of March 23, 1863, reported "A chatty letter from Gottschalk gives some amusing anecdotes of his Western experience. He says that he was giving (with Caroline Patti) a concert in a little city in Wisconsin, and there at received a polite note, written in a lady's hand, containing the following request:—'Will Mr. Gottschalk oblige thirty-six young ladies, who have studied his "Last Hope," by playing said piece.' This is fame."

Perhaps Maria and her latest beau, Capt. Herbst, went riding by Kendall Green. She certainly seems to have changed her mind about the young officer.

Washington June 5th 1863

Dear Sister Emma

Yours was received with a sigh of relief for I had watched a long time and feared you were ill—I am writing this with a large poultise on my first finger—I broke a pitcher and in picking up the pieces I cut myself. I did not think much of it and cleaned some paint using pummice stone occasionally and I suppose I must have rubbed it into the cut for when I was through it was very much swollen and quite painful—It is maturated and I expect I will lose my nail—So much for my invalid friend—We have made a change in our family since you were here. Miss Felord has left for New York on account of the warm weather and H[attie]. F[lorence]. and I have the back upper chamber commanding a view of the Capitol Patent-Office and quite a few streets—there being no houses on the lot back—Aunt Josie has gone too and there is quite a vacancy (two ladies) We have another gentleman to room with Mr. Whitaker—Mr. Gates of Bridgewater—All Massachusetts people—He is a young man very moral and I think one of the best—He was a pupil of Mr. Conant—This seems to unite all—I have not been away much since I last wrote—it is so dusty and warm that it does not pay to go out much—every article has to be dusted and shook afterwards—You have had as much heat North as we have here only I imagine not so constant—this week it is very cool and pleasant. Although confined in this way to the house I must say I have seldom passed a pleasanter three weeks—You will remember I wrote you about Capt. Herbst—He has returned from Boston and called a few times. I have changed my mind very much since I gave that last account.

Emma one of the greatest favors you can confer on your sister just at present is to send that part of his letter, in which she speaks of the gentleman, to Washington. I would like to see it I wish it very much indeed. I have quite an interesting story to tell but—shall be obliged to write the sequel at some future time. Oh if you were only within hearing—you would be amused—I dare not commit all to paper—I have been to ride once barouch & span and am engaged for number two as soon as it rains and the gent is in the city. He has gone and OH! the void that is in my buzzam! I shall have much to say perhaps. I wonder how you look here after such a mess of stuff—The case is not desperate so dont fear—One more word. I dont know but that I shall be a little inclined not to ans- your next unless you send the desired article.

The soldiers are fast dying in the hospitals from their wounds—We have every opportunity here to see the horror of war—It is coming very near you in the death of your close friends. Ciz has been sick but he will not give up while he has any strength—I think he is so noble and good—Do you really think the draft will go into effect we do not hear very much of it here—I have long known your feelings in relation to your beloved brother—I must feel doubly anxious now—God orders all things and a prayer of faith does not go unanswered—what a great consolation this is. I feel continually that he alone can be fully trusted—He hears all our little sermons and will give comfort if it is asked—Our steps are all ordered by Him—I do not understand all of what you write about "RxxWxxxxxxRxx" I have forgotten the signification—please enlighten me—I can imagine to whom you might refer but do not understand the term—

The High School is still standing—I read in the Chronicle that they were talking of a new building as of "yore" but had hopes it would amount to something more than mere debate this time—I would like to see the teachers again—I did like Mr. Williston so much—He was a noble man. Is Miss Pierce there still if you see her give my love to her—I would like to spend an hour in her company very well—Have your heard anything from Miss Willard (that was)—I remember those occasions at the Tremont Temple—I went once and enjoyed it very much—

Father has been teasing Mother along time to get a cat—but she is opposed to any such article and prefers rats—They make themselves very neighborly coming into the room whenever they choose and running off with all that is within their reach—Your kitty's mark reminded me of our old times with "Malty"—I believe you always have a kitty It would be a great rarity to see one here they are not very numerous—Pigs are much more so—

(1863)

It must be very pleasant to hear from your friends at the south although you could wish them in better company—My finger has pained one so much that I am ashamed to send this but fear I can give no better if I wait a week—I cannot take your whole heart for I know you will want it back for someone else sometime—I cannot send you all mine just at present but be assured that you have good share of it. You will be disappointed at this note but I will try and do better and make up next time.

Your affec. Sister-
May

Love to your "pere et mere" as they say here—

Surprisingly, Maria, who was privy to many of the goings on in Washington, seems not to be aware that the draft has been in effect for almost three months. Perhaps her interest has been monopolized by Capt. Herbst, who took her riding in his barouche, a four-wheeled carriage with a half-hood that can be raised or lowered for privacy, and span, a pair of matched horses. Small wonder that Maria looked forward to her next opportunity to go riding in such high style.

Nevertheless, Maria expressed concern about the hospitalized soldiers and her fear was not without foundation. Disease, more than bullets, felled the troops. Newly-designed, horse-drawn ambulances delivered the wounded to doctors, who did not yet practice sterilization. Surgeons used the same knife, which they might wipe off on a convenient rag, to operate on several people, thus spreading infection. As a result, fewer soldiers died on the battlefield than in hospitals.

As Maria's next letter also suggests, dysentery was a serious and dangerous threat. The Union Army reported 1,700,00 cases, including 17,748 men who were discharged with diarrhea and dysentery. Some died from these illnesses. Confederate army records document proportionally similar figures.

Washington Aug. 5th, 1863

My Dear Emma—

You may be surprised when you receive this to learn that I have been very sick for over three weeks—or perhaps Uncle Emery told you—I was taken with Dysentery the 11th Sat (the day Cousin Carrie died) and for two weeks was dangerously ill. Father doctored me for a few days but all felt I was too sick and he called a physician. I do not remember ever suffering so much before and could scarcely get a few minutes sleep, half an hour once or twice was the longest and no more for the rest of the night. Mother only left the bed for five days to get a mouthful of food I needed her so often (every 10 or fifteen minutes). After that she found she could not be with me night and day and I had watchers until about a week ago. (How thankful I am that such a <u>faithful</u> Mother was provided by Him who doeth all things well. There is no difference between her attentions and kindness and that of my own dear Mother. Few can say this but I <u>can</u>.) Father did the running and they were pretty busy. I feel the Lord has brought me through it all and raised up many kind friends. I never felt that All-sustaining Power as I have during my sickensss. I know the Lord has been preparing me for it and I trust I shall go forward with greater Zeal and a firmer trust. Dear Emma <u>pray for me</u>—that I may not falter—I had <u>longed</u> to hear from you and watched the Mail Carrier every <u>day</u> until I was taken sick and yours did come Monday and they would not let me read it and I did not <u>feel able</u>, but longed to see it. they did not consent until one <u>week ago</u> and it was there that I first heard of Carrie—It did me more good than medicine to have such a privilege for I enjoyed it much. I had expected to hear the sad news daily but had not the courage to enquire—Today I walked a <u>little</u> for the first time. I shall try to go down stairs Sunday. I <u>have</u> only been off the bed three times now but will gain fast as soon as I can use my feet. I wish I might visit Mass. but fear I cannot as I am very weak. Hattie & Florence have both been sick and weak with the same trouble. It is very prevalent and some cases are fatal. The weather is excessively warm so that we can only keep still and as cool as possible. The nights are mostly cooler than the days and this makes it more overcoming. I must not write much more for I am tired. The captain has not been here since he went North. I believe he is in N. York. You need not puzzle your brain out anything between the gent and myself for that can never be feeling as I do now. He is not a Christian man (I believe) and is not altogether suited. I like to talk to him. Mother and I have had considerable fun. Do write soon for I enjoy a letter very much. I would write more but am not able. Love to all

      Your affectionate friend and sister,
      Maria

(1863)

The draft is going on here. I have three or four friends drawn. Will Ned go? I have just had a letter from Ellie Appleby who is in Baltimore. She has been sick all summer and gone there for a while. She says Evie Cutter that young lady who played the piano so beautifully in N.Y. has lost her only brother and the last near relative she has in the battle in Louisiana June 23. It is a very sad case. All alone in the world, an orphan.

I will send the letter and photographs next time. I don't know yet which to keep. I want all. (I don't mean to be selfish)

Many of Emma's relatives and friends served in the army, including William H. Whitney, but her brothers did not. While Ned's health may have precluded his serving, Alfred and Bill, influenced by their father, may have paid a surrogate to serve. The unfairness of the draft continued to spark protests and late in September, mobs rioted in New York City, setting fire to buildings and laying siege to several blocks. The police restored order only with great difficulty.

On a personal level, however, everyone was sensitive to the sacrifices of neighbors. Susan mourned the death of a young man wounded at Gettysburg, the bloodiest battle ever fought in the Western Hemisphere. According to one account, Confederate troops, searching for shoes on July 1, met up with a Union cavalry. For three days, the armies clashed on the Pennsylvania battlefield, until General Robert E. Lee retreated. It was the turning point of the war; the South was unable to raise troops to launch another major offensive.

Damariscotta Sept. 1863

Dear Emma

You can't guess what I have got for a writing desk. It is the kitchen table. Mary has gone home to stay over Sunday and WH has gone to church. I am left alone to do the work and take care of the children who improve the opportunities for mischief in a way that makes me almost frantic. Just now they have retreated to the barn, where they seem to be most contented because there is more liberty and more dirt. It is a real relief to be rid of Mary a little while, the "change of scene brings change of pain" I cannot do without her long. I have (even Sunday) had to clean out a few of the dirty places I tumbled over. I see some things that make me sick at my stomach but I have to "grin and bear it" Mary has been real homesick for some time. She feels lonely here, having no congenial society (like myself) she says she would not stay up here, only that she can earn more. she dislikes it so much, not but she likes me well enough, only the place. I don't much blame her. If she gets a chance to work down home, she will not come up again. I suppose but that is not very likely—Girls are awful scarse here, and what there are, aren't worth much. Mary heard of the death of soldier in the hospital this week, who I expect is some particular friend. She seemed to feel very bad, that is, as much as she was able to feel he has written to her since she lived here. Her whole mind however seems to be taken up in getting herself a new Thibet and a new calico dress. I have had to hear and discuss the respective merits of those articles for the last six weeks, till I am sick of the sound. But I dare say you have heard enough about her, and it is not a pleasant subject for me to dwell upon. I am glad mother has a good girl to relieve her from the burden of the work, glad you like her so well hope she'll continue to please. You don't say how much you pay her, nor whether she is Irish but, I presume so by mary's recommending her. —Your letter was very entertaining and amusing, especially the part about aunt Hester. I wish Gus had been in Port Hudson. I am afraid he did not get a taste of the rat. horse and mule. I mean to ask Hattie Melcher when I see her, who S.G.S. is She sat the table with the officers and knew them all. One of them was particularly kind to her, perhaps it was he. I see by the papers that the Feds think of calling at Mobile. If so, perhaps Elisa Jane may see some of her old friends again. I hope W.H.W. will be spared to come home I am sure but it seems as if the best ones were taken. I see John Tucker's brother is dead. he was a friend of W.H.'s. There was a military funeral here this week, a young man who was wounded at Gettysburg, died at Washington & was brought home. WH is to call on another today who is now of the returned nine months vols. he is almost gone with chronic diarhea. he sent for WH to come. There is a great deal of sickness here, mostly summer complaint. H was called up at 5 o'clock Monday morning to see a woman who has since died. He spent all that day nearly in visiting the sick. Today he attended the funeral of John Hopkin's child, 17 months old, who died of dysentery. it was their only one, and the fifth child he has lost, besides his first wife—Contrary to all expectations Dr. Dixon rallied from his sickness, and is now able to sit up. His attending physician said it was one chance out of a thousand,

(1863)

his disease was stoppage. I hope he will get well again for he can't be spared from his place. There was universal anxiety on his behalf—

Clara Woolward's husband is in N.Y. and she is going on to stay while he is in port, as he can not leave the ship—I presume he will have to send on his $300. The ship was very badly damaged. it met two very severe hurricanes and it will take some time to put it in order—Tessie Colten is gone to thomaston to make a short visit. I miss her a good deal. she comes often, and always asks about you—

Callie Austin is at home again as the weather was too uncertain for her to go with her husband. he has gone to Liverpool. She was in N.Y. during the riots and saw something of it. (We also had letter from Mr. Richardson about it) Callie came up to see me this week. She didn't wait for me to call on her. She seems just the same as ever. I always feel when she is about that I have one friend. —

Last Monday mrs. Wales and I went making calls down the Bristol road. we had a real good time. when I came home I had a pocket full of apples and plums, which had been given me at different places on the way. Friday Mrs. Hutchins and I dragged the baby up to Mrs. Browns, but did not find her at home, so we went all over the grave yard. We had a pleasant time, but I got awful tired—Mrs. Hutchins has a sister & two children visiting her from Boston so that I see very little of her. Mrs. Wales expects her husbands two daughters next Wednes. in the boat. I wish Ellen H. knew them they would be company for her. I hope she will come I should be real glad to see her. I am glad anybody wants to come enough to take pains. I think if I lived in a place that was easy to get at or pleasant after one did get to it, I should not want for visitors. As it is those who do come, prove their friendship I shall try not to depend too much upon Seeing Lee lest I may be disappointed I shall try to make her visit as pleasant as I can. There is a Musical Convention going on here now and they are going to give a couple of concerts in the course of week. She will be just in time I expect of course it is a one horse affair but I shall be glad when it is over for W.H. is gone every single night of his life til ten o'clock and I get awful lonesome evenings.

Why don't you want to go to alfreds. I shoud think you would like to go & stay with Mary she is so pleasant.

How does Will seem now he has got married it seems so funny to me I can't farm any idea of thine.

I believe I have for once said everything I want to and that it is lucky for I have no more room. Give my love to all. Much to yourself. Sue

W.H. went to Association last week he did not have an extra good time.

I have not done much in the way of sewing this week so much running out and callers. Besides "much of my time runs to waste" when I am taking care of the children, and cant seem to do anything. I have to keep jumping up to wait upon them. It is getting cool weather fast and I see before me formidable piles of sewing. How shall I surmount them? But I try not to worry about it. when theres a will theres a way. and I suppose I shall get through somehow. it seems as though everything was dirty & ragged and gave way all at once—Mary took Allie to walk over the bridge the other day. he was so tired that he could hardly get home. when he did, he explained, "don't take off my Garibaldi. let me lay down with it on" the poor thing then went to sleep and slept 2 hours I have been trying to teach him a little. You will see what success I had. There was a funeral procession went by and he saw the hearse. he wanted to know about it so I told him that somebody got cold and was sick and died and had to be put in that carriage and buried up in the ground & their soul went up to God. and that we should all die some time. He listened very attentively and then said, that he didn't want to be put in the ground. I told him I guessed he wouldn't have to that day. But by & by I missed him, and found him out to the pump, pumping on his hands I asked him what he was doing that for and he said he wanted to get cold and die. I said what for? he said. "So I can ride in the team" I thought after that I had better give up awhile. He will be 3 years old this week and it seems but a very little while since he was a baby at home—I should think Ellen H. had rather a hard time of it hunting up folk that lay, all to no purpose. I have seen those kind of quilts like Julia's. Mrs. Shaw, where I used to board in China, had one for which she took the premium at the State fair at Augusta, it was splendid—Mrs. Hunnewell and mrs. Marshall also had them, not quite so elaborate—They make elegant patchwork quilts here. I saw two last week, which were being made for a young bride they were of pink and white, very handsome—but not so pretty as white, of course Mary's pink & white one has been a treasure to me. Clara Woodward has one of those sinks like Bills I guess, in her first set. did you know Hattie Hussey who sang in the choir. she had lost one eye. she went to Boston this week to have an artificial one put in. Melville Hitchcock has one, which they said is impossible to tell from the real one I wish Stanly would get one. I have got me an "invisible net" but I don't wear it because I don't know how to fix it—Do inform me if you can.

Have you seen those pictures in the beginning of Sept. No of Harper. I almost killed myself laughing at them. WH buys it for me now.

Give my best to Julia—

After calling on her neighbors, Susan returned home with arms full of fruits. In the city, etiquette required women to arrange in advance when they would call, and then only during established visiting hours. In the country, life was more casual and spontaneous.

Susan was not present at the August 20, 1863, wedding of her brother William and twenty-three-year-old Julia Battis of Roxbury, Massachusetts. He was twenty-eight and gave his occupation as civil engineer.

Apparently Emma took Susan's advice and paid a visit to Alfred and Mary, for that is where she received her mother's letter.

Cambridgeport   Sept. 14, 1863

My Dear Emma

Father received a letter from your W. today and is going to send it to you tomorrow so I thought I would send a few lines with it.

I received your letter informing me of your safe arrival at Alfreds, which I was very glad to hear. I was very glad to hear also that Mary was better. I hope she will continue so and try to be very careful and not do anything to make her sick again. I do not feel troubled about your being mistreated while you re at Alfs. i think you will have a nice time.

I received a long letter from Sue this week it was much like her last weeks letter, only more homesick or complaining in style than that of anything Miss Cotter that she spoke of that was to be married, was married and sent cards to the Rev. W.H. Evans not mentioning Sues name at all, she told WH she did not like the looks of them and she did not think he was to marry them as nothing else had been said to him but WH did not think as she did, and went, but Sue would not go when he got there Wm Shaw was there and married them. WH was not even asked to pray. he staid till it was over then congratulated the Bridal party. She says and they had the impudence to ask why she did not come, she said WH felt real bad about it, but she was too mad to feel bad, they sent a nice slice of cake but Sue says she was not too mad to eat it. She rather enjoys the breeze and indignation their friends manifest about it, one old lady called and showed her sympathy for them by giving her a V greenback and for W Evans, Sue says this was touching as we knew she made a sacrifice to do it, but she would have felt hurt if we had declined taking it. she (Sue) feels tired and careworn, Eddy is cutting teeth and she is broken of her rest a great deal, and she has no one to take any care off from her. I hope ellen will go down. I was in Boston wednesday and saw Aunt Rebecca, and she said she thought she would go. I hope to see her before she goes. Julia intends to send cakes and I shall try to send something. I bought a rubber ring for the baby today. Will went to Portland Monday night and J. to Roxbury, W. returned today and is to go back Monday Morning. We miss you very much, katy say, she is singing around the house so much, it is lonesome by the way you left your stocking hanging over the fireplace, well you will have to borrow or wash out one pair while you are wearing the other, you did not say wether the things you carried were acceptable. I suppose they were. But I think I hear you say you do not say anything about the wedding, well Addie was married yesterday, at about ten o'clock, by the Rev. Wm Hill President of Hanover College. W Ware was absent, and though a telegraph was sent for him he did not come. WH was a friend of Uncle T's they had not as much company as they expected as Will's folks did not come, accept his Brother, Calli Lowe dressed her hair, though she was not at the wedding. I went early and offered to assist them, but Mrs. Clark said they were near ready but asked me to come in again and see Addie by WC seemed kind of nervous, and I thought I would not go in again. Mrs. Munroe went over a minute or two. After she was married Mrs. Clark over for her. She did not think of me. Mrs. M. said she looked very pretty. Uncle Bed cried and then Addies mother and Aunt Julia said they could not help crying though

(1863)

they had promised not to. but I must close with much love to alf, Mary, and you.

I am your loving mother,
S.S.B.

Martha Brown came to spend the evening with you Thursday eve.

Greenbacks, such as the one a parishoner gave to the Reverend Evans, were introduced in 1862 to help finance the war. By the time the war was over, the North had issued $450 million in paper money, unsecured by metal or specie. Backed only by the people's confidence in their government, the value of greenbacks waxed and waned with changing military prospects.

The war also had a profound impact on women. A more liberating and lasting influence occurred when religious people came to see teaching and nursing as service professions and, therefore, an acceptable way for women to contribute to society. As a result, women like Maria, who probably would not have worked outside the home before, came to be challenged and changed by new opportunities. Maria, offered a teaching position, confided to Emma her pride as well as her fear of failing. The skills women learned—to organize, to speak in public, and to exercise control—were transferred to such other causes as suffrage, labor movements, and temperance.

Washington Oct. 14th, 1863

My dear Friend,

I so often begin my letters with an apology that I am determined to do so no more but write what I have been doing and allow you to excuse or condemn me as you think right. I have been hoping that you would write every day looking for some word—I am quite well now, never was so fleshy before. I have only written to mother four times since she left for Mass. beside this nothing has gone to my friends—

My right side troubled me for weeks after I was able to walk about and I was so tired and good-for-nothing that my mind could think of little else beside my ease. Another unfortunate thing happened almost the loss of my eyesight owing to reading while lying in bed, for reading, writing or sewing—I have thoroughly rested them & now it never was better.

Two or three weeks were employed in preparing Mother's

and Florence's things for a journey North. We had finished F's entire outfit at last decided it would be much better that she should stay and attend school (both go now). The care of the household now for four weeks has devolved upon me—4 borders and our own family and the house—Now I have a bit of privacy—No one must know it. Your sister M. has become a schoolmarm a real one—I am now teacher of a boys school sixty in number—have only had bout two weeks experience—I think I shall like very much the school has been without a regular teacher since May and only conducted by a sub-assistant who did not exercise any authority. I have not yet written to Mother & intend to surprise her when she comes. I never dreamed of such a thing until one day Father came home and said a gentleman of our acquaintance here had been in to see him and inquired if his daughter would like the school—Father had heard me say I would like to teach and told him, he thought I would have no objection but be pleased. Mrs. Townsend (who has two boys in the school and feels that they have been neglected) went immediately to the Trustees & requested them to call upon me. Teachers competent to take the school were very scarce—Mr. Miller the Trustee came and begged me to accept—if only for a short time. I did and am receiving a salary of $350 a year. Not much but something. I have to rush around in the morning to get all the chamber work done I assure you—Return home at 3 ½ or frequently 4 o'clock and make pies once or twice a week and dessert for dinner—Next week I shall issue a circular for music scholars—I have excellent names for reference—Dr. Sunderland—Chaplain of the Senate. My minister Mr. Howlett. An excellent letter from my music teacher and Hon. Horatio King's name together with Mr. Whitaker & Conant.

Have I not business enough in my hands for the winter? I am glad for I do not like to remain idle. I should probably go North if it were not for my school. I cannot leave it. I have told no one because I may fail in governing them or in pleasing the committee in which case I would rather it should not be known. Please keep dark.

I have had some glorious rides. A gentleman here who owns a carriage kindly offered me a ride twice a week when he comes up from the Army. he is no beau of mine only a friend of mothers. I have respectfully declined taking any more as he was getting too ammorous—I have seen all the country around Washington—It is beautiful—There are many fine county seats. I don't have much time now-a-days to think of the gents. I suppose you would like to know the where-abouts of the Captain. He came to W. just about five weeks ago and called once. It was very affecting particularly as he was about to start for Texas to return he knew not when. I didn't see the point and he started off a little offended I imagine. He is in Texas probably now. Mother met him in Boston the day before he started. Joy go with him!! Yesterday I had an invitation to a Concert from another gent. —Gilbert Towles—but as he called altogether too often for my pleasure or wishes I felt rather compelled to decline. It was a great disappointment as it was the best concert given since I have been here. To much and no more on this subject. I am to be an old maid now sure. I have great sports Father is in the Pension Bureu and likes it much better than the War Department. I hope when Congress assembles he will get a still better place. Father says Can he have one of your photographs he has an album.

Hattie & Florence are quite large girls both attend school and like much—Florence was thirteen yesterday and Hattie sixteen last month. On the 11th of next month I shall be twenty one What an old maid and that is not the worst of it.

We have five little kittens three weeks old they are very cunning, I think (don't you see a sign). I got all ready to go North and had my clothes ready to put in the trunk two months ago but was disappointed in my campaign not going & I was not able to go alone. I was quite disappointed at not being able to see you but was so unwell that I felt I should enjoy going about little. It is after eleven now I wanted to write you & have stolen the time but must rise early in the morning so as to be ready in time. Many kisses from your aff

Maria

Do excuse this scribble for I cannot copy it. Patience & perseverance will overcome difficulties. Give my love to all who may enquire and to where it should be delivered my regards to the rest. I have not your letter with me so I cannot answer it. Yours in bed—

M.

Don't lisp a word to mother.

10
(1864)

*M*aria's opportunities at school and her busy social life contrasted sharply with Susan's bleak circumstances. Housebound during snowstorms and the frigid Maine winter, Susan ached with arthritis and was overwhelmed by loneliness, bickering children, trouble with household help, and fear that at any time W.H. could be drafted. She might have derived solace in shopping, for she appreciated nice clothes and women attended to fashion in Damariscotta, a wealthy ship-building community, but she confided to Emma that merchandise in the local stores was too expensive for her pocketbook. Shopping on a poor minister's salary meant counting out pennies for purchases, borrowing from her mother and Emma, and haggling with itinerant peddlers. With all of these hardships, she was grateful for the luxury of apples in winter.

She was pleased, too, with her son's new outfit, surprisingly, a Confederate gray, "secesh" being the nickname for Southern rebels. Union troops were called "bluebellies." Her reference to Blue Noses was to the Canadians from Nova Scotia who lived in Maine, sometimes called "Bluenoses" because of the purplish potato they grew.

Damariscotta Jan. 3, 1864

Dear Emma

Today is an awful cold day, we had meeting in the vestry all day, but few went out in the A.M. I went out all day. I have not been out but half a day for once a month, and last Sunday not at all—Seemed real good to hear preaching again—Besides being cold it was very slippery and really dangerous to walk. I managed to get along without falling down but it required all the skill I possessed, and round the corner the wind was terrific. W.H. fell nearly down once, but as might be supposed, recovered himself before he got wholly down. It has been storming most all the week, and rather warm till today—Well, I have got my girl again, thank fortune, and am relieved of my drudgery, but I have wished several times since, that she was back again to her fathers, for things go on in the old way. The very first thing she did was to wash the dishes with an old rag, that I used to wipe up puddles, to do her justice I will say that it was the color of the dishcloth she left and hung in the same place, but where should you think was her nose? I had a nice new white one but that is the same color now, so that Allie has since used it for a similar purpose, isn't that agreeable to think of? She came on Monday about 1/2 past 9. I had just finished washing, and was wringing out the clothes to put out. She had had a slow fever and was not able to come up before. She seems quite well now, though not so strong as formerly, and rather more smart and independent in her manners. Sarah came up at the same time. She has given up going to sea, and wants to get a place up here this winter. She says there are plenty of places, but I hope she will have to hunt for one. Her beau has enlisted, and gone off, and Mary's as far as I can find out died in the hospital at N.O. I was in hope Sarah would not be round this winter I do not think Mary is half so good, when she is about. As I had nearly got through washing I told Mary if she would do the odd jobs, I would put out the clothes as it was an awful cold day and she had been riding and was chilly. I feared she would take cold, but I took cold myself. After dinner I went down street to get some things I felt obliged to have and that night I was up several times, and felt real sick. Besides that, the baby was awake several hours, so that I finally dressed myself and rocked him to sleep—I have not felt well at all this week and have been up with him two nights since. One of my shoulders is very lame so I can scarcely move my arm and for two nights it has ached so I did not sleep well. I expect it is neuralgia—I am glad that I do not have to do the work—As might be expected, I have been very blue indeed, almost to desperation, today is the first day I have felt like even smiling. The baby is better he has been cutting teeth and has had diarrhea, but I administered as a last resort some "Soothing Syrup" which wrought a happy effect— he has one if not two more teeth. The ironing Mary did, caused me to groan not in spirit but in the letter, and other things ditto. "How many trials we do enjoy!" But to turn from these. I wish you all a Happy New Year. There was nothing here to mark the day—Nobody got any New Years Presents—though W.H. expressed his willingness to give me one if I would specify, but I could not. I wanted something unexpected. I mentioned a muff, but that was of course out of the question—I hope you all had something but think you ought to be content if you did not, you fared so well for Christmas. W.H. did however buy me a new "Harper" and half a bushel of apples, which latter smelt of the money I can tell you. It seems as if I could not get along a day without an apple but they are an expensive luxury—I bought a very pretty pair of slippers for a C. present for W.H. I gave 1.25 they look something like velvet carpet, there is a border of purple roses and on the foot an orange colored pansy—I bought me a blue flannel skirt very thick 62½ a yard, almost 2.00 for the skirt, 3 yards of crash 17cts. a yard and I came across a splendid piece of twilled white all wool flannel, it was over a yard wide and very thick. I got 1½ yd. to make a blanket for the trundle bed, it was 1.00 a yard. I got some red and brown yarn for another pair of stockings, for Eddie, and Mary went right to work on them and has got them done they are real pretty. all I got that day so few things cost 4.25. It takes a heap to get very little. Everything is dear. Cotton flannel is 42 cts a yd—I finished

(1864)

my brown dress and wore it today. I made the sleeves trimmed and put them in, and plaited the skirt and put it on, pocket etc. I found it a good deal of work sewing on the velvet but it looks real pretty—I did not know how to plait the skirt not having seen any new fashions, but I plaited it in large box plaits. I felt quite grand with it on but "pride must have a fall" I caught it and tore quite a rent right on the bottom of the skirt behind so I shall have to go to darning tomorrow. I should think your green dress would look fancy, but it is well enough for young ladies like you. Nettie Hussey has postillions like yours on one of her dresses, and Mary's new dress has very much such sleeves I should think. I dislike anything in the rear exceedingly—Mine has two points before I wish you would send me some pieces of your dresses and mother's and pa's dressing gown. I want to see what they are like. A great many folks here have fans on their bonnets with feathers coming out of the spread end. I think they are very pretty. I would get you to make one for me if you were here, but I dont want to be too fashionable. Clara & M. have brown hats with brown velvet fans, a jet across the small end & a black feather tipped with magenta out of the other. I have seen some plaited in the middle just like butterflies. There is quite a display of the fashions this winter here, a good many circulars like yours, and lots of hateful light shaggy sacks. Scarcely anyone wears kid gloves. I suppose you do of course. I should think your bonnet would be real pretty. Fanny Flye wears French blue velvet plaited in her bonnet. The Sing meets there this week and W.H. wants me to go, but my time for such things is past. He says his club goes ahead of yours for they sing sacred Choruses and Opera Music quite difficult. I expect it is quite an affair, and is largely patronized by the upper ten as you call them. But all they have is apples.

 I have only time for a few lines more. I have done quite a little in the way of sewing besides my dressmaking the blanket, towels, and my skirt and a heap of mending. One day I papered the room behind the lounge as we could not match the paper I had to piece it forty leven places some not bigger than a quarter of a dollar, it took a good while then I washed ironed and put on the baby basket covering which was up in my front room awful dirty, that was a fussy job. You had better believe—One day a pedlar came here to buy gold. I hunted up two or three old things which I thought worthless he gave me 13 cts and a silver piece about as big as a fourpence. I made him give me 10 cts for it I got in all 23cts. I mean to get something for the children with it. I send in this 50 cts to pay Hayes for express of the box etc. and crackers, if anything is left take it for your sack, and much obliged I meant to have sent it before but could not. Allie looks nicely in his coat and cape, he dont wear them much but it is a consolation to know that he has got it, he looks like a volunteer in it, only it is gray-secesh color. Speaking of volunteers, I do really hope if you do like W.H.W. you will not commit yourself to any one else if there is the least prospect of anything ———— Remember my experience and profit thereby. I have felt very sad at times thinking upon the past, still I am sure I was led in the best and right way, though perhaps not as I should have chosen. But this openess you will not speak of—I must close, and hope you will excuse this wretched letter it is written in great haste. Children are full of mischief Eddie has just smashed the looking glass and something goes daily— Give my love to all the folks and pray do not think that I do not value or miss your letters, for it is a mistake. Goodbye dear Emma, Sue

I should think Mr. M Lee Smith had better give his money towards the volunteers than giving suppers or buying such expensive clothes for his family, but I consider them vulgar people anyhow—I think it is wrong in such times for Christians to be so extravagant in their dress indeed it is at any time but I have often expressed my mind on this subjects. Perhaps you think it is because I cannot and maybe so—yet I might dress better and more showy if I chose. I had rather give my money to the suffering or some of the various commisions. There has been any number of agents here lately. They will have a public meeting for the Freedmen's Commission this week did you go to the fair I wish I could have gone—Who was the beau? I dont know how many volunteers we have more than half. the agent has gone after Blue Noses I dont know as he will get any they has postponed the draft. Spinning out the agony for me.

Not yet thirty-four, Susan already regarded herself as ancient. With a wistful wink at the memory of a possible past love, she advised Emma not to compromise, but to wait for W.H.W. (William H. Whitney), if that was who she truly cared for. Maria also mentioned Will, suggesting that at twenty, Emma was in love.

(1864)

Washington Jan. 29th 1864

My dear Sister,

What has become of you? it seems an age since I have heard. I know you must have some good excuse for not answering my last, are you sick or not? I only wish I could get beside you for one hour if not longer it would do me so much good. I feel quite anxious about you and my mind dwells so constantly in your home that I fear all is not right. I have thought for several weeks I would write again but my time is so fully occupied that I have really found no opportunity. I will give you a little account of one day—Rise at Half past six and after breakfast help do the chamber work, before school, half past eight. From nine until twelve and frequently the whole noon until then am engaged in my school of sixty-seven boys (for the last month; today the number is reduced to fifty-four) You may imagine that one's brain would be pretty thoroughly turned at the close of the day. Dine about five and for three weeks have attended quite regularly the prayer-meetings held in our church. There is quite an interest felt. Hattie and Florence seem to feel deeply particulary F. they have risen for prayers twice. Oh! how much I wish they might become Christians. This is one reason why I write you. Pray for them. Hattie is so fond of life I sometimes fear for her. Ronnie is still with us and she will probably remain until next Summer. She was on her way to the Capitol accompanying me as far as the City Hall, where I was to be examined, when she remarked that she had a good mind to try just for fun. She went in and passed an excellent examination and next Monday will take a position at my school with those who are awaiting admission and will begin her duties as teacher in the room above mine. She passed for a Secondary School but as there is no vacancy, she has accepted this for the present. She will remain with us, she is excellent company for me.

Washington seems no livelier to me now that a busy country town, I go out so seldom. I have very sad news about Ellie Appleby. Yesterday her father was buried, it is not a year little Mollie breathed her last. The house seems so desolate now. He was a Lutheran minister, but his health failed him and he was compelled to give up preaching. The funeral services were very interesting.

Tonight—Ronnie and Mr. Gates attend a lecture by Henry Barnard of Conn. He will lecture this week before the Teachers'

Institute. I should have gone but yesterday I strained my voice, I suppose and caught cold so that my voice became whispers for one day. The evenings here are very misty and damp, so that people have to be careful. You probably have heard startling reports of Small Pox in this city. There are many cases but no more than there have been for three years past. Father has vaccinated us all. The law has been passed causing all who have not been inoculated for five years to proceed immediately to a doctor or suffer a serious penalty. It is not so severe here as in Baltimore. Would it not be awful if it should get into the army? The very warm weather is quite unfavorable—there has been no mud to speak of this winter, one beautiful Fall, with a few cold days. I have just been in Mrs. Whitiker's room. mr. W. says send my regards. He is a very nice man.

Emma it does seem as if you would never write. I have waited so long—I have blamed myself because I wrote so short a letter but then I had no news as is also the case now.

We occasionally get a Cambridge Chronical and it is treat although there is little of it but the advertisements look so natural. Mr. W. takes the Boston Journal. I wonder how our Southern friends prosper. What do you hear. Well; a new idea just struck me. You are getting ready for the arrival of our friend in a busy way—I do not wonder you have no time to think of your friends. How many of our classmates are married and engaged. I sometimes get frightened at shadowy premonitions of the future but that is all the good it does. I settle down again in the regular old track. Father teases me considerably and says i grow old fast—I suppose I am getting on the schoolmarm expression. I have not had any photographs taken yet. You must not be surprised some day to see a ghost appear in your letter in the cad form. Since I last wrote I have had my teeth filled and fixed nicely—It was not at all painful—I am quite disgusted with myself for waiting so long.

I wonder if Will is with you now and how all are. Give my love to your Father and Mother. I wish I coud see them. How is Sue and her little ones or big boys now?

Que-prenez-vous de mon papier? It is something new. i have been investing in a small scale. It is beautiful to write upon.

Half past eleven and I must go to bed so as to be frech tomorrow. <u>Do write soon.</u> If you have any mercy on your loving sister

Maria

(1864)

"Washington seems no livelier to me now than a busy country town," observed Maria. The capitol suffered by comparison with "Athens of America," the Boston/Cambridge community from which she had moved.

A French engineer, Major Pierre Charles L'Enfantin, designed Washington, the first planned city in the United States, in the pattern of a checkerboard with spokes radiating from the center. The city was built in 1791 on marshy swamp that had belonged to the Powhatan Indians and remained pretty much a country town until the Civil War, when government expansion nourished a building boom. At the time Maria was writing, neither the Washington Monument, which had been under construction for more than fifteen years, nor the Capitol Building were completed. Throughout the war, however, President Lincoln insisted that construction crews work on the Capitol Building as a symbol that the country would be made whole again.

> Sunday Evening.
> Washington Feb 21st 1864

My dear Sister,

I have such joyful news to write that I cannot wait for you to answer my last. tonight I have a severe cold and dare not venture out in the damp evening air, so I will pen a few of my thoughts to you. I wrote that Hattie and Florence were deeply interested in the subject of Religion, both feel now that they have found a precious Saviour, and are surprised that they did not see the way before, it is so simple. Florence says "Last night after I retired, I thought in how many ways God has blessed me, with Father and Mother, everything to make me happy, and I had never realized that He was the giver, and never thanked Him." She seems to understand herself and expresses her feelings in a beautiful manner; F. always was a good child, everyone who has seen her any length of time has observed it; we think her judgement is excellent, upon what is said to her by those friends who have spoken with her. Hattie has always possessed an entirely different disposition, but we see a happy change in her. She remarked yesterday, "Florence always was good, but I have so much more to overcome." Emma, rejoice with me and give praises to the Lord for his wonderful kindness. I feel condemned when I think how little faith I possessed. How rejoiced my dear Mother would have been, could she have witnessed the change before she died, her children, Hattie particularly were the only cause she had for anxiety in leaving this world. Does she know of our happiness? I love to think so anyway. The interest is very general among the S.S. Scholars, special prayer is made for some one unconverted, every evening. Friday eve. Fred McLellan was the subject. I believe he is rather skeptical. Thursday, there was a young drummer boy from the hospital opposite the church, who seemed agonized on account of his sins; he would not give up but persisted in praying for himself when others were not praying for him; he acted so singularly that many thought him deranged until all at once he burst out "He is coming" "Jesus is coming" and began to sing. Since then he is evidently a creature in Christ. Last week one of my dear friends passed, as she expressed it, <u>Home</u>. Her death was beautiful, longing to be with Jesus and <u>see Him</u> as he is. She was an orphan and a few days before her death counted her friends in heaven. The day, on which she died she left a message for each one of her friends in the Church. I believe I have never written to you about her for she is comparitively [sic] a stranger amongst us, yet everyone loved her the short time she was with us and she loved everybody, her name was Sarah Swan. We had become very well acquainted meeting at S. School, church and Sewing Circles. her life was beautiful. Father writes that there is quite an interest in Cambridge, well do I remember those Monday evening prayer meetings. Who attend them now, it seems as if most of those who used to take part had gone to the war. Where is Martha Burage now and has she joined the church; you know at one time she thought of it.

Mr. Williams was on last week, I was very much disappointed in not seeing him, we were all away at a lecture. He went to the church and saw the children. I had made an engagement to attend the lectures before the meetings commenced, although I do not go out much evenings and do not know as I should go to the meetings all the time. I get very tired during the day in my school. Give my love to all my friends, tell Mrs. W. I should have called her had I known she was here. Ronnie is waiting for me to go to bed now so I must soon close, she sends her love. it is very pleasant for me to have her here. We go and come from school together. We are longing for next Summer.

Have you a class in S. School now and who are in it. I have eight or nine little boys. Do write soon for I am anxiously waiting. You <u>must</u> have your mother's photograph. I would not let

(1864)

another week pass without it. You will always regret it if anything should happen and you had none taken recently. From

Your affec. Sister
Maria

As her letter indicates, Maria and other religious people believed that they would be reunited with their loved ones in the hereafter. Indeed, to preserve the body for posterity, embalming became popular at this time. Some ministers also wrote treatises on the afterlife, describing in detail the reunions of family and friends in Heaven, how their houses would be furnished, what they would eat, and the activities appropriate to eternity.

It is interesting that Susan, immersed in church affairs through her husband's ministry, wrote little about religious matters. Rather, acutely conscious of her own shortcomings, she tried to live an exemplary life, fulfilling her responsibilities to family and community, both of which threatened to strain her endurance.

Pregnant for the third time in four years, Susan was exhausted and frightened. Although it is unlikely that she and her husband practiced birth control, many middle-class couples were able to plan their families with some success. The first reliable condom was manufactured around 1844, approximately five years after Charles Goodyear vulcanized rubber. By mid-century, when condoms replaced coitus interruptus as the most popular form of birth control, the birth rate began to decline. Coincidentally, medical books also for the first time accurately reported the fertile time in a woman's menstrual cycle.

Damariscotta Feb. 28, 1864

Dear Emma:

I owe you many thanks for your kind letter, so full of interesting accounts of the meetings and "goings on" at home. It makes me almost imagine I am there. I enjoy hearing about them so much. You are very fortunate to have so many opportunities. I look back to mine with much pleasure, doubtless you will in the future. You say if your letter is not enough, there will be enough beside to satisfy me but my hunger is of the kind that Shakespeare describes it "grows uppon what it feeds on." If I got 2 letters a day I should not be more satisfied. Writing home is one of the sunny spots in my existence, though I labor under many disadvantages. I can't shut myself up in my room with a portfolio, clean paper, and one to molest, but I have to fight my way amidst screams, battle mischif, and interruptions of all kinds. Paper daubed with molasses or ink as the case may be, and I am so low that I can't sit but little while to do anything. I began a letter this morning, but they tormented me so I had to give it up, and when i came to read it over it didn't make any sense and I threw it into the stove. Things are going on about the old way here only "more so". I don't seem to make any progress forward or backward. The children's cols hang on yet, and I am about half sick myself. I have been awake with that baby 4 nights running 2 and 3 hours at a time, he wakes about midnight. I stand it as long as I can, and my limbs ache so i can't lay in the bed so I get up and rock him an hour or so til he goes to sleep, then I go back, but do not always rest for one night I had the nightmare awfully, and last night allie was so croupy I did not dare to go to sleep. The baby wakes with a coughing spell, and keep awake. Soothing Syrup don't do any good, keeping him awake in the day time don't either. he is bound not to sleep. W.H. fusses because the baby acts so, and he won't go upstairs because it is cold so I am between two fire's all the time, though I must say W.H. does take care of him some of the time, and will do most anything but get out of bed for him. I get about desperate, and make up my mind that I can't live another day, but somehow in the morning I seem to feel a little more courage, he is often cross in the daytime and into every kind of mischief. I have to keep running all the time to repair and prevent damages and even then dont keep things from generally going to ruin and smash. Allie too is occasionally mischievous though I can manage him well enough—I have stuck pretty faithfully to the old lounge this week, though it is full of lumps and not very comfortable. I could not do much in the sewing line, but I am not very much driven there is enough that I ought to do if I could get spunk to cut it out but I am too low to stand long, and the children steal my scissors and work, so I give it up. I spent an hour yesterday blowing bubbles for the children with an old pipe aunt Hildreth gave me they were highly pleased. I show them pictures and tell them stories, and sing to them. Allie is charmed with "Darling Nelly Gray" and when his father sang "old uncle Ned" he cried hard "because the poor old man had to be burried up", "Aint you sorry" he said. I enjoy playing with the children, but don't dare to give them much

(1864)

attention for fear they will miss me too much by and by. I have been reading "the Color Guard" it was written by one of W.H.'s college classmates, a clergyman, who enlisted as a private soldier in the Mass 52nd and it is very interesting as giving an account of Bank's campaign & seige of P. Hudson. There is not much battle about it, but the descriptions of the forced marches and hospitals scenes are very interesting. I wish I could get more books to read as the time hangs heavy on my hands. I read all the papers and W.H. buys Harper every month, but still I could read much more. Preparations for the fair are going on bravely. I made a prodigious effort this week and made two butterflies like what I used to make long ago. They were very pretty. I wanted to make a cat and dog, but could not muster spunk enough, so I sent some money. By the way my funds have been replenished this week. 5.00 the result of two marriages (hard times you know) Thursday eve. just before meeting a young couple appeared and were "jined" and W.H. had hardly gone before another middle aged couple appeared, they waited till he came home. Both lived out of the village in different directions. Wasn't it rather singular coincidence. I thought of getting me a new calico dress, but believe after all I shall wait and have my carte de visitee when I visit home again, if I ever am permitted to do so but I am afraid that will not be very soon. I feel rather poor this year, though W.H.'s salary has been nominally increased $100. he will not probably get it, and things are so awful dear and our expenses grow larger. But that gives me little concern, if we only keep out of debt. W.H. is going to give his school bill to the town towards the counties. There will be no danger here of a draft on the 2 calls, and we have 7 or 8 on a future call. I am thankful for that. Mary is exceedingly dismal and cross today. Sarah has just heard that her beau is at the point of death in Washington. I think Mary feels it most, but it does not express itself in the pleasantest way. She is snappish and sulky to me and the children. She has got a bad cold too. I have just left off an hour or two and been trying to amuse the baby, he was awful cross. I made a horrible compound composed of molasses, onions, hot tea he wouldn't touch it but Allie would, so I made a little Slipping Elm candy for Eddie and they were both suited. You ought to have seen their faces. Yesterday I made some more soft soap, but didn't have such good luck as I did with the first. Eddie got a little speck of the "Concentrated Lye" which was on the table, and ate it and it took the skin off of his lip and tongue and made him as cross as time all the P.M. he is better today but coughs badly. I don't know but he has got the whooping cough. The measles are all round as well as other diseases. Agreeable to think of isn't it? It seems as I should give wholly up sometimes. How long are you going to stay at Alfred's and what are they going to do after you are gone. I don't see why in the world her own sister don't go and help her. I don't think you ought to be detailed as Bridget all the time. I felt dreadfully to think they lost their baby I have not told the children yet. But I must close I feel as if this was a wretched letter written by a wretched individual but you must excuse all faults and give my love to all from yours truly. Sue

Susan mentioned that she hoped to pose for a carte de visitee, a visiting card, 3½ by 2¼ inches, with a small photographic portrait. It was introduced in Paris in 1858 and soon became popular everywhere.

She called Emma, who was helping out at Alfred's, "Bridget," a colloquial expression derived from the many Irish immigrants who found jobs as domestics. But Alfred had no intention of taking advantage of Emma. He had asked his mother only how to care for Mary after the death of their infant and Emma volunteered her assistance. He responded, "I am much obliged to you for sending Emma, can you spare her? I did not intend to have you send me anything for Mary only send me recipes that I may know what to make for her when she is so weakened by Diarrhoea and Vomiting as Cracker distressed her, toasted bread sours on her stomach. I think only of Farina, Rice etc. We have apparently a very good Doctor (Homeopath & [undecipherable]) but still I found I knew all he told me but had not the medicines to give to Mary—

If Emma has time before she comes up to step into Bayley's (I'll ask father to do it) and get me a small bottle of Alcohol to bathe Mary with as she is sometimes in the hot days (when sick) very cold and shivering the doctor gave me some Extract of Cayenne to mix with half alcohol & half water to bathe her to get up a warmth. do you think it would be beneficial, he told me to rub it onto the back up and down the spine."

Mary's illness on the heels of what appears to have been a difficult delivery and loss of her baby may have been in Susan's thoughts. Her depression is reflected in, among other statements, the comment that while she enjoys playing with the children, she is afraid of giving them too much attention "for fear they will miss me by and by." This was a common attitude during pregnancy, when women customarily prepared for their own death by drawing up wills. The mortality rate —one mother died in every one hundred fifty-four live births, and many others were maimed for life—meant that most women knew of friends or relatives who had died in childbirth.

As her pregnancy progressed, Susan was confined more to home. By her seventh or eighth month, a woman often took to her bed. Modesty dictated that she also restrict her activities in public. This represented a considerable loss of freedom since, in the antebellum period, pregnant women enjoyed a full social life. The ban was so pervasive that a pregnant neighbor was reluctant to visit Susan lest she encounter the Reverend Evans. When Susan's pregnancy became obvious she was even reluctant to go through the village. For that reason, she was especially thankful for the visits and favors of her neighbors, which extended the boundaries of her world.

The childbirth experience bonded women; labor and delivery was a cooperative event. Neighbor women brought food, took care of children, and helped during the delivery. Even when a physician was present, he was very much aware of being watched by the women. Some physicians complained about interfering neighbors; a few had to pack up their offices and move out of town after neighbor women witnessed their poor treatment of a patient during childbirth.

D. March 20, 1864

Dear Emma,

I havent written to you; for quite a while I know, not because I didnt want to, but I have felt unequal to it. I can make out a list of my sufferings to mother, but I do not wish to intrude them upon anyone else, and I would not to any one, only that I must write something, and after have nothing else to write. I am much obliged to you for your last letter, as I have it not handy, I may not be able to answer it in detail, still I was much interested in your account of matters & things in which you were occupied. It served to divert my mind for a time at least from my cares, and yet when I think how much you are enjoying, while I am struggling on alone, I cant help almost envying you, and feeling sad at the contrast, not that I dont wish you to be happy of course, or to complain of my own lot. I have had my day, and I hope it will be a long long while before lifes burdens press upon you as heavily as I feel them. But I have said enough on this score—I was very much pleased with the little things you made for me, they were beautiful. Lissie was up here one evening this week and said Callie was delighted with her present and thought it real kind of you to think of her. She has a good many little presents sent to her. Her friends feel a great deal of anxiety about her. She is so very large, and she is hardly able to move about. She wants very much to come up and see me, but doesnt like to meet W.H. I would go to see her if I didnt have to go through the village, but I hope we shall meet by & by if all is favorable. her husband is expected very soon, and she is quite impatient at the delay she had hoped to take the next voyage with him, but according to present indications, is not likely to. I felt so lonely that I asked Lissie to come up and spend the P.M. with me, and so on Friday she came. I should have enjoyed her visit but the children were very troublesome that day, and I was quite unwell, and she was so nice and particular, and everything I had seemed so dirty and out of order, that I really felt sorry I asked her. I felt so tired that night that I laid down with my clothes on, till W.H. came home from the sing (10 o' clock) he helped me get to bed. Still Lissie was kind and cheerful, and helped while away a stormy afternoon—she is one of the best girls. i wish she could visit Cambridge and attend the meetings. She is so much interested in religion she is very different from other young ladies here. She said how much she wished she could have your photograph—She said Alfred enquired about you in a recent letter, he is in Mystic, Conn. and is I believe doing well. Russell has boarded at Lissie's this winter. He is engaged to a young lady in Waldoboro she says. He has been to Augusta, and had thought of enlisting but I dont know whether he has or not. He will be a great loss to this place, he is the best and most popular teacher we have had though he has some enemies. he makes himself at home here, and walks right in where I am, and the children (sometimes to my discomfiture, but I have to grin & bear it)

Abbie Hutton's brother, Liet Reeve, has been home on a furlough he is a classmate of Russells. he left yesterday and Mary Hilton went with him. She and Abbie came once to bid me goodbye. She is a nice little girl, and has been to see me a good deal. She has been here almost two years. I shall miss her, and Abbie is quite sad about it (she is not very well)

Jeannette Webb called on me one day this week, and brought a little pair of blue & white socks which old Mrs. Hanley knit for me. I enjoyed her call very much. I went over to Mrs. Wales

(1864)

one afternoon and staid quite a while—Mrs. Hutchins comes in almost every day, and Mrs. Clapp came in one day she is a very kind woman. W.H. has been full of business this week. He has had to make out his school bill and report, which was quite a job. He <u>gave</u> in his services to the town this year, as the expenses have been very heavy owing to the high bounties, etc. and he is not reqired to pay taxes. He hoped to withdraw from his position but discovered to his consternation that he had been elected for 3 years ("for the war," I said) What he will do I cant tell. It is a very laborious and thankless office, compensation almost nothing in proportion to labor expended, and he makes enemies and gets found fault with because he does what he thinks right without reference to what people think or say. Yet all concede that the schools have never been so good here before. He had 2 funerals to attend besides, and visit the bereaved families besides. Old Mr. Hitchcock on the Bristol road one day and Judge Chapman the next. His body came from Augusta Tues. night. W.H. called Wednes. A.M. and his wife desired a strictly private funeral. (He was preparing a funeral sermon for Sunday) Thursday A.M. some one called and told him they had concluded to have it in the meeting house, and wanted a sermon that day at 1 o' clock. Upon such short notice he was obliged to take out an old one and then run round and invite Bulfinch and attend to other matters. The services were very long and he was about tired out, besides having his feelings very much wrought upon, for he was deeply affected at the death of Mr. C who has been one of his warmest friends and supporters. He was a fine man, and a great loss to his family & the public. His death made a deep impression here and there is some reason to hope that good may result from it. There are some encouraging signs here, still we hardly dare hope. Yet, W.H. and some of the members are feeling much, and praying for a change. They are going to try and get a church meeting this week, and discipline some of the members. Will probably be excluded who have been engaged in <u>open</u> wickedness—The Fair came off last week, 3 evenings, one <u>was</u> a sale, the other two, tableaux music & comedy. It was pretty well attended and they got clear about $500 and would have had more, but the weather and giving were very bad. About $50 of the money was abstracted by some of the Committee, and there is now a great fuss and stew to find it. The whole was rather a disgraceful affair and those who were in it wish they had kept clear of it.

W.H. is thankful he stood aloof, Bulfinch & the Cong. minister of Bristol were there. The stage has not been in any night till past 9 o' clock, and the going is awful. One night it did not come in till 3 o' clock. The cars run off the track and were detained 3 hours, and the stage got stuck in a mud hole and they had to wake up the folks in the nearest houses and get 2 yoke of oxen to get it out. But we are hoping the going will be better soon. The Queen begins her trips, by the first of next month, and there is a strong probability that there will be a steamer between here and Portland this summer.

Susan's war cake recipe called for apples, but women made do with whatever they had on hand. The following recipe is from Marjorie Mosser's cookbook, *Good Maine Food*:

WAR CAKE

2 cups brown sugar   1/4 teaspoon cloves
1/2 cup hot water   1 teaspoon cinnamon
1/2 cup raisins   pinch of salt
2 tablespoons butter 1 teaspoon soda
                     3 cups flour

Boil sugar, water, raisins, butter, spices and salt 5 minutes. Cool; then add soda and flour. Pour into a buttered cake pan and bake in a moderate oven, 350 degrees.

Sarah has not got any plans. she is waiting to hear from Bath. I made a new kind of cake this week, all the neighbors have been making it. it is called War Cake, or "Dried Apple Gingerbread." It has the appearance of fruit cake but is only an imitation. I wish you could see the boys play. Eddie gets the wheelbarrows and says "Allie, ride me to Bath" Allie obeys. Then Eddie tries to ride Allie in it. that is the bright side. They have sad battles sometimes and make me almost crasy. [sic] Allie asks such curious questions such as "Mama has God got any legs? and why not?" He will pin you up so close you cant get away from his questions nor answer them either. He has been very naughty this week but he thinks if he is not actually committing sin at the time, that he is a good boy. I have not done

(1864)

any work to speak of. I have not been able to but have had to be on the lounge all I could. My spring work is beginning to call me, but I cannot do it and so I have to keep still and try to be patient—But I cannot write any more now, I am paying you back in your own coin and making a pussle for you to read. I would like to write a good deal more, but I am tired and the children are teasing me so I shall have to quit. I will try and put in a line to mother if I can. I shall not attempt to come to Cambridge this summer, and if my friends wish to see me they must prove it by coming where I am. As for the "little girl" I do not think there is any danger of one. I shall be thankful to have anything. But I never shall stop writing if I keep on, so I'll stop short and say "goodbye" with love to all from Sue.

P.S. Another call for men, and few if any on our quota, but I try to take it easy.

Gymnastics are taught in the public schools in Bath. I think it good for the health if not carried to excess. I hardly think I should care to engage in it though perhaps I may when I have had 9 children. At present I have excercised enough very likely that old lady missed her former exercise. I am glad you like it. I should think you would look real funny. Pity about W. Hammond wasnt it? but I dont see as he was to blame Emily W. has not a surplus of manners if she is a rich man's daughter what sweet pet that alligator must be. I have felt real anxious about the folks there has been so much sickness I feared some of you would be sick I hope they are better I am almost afraid it is very gloomy all the time so I have very hard work to be cheerful at all Mary does quite well now but I have to be careful and keep the right side of her.

Susan concluded her postscript with a comment about Emily W., calling her an "alligator," a term for someone who binds or ties down another person.

While Susan was anchored in the Maine wilderness, confined to home during her pregnancy, Emma visited with friends, attended lectures, skated, and went sleighing. In short, she seemed carefree, taking part in Cambridge's busy social life. The contrast was not lost on Susan, who admitted to envying her sister's lifestyle.

Yet in June, when Susan's baby was due, Emma scurried to Maine to help out where she was needed. Writing to her there, her Mother appropriated Father Barbour's official stationery.

United States internal Revenue Office
No. 449 Main Street
John N. Barbour, Deputy Collector

Cambridgeport   June 15th, 1864

My dear Emma:

I was much pleased to receive your letter, and also find you got along so well. I did not expect you would both go off without being seasick. I think from your discription you must have had a very pleasant journey. I think that sail into Bath, early in the morning is very fine, I enjoyed it much, then you found them all well. I was so glad, let us be thankful to our Heavenly Father for all his mercies to us, after you left Mrs. Munroe stopt awhile then Father came in, he had been to Mothers he found her downstairs, as smart (as he said) as a biscuit. Aunt Abby had gone out with H. to ride. Aunt Maryann was there, Father told her that I was left all alone, she said directly she would come on the next day and spend the day with me if it was Saturday, he told her I would be real glad to have her, and to come early, and I was and had a very pleasant time only for one thing, you know I would rather she would come when G. was at home, she sat with me in the kitchen until I got my pies and cakes baked (for she did come early) then we went out to see the garden, canker worms and catterpillars included after dinner we went out on the street and got my photographs, she selected one, the standing ones she did not recognize, seemed to enjoy herself much, and returned home with a nice little boquet I gathered for her about seven o'clock. Sunday it was real lonesome so few of us, we sat until half past eleven waiting for Katy but she did not come, so we shut up the house and went to bed but she was home at five o'clock (before I was up) in the morning I went down and let her in, she said she staid to the Christening. I do not know what they do have a good time I suppose, she and Michels brother staid with the baby, as God Father and Mother I suppose this seems to be thought a great honour among them, she said she had to work real hard and Bright thought she would be glad to get back, she went up Tuesday even to see how she was getting along and wants to go Friday afternoon and sweep for her Monday I went to the prayer meeting after which mrs. Leeds and myself went and made that call after the Golden Wedding it was a fine day and we had a very pleasant call, as

(1864)

well and walk though it was long. Tuesday I went in and sat with Aunt Julia a while, in the evening Father and I went up to Aunt Lovica's and spent the evening we had a very pleasant visit, they had heard from Jimmie the day before he sent to his Mother to get him some new army pants that his government pants (shoddy) were coming all to pieces, Shame she said to Miss Ballard and another young lady who had a brother there went down to visit them and said they saw J. that he was puttying cracks in [undeciferable] carriages and painting them, he said his hands were so black he could not shake hands with them, however, he was mighty glad to see them. Auntys folks have none of them been down yet they are hoping he will get to come home Class day and spend the day and night, by the way Willie Munroe came in Saturday and gave me one of his cards invited me to come up to his room Class day and he would get me a seat to hear the oration and poem, he invited Mrs. Leeds also and if she goes perhaps I shall though I do not care a great sight about it. Mr. and Mrs. Munroe have reserved seats, I suppose there will be a great crowd which you know I do not enjoy much. Monday eve Freddy Lewis came in and sat till nine o' clock she came to beg a piece more of that calico trimming we gave her to trim a white apron. I found some and gave it to her, she said they heard from Abby the week before she seemed to be enjoying herself, some of her scholars are pretty hard cases, but not all. Last Sunday Mr. Shute visited the sabbath school and spoke he is an agent for the tract society for the Army he spoke of the need of religious reading in the Army and asked the children any of them that felt willing to take a paper of which he had a number with him, and go round and see how much they could get in small sums quite a number of the girls and boys took papers, and this week have been round from door to door and some of them have raised quite a little sum, there have been six or eight here so I try to manage to give a small amount to each that they may all be encouraged in their good work you would like to see how pleased they look if you give them five or ten cts postal currency, they say now I have got so much but to your letter, I was glad if the articles you carried gave pleasure. I was sorry, we forgot some things, those you mentioned also maple sugar I stowed away to send, I was so glad Ned thought of the candy; then your waist lining that was my fault, for I got the muslin waist out of the drawer, and did not see the lining however, I hope you will manage to get along if you could not do better you could buy a little piece of cotton and make one, but if M. can spare one of her to you i suppose you would like it better. I shall want to know if any of the little clothes fitted when you write again stocking, dresses, & wether the collars were what was needed or anything you can think of to tell me. I was sorry the Horse caused strife, I think however Sue adopted the right coarse, in taking the ownership to herself and let them take turns riding Father supposed she would do that. I hope you are having a nice time I know there will be enough to do, but many hands make light work, and if you was glad to have M. go I know you will be ready and willing to do it for Sues sake perhaps she did not think as you said she was playing second, but my how I hope she will be able if she gets another girl to get one more agreeable. Will went over to Roxbury Friday he called at Mrs. Burrages and took tea, little Henry was sick abed with the measles, he was taken just a fortnight from the time he came to our house, they had a telegraph also that day, from Washington, stating that Henry Burrage, had been wounded, and was on his way home they had no particulars. I supposed when W.H. went to G. Mond and told she would come right home, but she has not come yet. Alfred says they will come to night. I wanted to go over there today but Father did not think it necessary so I did not go. I hope to hear soon Will said he could not be here for several days. I hope he is not badly wounded. to day is the first real warm day we have had since you left it began to grow warmer yesterday I am cutting and fitting my new thin dress this week I shall make a full waist and jacket sleeves like yours but I must close now think how lonesome I am and write every thing you can think of and more too, tell Sue and Mary I hope they will have a nice time as well as yourself and perhaps Sue will think it a good time to visit us when you all come home, but she knows best with much love from Mother, S.S.B.

P.S. Robert Fullers children have all had the measles and were very sick but have all got about again. Sarah has had the mumps she left I think in England, poor thing.

After the birth of Charles, Susan's health was broken. Physically and emotionally spent, she was unable to care for her three young children. Allie, the eldest, was easiest to manage and the new baby needed to be nursed, so she arranged for Eddie to visit his grandparents. Emma returned to Cambridgeport, with her nephew in tow.

(1864)

Susan missed him terribly. Longing for his return, she strived to regain her strength and spirits.

Damariscotta Nov. 2 1864

Dear Sister Emma,

As I have little leisure before bedtime and do not feel like sewing I will employ it in writing to you, though I may only write part of a letter. I received mothers & fathers last night and am very glad to read them and to have the photograph of Ned, tell him I am very much obliged also for his truble in sending the ale. The vessel came in today, and the box was all right. I was very glad of the corkscrew, for ours was not large enough for the bottles. It took all of W.H.'s strength to draw the cork. I liked the ale quite well, and hope that it may prove strengthening to me. I shall take a little every day. I am very much obliged to you for all your kindness. Tell father I shall not dare to give a picture to mrs. Hutchings unless I give Mrs. Wales one, for she has done equally as much for me according to her ability, and she is very sensitive and would feel quite hurt I am sure, if she knew Mrs. H. had one and she had not.

So let him send one more for her. I am sorry I did not write before about Allie, if mother felt anxious to hear but I have not had much time, and he was not any worse. I do not think however that he has been so well since his fall, he has a real bad cold now, and last evening he said he saw lamps all over the room and he was afraid of them and the figures on the carpet were going up to the ceiling and he was going to catch one of them. I think he must have been a little dissy. He has seemed rather more nervous and cross since his fall I got so frightened that I did not get over it for several days. Little Charlie is real cunning now he will soon creep I think, he is very active and noisy. he seems almost exactly like Eddie all over again. He knows where the clock is, and Allie. and when you say "stop"! and if any one coughs he will hide his head under my arm he will pull up the tablecloth or his dress to play "peek-a-boo" with us. He is pretty good with Sarah, but cries after me some. I have him a good deal. Allie does not like her nor she him very well. he will not mind her a bit, and she dont like to coax him. How cunning dear little Eddie must be. I have wanted to see him so much for a day or two past that I didn't know what to do but I am glad the dear child is where he can receive so much care

Emma's World

and attention. Allie often wishes he could see him. It seems to me as if Charlie was Eddie, and I had never had but two I have about concluded to call the baby Charles Albert for Mr. Hale said one day that he thought perhaps it would make us unpopular to call him after anyone, and I felt so too and had all along so I thought I would change it—we all went over to make a call at Mrs. S. Halls, and they made us stop to tea. We had a real pleasant time Austin asked after you, he said you went over there with me to tea. I remembered it very well. Mrs. Hilton, Mrs. Campbell and Annette Curtis came here the other evening. Mrs. C. brought me 4 pounds of splendid butter as a present, and the next day she sent me 2 quarts of milk, we indulged in a squash pie, some dipped toast and had milk in our tea for three days. Poor Allie is badly off for his "pug-feels" he will not drink anything but water, though we offer him tea and cocoa. he dropped his picture plate and broke it today, and was most heartbroken. he cried but I told him he had another, with Old Robert on it, so I brought out the old one and he was comforted. I went out and made some calls yesterday I called at Mrs. Farnhams. She was out, at Mrs. A. Flye's, and she was out. I saw Fannie she asked for you I called at Mrs. Cotters and at Mrs. Wins. I called on Abbie metcalf the other day she is just getting out, she has been very sick. She said she should certainly have called to see you, but she supposed you were going to stay much longer. Do you go to the Gymnasium now? They had one here in summer. I saw some church bells and rings like yours in Mrs. Morse's house.

This afternoon there was a female prayer meeting at Mrs. Clapps I went, and they had a very good meeting. There seems to be a good deal of interest here, there is one more hopeful conversion, and several thoughtful. I hope there is going to be a revival.

We had tickets to a concert by Comical Brown sent us last night. I did not wish to go but Sarah went. The Methodists are to have an Antiquarian Supper Friday night and W.H. says we are expected to go. I can feel safe to leave the baby with S. evenings so I may go out more than I used to. I like her quite well. She is real handy and kind and affectionate. She knows how to do most everything and is very quick and smart, but is not very strong. She reminds me very much of Mary Evans, but is more intelligent and refined—We have been cleaning house today and shall do so the rest of the week. I feel rather tired, not being

(1864)

used to the business, in fact I am rather slow and clumsy about all kinds of housework, it is so long since I did any. I had a dreadful disappointment this week. You know the vessel that has been building in sight of our house. The first piece was put up when I was sick in my room. I have watched it with deep interest, and dreaded to have it go away I really loved it. She was launched last Monday and we hurried through the washing, and the folks went off but me. I preferred to stay and see it from the window. I stationed myself upstairs and was looking out when I thought maybe I could see it a little plainer from the entry window So I got up and laid Charlie on the bed, and went to the window the curtain was down, and when I rolled it up. She was gone! I could not help crying not for the mere disappointment of not seeing it but the associations connected with it were so deep they seemed a part of myself. I cannot look at her empty place without a pang of regret. It may seem foolish to you but I am weak and childish yet. No money would have paid me to miss seeing it and yet it was my own fault but I am getting over it now but I cannot write any more tonight I may add a line tomorrow.

Elisa Upham sent me a squash pie, Mrs. Tukey some fresh pork, and Mr. Norris did two splendid loads of chips. The people are very kind to us

Thursday—I thought I would write a line or two more we have been cleaning all day it is five o' clock, and I have just sat down, I expect to feel tired tomorrow we cleaned the entries and parlor, there is so much to do and the days are so short I don't get much time to sew. I have been out a good deal in the P.M. and evenings I am too tired to write. Sarah helps me a great deal, but I don't like to take all her time. She has had sewing of her own. I concluded to Keep the proofs of the children and send good pictures to aunt H. and Aunt Lovika the one I sent has Hildreth on the back. I thought you would know what it meant. Dear Emma you can't tell how grateful I feel to you for your kind care of dear little Eddy. I feel far safer to have him there than here, though I miss him very much and last night could not sleep for thinking of him. Yet, Charlie seems in a great measure to fill his place, he seems very much like him he screams loud and acts real witch-y But I hope we shall be able to break in his surplus spirits, before he gets as far along as Eddie did, and not let him gain on us to much. I hope I shall be able before long to have them all together with me. When Charlie gets a little older, but sometimes I think I never shall see that time again. I feel sometimes almost discouraged I feel so weary and weak. But I try to keep up courage as well as I can. I suppose you have not seen the Lieut. or Capt dear Emma, before that subject is dismissed. But I must say goodbye now dear sister though I have much more to say. I have no time. God bless you always, live near to Christ, and you will be happy. If I have, as I know, I often have seemed to chide you, to intrude my opinion upon you, forgive it, it was meant kindly, but you are far better than I and the tears will come when I think upon your goodness, but no more. Love to all from your Sister. Sarah is real pleasant she runs around and waits on me lots. I like her very much indeed. I hope she will be contented.

Dear little Eddie

How your mama would like to see you. Do you want to see her and Allie and papa and little Charlie. Oh he is so cunning and pretty. he can shout real loud now, and he knows ever so much. Poor little Allie hurt him but he is better now. One day he took a walk with mama and he saw a pet dowwie and some hens, and he took his Dicky that Granma made him and said he was going to give his to Willie Hilton, he got an old piece of cloth and sewed red and blue stripes on it to make a soldier coat for him, but Willie was gone away so he tossed Dick into Mrs. H's entry, but mama picked it up and brought it home. Allie wants mama to make him a flag and she is going to when she gets time. Last night when Allie went to bed he hung up his sock by the fire in the kitchen, and said he should find something good in the morning and what do you think he found A cooky and an apple! Now little Eddie mama must say goodbye. How she would like to kiss him. Be a good little boy for Mama.

11
(1865)

*B*y the new year, Susan's health had improved very little. She was discouraged and impatient; it seemed to take her a long time to recuperate. Moreover, she had a tendency to set very high standards for herself, then judge herself harshly when she didn't always meet them. She knew she wasn't strong enough to care for three children, but she sadly missed Eddie, who remained with Emma in Cambridgeport, and recurring thoughts of him haunted her. In her weakened condition, she found it difficult to make choices, preferring to leave important decisions to W.H.

Emma's World

January 24, 1865
Newcastle, Me.

My Dear Sister

Your long and interesting letter is before me and I am sure I can do nothing adequate in the way of answering it but I will try to the best I can Allie is at my side writing a letter to Eddie, and keeps teasing for one thing or other. Charlie is asleep but for how long is uncertain, so you see circumstances must affect me somewhat. I have been ironing this morning and did some yesterday we dry our clothes upstairs now in the very cold weather and very deep snow, and as they freese it keeps the ironing dragging about longer than I like, that is of course only a temporary inconvenience. The snow is several feet on the ground and in some places is drifted very badly, the weather has been bitter cold for a day or two, but I suppose I do not know much about it as we keep our rooms quite warm and do not get up till the fires are going. Monday morning W.H. wished to go to King's early and did the washing I laid abed with the children he left at 9 o' clock and did not return till Tuesday noon when he brought a minister back with him to dinner, it was so cold they had no meeting, but he accomplished some business (I don't know what) that atoned for the discomforts of his cold trip. While he was gone, we got our meals in the sitting room with the coal fire which saved so much trouble. We had no services on Sunday as the roads were wholly blocked up in the P.M. there was a path shovelled to the meeting house and I started bravely out, but when I got to the vestry, there was no one there but Mr. Wales and his boys so back I came I have not been to meeting since New Years day, and then only half a day. the weather has been very stormy since I came home. The church are now to have two preaching services, instead of Sunday School in the P.M. as they have had all along, and W.H. has given up his Bible class and they will have a prayer meeting in the evening instead of preaching. W.H. thinks it will be a little easier for him as the labor of getting ready for S. School lesson was considerable added to preaching twice, his work is hard any way—and he has many obstacles to contend with, but I think he will remain here for the present as regards my own feelings though I would much prefer to be nearer home, still I am willing I think, to stay as long as is best. I do not wish to have any choice in the matter. W.H. is very much disenchanted

(1865)

and discouraged at times, but I do not see any special reason for it or any more obstacles than he would encounter in any other place though not perhaps of the same nature.

The people mostly are very polite and kind. I think the visit of the S. School here was mutually pleasant and agreeable. To Allie it was a source of great pleasure and he has talked much about it since. —Annette Curtis was in here the other evening and offered to take home my new dress and make it, she returned it last week splendidly made, but unfortunately, it is so tight I shall have to alter it. I ought to have tried it on after the dressmaker sent it back, but as it fitted well in the shop, I supposed it was all right. I suppose she is used to fitting tight for genteel people who wear corsets. I have not got a piece of any sise left to alter my dress though I had a large pattern. I think after all I can suit myself best. I cut Sarah's new dress for her and it fits pretty well. I thought it would save her something and what a girl works hard to earn it seems hard to have to pay 75 cts or more just for cutting a dress. She had to pay 25 cts. just to have the sleeves cut, as I had no pattern that she wanted. Sarah is very kind and appreciates all I do for her much more than I deserve. Her little kindnesses are so gratifying when I feel tired or desponding, and yet I am tired with her sometimes. she is so sure that her way is the best way, and so quick to take perfect equality with us (while I have been obliged so long to keep Mary Plummer and others at a distance) that I fall into the old track sometimes) that at times I find it difficult to steer straight. then I never can give up the whole care of my work, but if anything goes wrong the whole blame has to come right back on me but perhaps such discipline is best for me and I am complaining such a habit of writing home my little petty vexations that I find it difficult to restrain them now, but I feel in my heart that I have no real trials except with myself. Sarah has crocheted me a sweet pretty Roman Scarf, and gave me for a Christmas present. it is black in the middle with Scotch colors green & purple with white & black harion stripes on the end. I chose and designed it, but she wished to present it to me though I expected to pay for it. I think she loves me dearly. though I cant see why she should for I am so often unamiable to her and set such a bad example, and she is so susceptible, like that I fear my influence injures her, sometimes I think I ought not to have her with me.

I find Allie no small trial he is beginning to be disagreeable and unmanageable. he has the "show off" style, and likes to use big words etc while he is so artful in trying to gain his ends that his artiface (clearly seen through) seems rather disgusting. After all I see in him so complete a mirror of myself (singing and music has great power with and over him) that I am constrained to try at least to have charity for him if not his faults. But I have used all my time and paper saying little or nothing I expect to go out making calls this P.M. if I have time will add more when I come back. I never have time to write half all I want to Lissie Cotter has gone to thomaston to make a visit I dont see much of her this winter Clara is spending the winter in New York. Mr. Richardson is to have a Singing school twice a week Sarah & W.H. will go but they will not be gone very late. I did not know that Ed Everett was dead till father wrote, we do not take the Journal and consequently I dont get much news, but I had not time to read it before we gave it up. I read the weekly religious papers Sundays. I got a beautiful letter from Aunt Hildreth this week and one from Pa and I wish I could write to him today but other things positively forbid. Dear little Eddie I dont forget him though I have not spoken of him long to see him little Charlie is very cunning he says and does lots of cunning things he stands up to a chair but I am sorry to say he is rather cross and is getting to plague us nights some. P.S. I have not time to write any more, though I would like to send something to Eddie and more to you I have not answered anything in your letter yet, but I hope to send half a sheet more. Little Charlie does not seem very well tonight but I guess it is only his teeth. I have not been very well this week, but I think it is only the result of a cold.

Susan often fastened upon such news from Cambridge as the death of Edward Everett (1794–1865), who had served as minister of the Brattle Street Unitarian Church, Cambridge. A former president of Harvard College, editor of the North American Review, congressman and senator from Massachusetts in Washington, D.C., Everett had been an unsuccessful candidate for vice-president. He worked hard for a compromise on the slavery issue and may have been acquainted with Emma's father through abolitionist activities. One of the country's leading orators he had preceded Lincoln at ceremonies dedicating the cemetery at Gettysburg. Lincoln's brief address was perfunctorily noted in the next day's newspapers, which reprinted Everett's with praise. After reading the accounts of his own long-

(1865)

winded speech, however, Everett sent a note to the President: "I wish that I could flatter myself that I had come as near to the central idea of the occasion in two hours as you did in two minutes."

Feb. 23 [1865]
Damariscotta

Dear Emma

It is Monday P.M. and I have just done the last job (or apparently, for there is always one more) I take the time now but I may be interrupted any minute, as it is, Allie is teasing and Charlie crying, so I may not get off anything very connected. I was so tired and sleepy last night that I gave up writing, and being a rather dull night & WH very tired, we went to bed at 9 oclock. We had just got into a comfortable sleep when we were awakened by the doorbell, it was about quarter of ten, and of course we were somewhat startled. We both jumped up, and WH rushed to the door "en deshabille" and demanded the mans name, which not being satisfactory, asked his business, rather demurring about letting any one in at so late an hour. As the errand proved to be the very natural and harmless one of getting married, we concluded to open house and they waited while W.H. dressed and I partly so, and lighted the sitting room. They were a young couple and rather green and seemed somewhat embarrased as well they might what brought them there at that hour we couldnt imagine, and they were to ride several miles further, they said. They were soon dispatched and went on their way rejoicing I hope. WH was amused because the man kept him waiting several minutes before the ceremony to draw on a pair of kid gloves and "nobody there to see". he asked WH what he charged. WH replied "I make no bill." Whereupon he launched forth $2.50 and asked if that would satisfy him "oh yes" says WH But he said to me he thought himself poorly paid for being routed out of bed, and it hardly paid me for my "scare" for I did not know but it was some robber or civil disposed person, we had a good laugh after we went to bed again. "What an episode" says WH. Well, I had a very busy week last week I did a fortnight's wash, ironed the same, papered the kitchen, made a big kettle of mince meat for pies and went to the S. Circle, besides callers as usual. The children had real bad colds and were rather cross I had to keep Allie in doors most of the time, as he had a very sore throat, but he got rather uneasy now it is a little warmer weather. I dress them up and let them play in the barn which works very well. Saturday i did my usual baking. I can see quite a difference in my work now the days are longer but I always seem to be in a hurry, it took us two half days to paper the room it looks real pretty and Mrs. Carleton who called seemed to be quite pleased she said she did not expect us to do it, but when we got the paper we did not know whether we were to stay or not. I thought if I was I certainly must have it papered for my own comfort, and if I wasn't, I hated to have anyone come in to such a looking place. It really looks like leaving now, for our house is engaged for the first of May probably to mr. Berry who is to have the refusal of the house at $100 a year. If we dont get a place by that time we shall be rather badly off but I dont worry yet. WH has several plans in his head, but "I dont know how they will work" Coming to Cambridge however will hardly be probable, it will be the very "dernier resort" as he is determined not to leave the State if possible. If no pastoral field opens he will probably take up teaching or something else for the time being, but all is as yet uncertain. I hope we shall be directed by the Lord and be willing to follow where he leads. WH says that while he was wasted here, he couldn't see clear to leave, but now of course they have made his duty plain—We shall be sorry and glad but on the whole WH thinks glad. I have just got so I can enjoy myself a little better I go to the S. School every Sunday we have a very interesting Bible class and we have got a nice Sewing Circle and very Social. I think there is a fuller attendance at church and a little more interest in meetings though WH thinks nothing to be relied upon. I hope there is going to be a change here, but I find when I think of leaving, that there are many ties here, and to go among strangers again is discouraging. But I must be resigned to things as they come.

There is a good deal of feeling in the Society about WH leaving but he thinks it best to keep quiet and hopes after he is gone, that they will come together again and unite on some one, but many declare they will not pay a cent, if he leaves. But people do act so strangely here I cant for my life find out what they mean, or who is friendly and who isn't. but I've spun out a pretty long story which perhaps wont interest you much but its "pro bono publico" I thought of you much last week hope you had a good time at the fair. They are going to have one here by and by. Glad you and your Captain are having such nice times give my respects to him. I received a very kind letter from Alfred which I will answer when I can. I wish I could tell him definitely about the S. machine but now we are so unsettled, we cant decide, whether we can afford it or not. I mean to have one I got real blue last week, I told WH that I was nothing but a drudge, work work all the time and no play thereupon he said he knew of a real nice girl that perhaps he could get for a few weeks till I could get some of my sewing done. Perhaps I may, though she lives several miles from here and may be gone before we can see her or she may not be willing to come. I shall have to have some help when i get ready to move though I shall be getting ready now all along. The Club give another concert at Waldoboro Friday but as the going is bad I dont think I shall go over. Little Charlie is getting very Eddy-ish he is very mischievous and so knowing! the other night I washed them all over in the "big tub". I usually change their shirts at that time, but not having his handy put on the one I took off. he immediately said "that's a dirty one" He can say almost anything now and he is very hard to get to sleep in the evening he is last week he wasn't very well and was restless nights I think he is getting more teeth Your last letter was very interesting. the letters from home do me a great deal of good WH & I were much obliged to Pa for his this week. You see I've rattled on to the end of my paper and could say more but feel as if I couldn't spaire the time. Goodbye with very much love to all Sue. Kiss dear little Eddie for me.

When I put Allie to bed I talk with him. the other night he said, "oh dear mother—I cant get good. I try but I cant, I wish you would tell me how." A hard lesson and he has just begun to learn it. He is spelling words of two & three letters How he will learn! I find he teaches himself mostly. he always wants me to read the letters to him that I get and write and oh the questions! innumerable about everyting. [Enclosed: Brown and green wallpaper. On back, "kitchen paper. WH's choice, 25 cts a roll, double the length of an ordinary one."]

The impromptu wedding took place in the sitting room, suggesting that Susan's house may have had no parlor or living room. In rural houses, parlors were sometimes eliminated in favor of sitting rooms. The sitting room, where families gathered, was more child oriented than the urban parlor. Magazine articles of the period discussed parlor values versus kitchen values, the difference between woman as consumer and woman as producer.

Emma's World

Making plans to leave Damariscotta, Susan experienced a surge of energy that had her sewing, cleaning, and entertaining neighbors. By spring, she seemed more relaxed, inviting friends in for a pot-luck supper.

Damariscotta April 13th [1865]

Dear Emma,

It seems a long while since I have written to you but I believe it is your turn to get one. I was real sorry I could'nt write a longer letter last week but I was very busy, and in fact am today. I cant ever tell how long I can write, or what may happen to interrupt me. Last week I had "Cynthia" two days to make allie's suit of clothes. Tues. and Thursday, the baby was very cross and troublesome last week, and we had a great deal to do. I had to help her cut and contrive the clothes, she was rather slow, but Sarah and I both helped her and we got quite a pretty suit made, Allie wore them Saturday P.M. and felt quite grand. They were made of the drab cloth, vest & pants that you brought down last summer I made them up on the other side, and trimmed them with drab braid and smoke pearl buttons. I shall make him some more clothes soon as he is getting quite ragged. I have been making some clothes for Charlie this week and Sarah is helping me. Last Wednes. I invited mary Harrington in to take tea. She is you know rather unfortunate and I wished to do my part towards lightning her lot, but I found it a rather thankless task. She is very trying to our patience but I think she enjoys herself. I hope so at least. Her new mother and she get along very nicely together they say, and I think from all I see of Mrs. H. that she is disposed to do well, though there has been and is still a great deal of opposition to the match in the family, and I suppose there is some cause, as she was very young and hardly suitable for such a position. Friday mrs. Hutchins had a little company and invited us in I had a real pleasant time. Saturday as Mr. H. was going to Portland Monday, I asked them and the "Wales" here to tea i had quite a pleasant time, though I didn't get (cook) anything. Cooked just to suit me. I think they enjoyed it. The same afternoon, Sarah had her "Society" meet here, there was 23 here and had quite a lively time. they are going to have a fair soon and send the proceeds to the soldiers. They went away at half past four which was about the time my company came. I had several callers in the course of the P.M. besides. After tea I had two more callers and at Eight o clock a wedding at the house, after which, WH went to singing school. Mr. & Mrs. H. went home when Sarah & I washed the dishes so you see that day was a pretty busy and exciting one. I was glad to have sunday come I only went out half a day. Allie was not well enough to go out, but he was out to play yesterday. both their colds are better, the baby kept me awake awhile last night so I feel rather sleepy today. monday mr. H. went away he and his wife both felt rather badly, more so than they ever have before. she is very miserable this spring and he was not well. After dinner I felt tired, and so we went in there thinking she would be lonesome but she had gone into Mr. Harringtons to see the old lady, his mother. I took the baby and went in a little while, and left Sarah and Allie with clara & M. Mrs. Harrington is a nice old lady she has been stopping there most all winter She is going away very soon. monday evening I went to the "Knitting society" at Mrs. Metcalf's they sent me a special invitation I had a real pleasant time. I made one square quilted & bound it for a quilt for it was a foot square. they are going to send a box this week, two quilts and lots of stockings hospital stores etc. We are invited to Mrs. Wales to tea today, and tomorrow P.M. we expect to go to Warren to see mrs. Richardson, and stop over Sunday. WH exchanging with Mr. Leland. We may also go to Rockland on Saturday. Tomorrow there is to be a celebration here of the recent victories. WH has got to make an address and there is to be a procession illuminations etc. I am sorry that we are going away for I would like to illuminate and besides look after Allie. I shall have to leave him with S. and i fear he will get cold, but W.H. thought it was best. We may not go till Saturday and shall probably come back Monday or Tuesday. I dont want to go at all, but WH thinks it would be pleasant for me. I shall begin to clear house next week and I am planning to get ready to come home in May, but I may be prevented so dont count too much on it. I want to see Eddie very much i dont know when Sarah will go home but I think not till after I start. I shall not make any definite arrangement with her about coming back. I cannot say all I would like to in a letter about matters. She and Allie dont get along very well but I know he is a trial, and of course no one can make the allowances that a mother can. I wish I could get along alone, but I will speak no more on this subject—Little Charlie is real cunning he runs alone now, and talks a little. He is much like Eddie. I saw a little boy Eddies size the other day and it made my heart jump into my mouth. I send 5.00 the avails of the wedding for Eddie. Tell Mother to get him something that he needs or keep it. Tell her too that I do not consider that I have half repaid her our indebtedness and shall do all I can in the future, but no more of that at present. I was astonished that Ellen Hoyt had a baby. I hope she will get along well now. I think of her often, glad that Aunt Nancy and Grandma, folks are improving.

I dont know what I shall do about a bonnet. Calin Cotter has got one without any crown. I dont admire the style, but it does well enough for young folks. Lizzie Cotter sent her love to you and wants you to give her a photograph. Callie Austin is near Caleao and is going to the Chin Chin Islands, and perhaps afterwards to Spain, they expect a letter from her very soon. Much obliged to alf for his papers. I have been trying to answer his letter but find it difficult to get a chance but I must say goodbye from Sister Sue. Love to all. I havent answered a word of your letter but you must excuse my haste. I am glad your are having such pleasant times—goodbye dearest Sister.

[Enclosed: "Just a word for mama's little Eddie. How she would like to see him. Does Eddie go out to play now and does he go to ride in the horse cars. Allie goes out and plays in the yard the other day he found your old spoon that you left out there last summer. he gets bones to sell there are lots of them in the yard he got a great pile and sold them to some boys for a handful of acorns. We didnt think it was a very smart trade, but he has got another pile now and he is going to get some pennies for them. Did Eddie see the pretty candles and light, Allie is going to see some tomorrow. shouldnt you like to see your cunning little brother he is a great boy now but mama must say goodbye now for she has not more time. Kiss to her little dear, and one from Allie he was real pleased with his letter."]

Susan regretted that she would be away with her husband when the town celebrated the final victories of the war with fireworks. Early in April, Grant broke through Lee's defenses and, with the relentless singlemindedness that had earned him the epithet of "Butcher" from his own men, hounded Southern forces trying to escape to the West. Lee's starving and exhausted army collapsed. Unable to resist, their gallant general surrendered his sword to Grant on April 9 at ceremonies at Appomattox (Virginia) Court House. Grant

(1865)

was as magnanimous in setting the conditions for surrender as he had been fierce in battle. Among other concessions, he allowed the Confederate soldiers to keep their horses and immediately ordered food for his 25,000 hungry prisoners. The last Confederate troops did not capitulate until May 26, 1865, but the war was virtually over in April. More than 600,000 Americans had sacrificed their lives.

Within a week, April 15, President Lincoln died, too, shot in the back at Ford's Theater, Washington, by John Wilkes Booth, an actor championing the Southern cause. The country went into deep mourning. Sorrowful crowds, tendering their last respects, lined the tracks along the route of the train bearing the body of the fallen leader home from Washington. On May 4, 1865, Abraham Lincoln was buried in Oak Ridge Cemetery, Springfield, Illinois. Susan's low spirits match the mood of the day.

                              Damariscotta May 4th [1865]

Dear Emma

I have not much time but I shall try to improve it. I meant to have commenced this afternoon early, but one thing and another hindered me. First Sarah went down street and staid longer than I expected, then after that I went down street to see about a bonnet and it was so pleasant I did not want to come home. I called in to see Mrs. Brown (Cox) I have not seen her since she was married. She was real pleased to see me. She had got a real pleasant home. I had Allie with me and he bought some candy for Charlie down street and he wanted to give it to him. Sarah had him in Mrs. Wrights, so I went in there and staid awhile, so with fixing the children and myself, the afternoon all passed away. I found when I went to the miliners that she had sold the Cobary bonnets, but she is going to have some more next week. I am going to have it trimmed with tan or drab and have blue inside. I wish I could have it till I come home but my velvet is getting to heavy to wear. I think Mrs. Skinner has pretty good taste. I tried to get a little hat for Charlie, but was not successful. It is a real bother to me to get anything and sometimes I think I will never try for when I do I dont like it. I often wish you were here to tell me I should think your bonnet would look sweet pretty. Sarah is going to have a white hat (or cap) trimmed with buff & black velvet. We have been cleaning house last week and this. We have got all done now but the sitting room and kitchen. I found it rather a hard business with the children fussing round, and I find everything hard sometimes. I feel all the care, for Sarah though she is handy and useful, dont have much judgment, at least I dont feel easy to leave things wholly to her and I cant attend to everything myself. But I did not mean to complain for we get along after a fashion. Some days I am almost discouraged, then I pluck up courage and start again. Coming home seems like a mountain to me I have so many things to do and make, if I had not said I should I believe I should give it up, but I dare say it may benefit me, and the children and then Eddie I have wanted to see him so for a few days, that it seemed as if I couldn't do anything at all. How cunning he must be, I think of all his ways and when I see anything that was his it makes me feel most sick for a minute. I dont look at his picture very often, it makes me feel so bad. By the way WH brought home a new proof yesterday that was very good it was larger than the carte de visite size I want him to have some taken from it, but I dont know as he will think it is best. Little Charlie is getting real cunning and he is pretty good most of the time. I have wholly weaned him daytimes, and I dont nurse him till about the time I go to bed I dont think I shall wean him now till I have been home, for I am afraid he will not be good nights. He wants to go out of doors all the time, and so does Allie I let them go every day when it is pleasant but he meets with all sorts of adventures I am sorry to say he gets into squabbles with the other children occasionally and I have to settle their quarrels. Clara Wales in particular is a great hand to fight with him. I dont know what I should do if Eddie was here, still I often feel as if I wanted him. Allie went to Sunday School last Sunday. I think I shall let him go all the time he behaves quite well only he is inclined to talk. We had quite a heavy thunderstorm last week, I felt quite timid it was at tea time, and Clara & Marcia came in. their mother was away. Allie seemed to be somewhat frightened he never was before, but he heard the girls talking about it striking the house. I felt sorry for I dont want him to suffer what I do, but I cant help showing when I feel frightened. I cant get rid of my cough though it is better than it was. I feel rather weary with the care of the children but I hope a change will do me good. How glad I am you had a surprise party and a present. You must have enjoyed it. Things are quite forward here the spring is very early, but I must close now for Charlie is crying and it is time almost

(1865)

for W.H. to carry this. I have not said half what I want to but you must excuse it. If you knew the obstacles I had to contend with you would wonder I did as well. But goodbye Love to all from Sue

Part Three

Emma's World: Completing the Home Circle

"The time is approaching when History will be attempted on quite other principles; when the Court, the Senate, and the Battlefields receding more and more into the background, the Temple, the Workshop, and the Social Hearth will advance more and more into the foreground."

Thomas Carlyle

12
(1865)

---

*T*he United States entered its most controversial era with President Andrew Johnson at the helm. Reconstruction was a misnomer; the country never regained its lost innocence. The Mason-Dixon Line scarred the national consciousness. Land reform in the South, the rise of slums in the North, range wars in the West, the arrival of successive boatloads of a variety of non-English-speaking immigrants, and the plight of homeless, jobless freed slaves tempered the joy of peace. Returning soldiers, like Emma's boyfriend Will Whitney, were war-weary and embraced civilian life; but ambitious politicians and self-aggrandizing businessmen turned turbulent conditions to their advantage, seizing land, money, and power. In the eleven states that had seceded, carpetbaggers competed for political spoils with recently emancipated Negroes and old-time politicians—no retribution was exacted from Confederate supporters—and in the North political machines, among them the Tweed Ring in New York City, usurped authority and peddled privileges for profit. On Capitol Hill, Radical Republicans refused to seat southern Congressmen, and a weak President, blown from side to side by the gales of partisan politics, faltered. In 1868, Johnson became the first President to be impeached, but the Senate acquitted him. With characteristic irony, Mark Twain christened the two decades following the Civil War the "Gilded Age."

Emancipated slaves were the country's most persistent problem. Many citizens, including President Lincoln, had hoped to resettle Negroes outside the United States. The most likely places seemed to be one of the Caribbean islands or Liberia, an African republic on the Gulf of Guinea, founded by freed United States slaves in 1847. But most freedmen refused to leave the country of their birth, so the South replaced Slave Codes with harsh Jim Crow laws such as the Black Codes. Mississippi, for example, passed legislation in 1865 making it illegal for freedmen to lease or to rent farm land; Negroes wanting work as farmers had to sign a contract which they could not break without going to jail. The North, fearful that thousands of rural Negroes would migrate to its cities, braced itself with prejudice. North and South, most white people believed the black race was inferior.

Native Americans, too, were a displaced, disadvantaged people. Individual states and the federal government consistently ignored treaties with the Indian nations. Particularly after the Indian Removal Act of 1830, Native Americans were herded and moved like cattle from place to place at the convenience of the new settlers. Their fate was the same whether a nation retained its own customs or attempted to follow the white people's way as the Cherokees did—even to establishing similar forms of government, accepting Christian missionaries, and taking up trades. Neither did it make a difference whether the Indian was viewed as a noble savage, as in the East, or a ruthless beast, as in the West. The era's expansionist, land-grabbing appetite was insatiable; mythic stereotypes of cowboys—the good guys—and Indians—bad guys—embellished the country's folklore.

The West lured many who desired a fresh start, among them flocks of returning soldiers unable to find work and others, like Emma's brothers Alfred and Ned, who sought greater opportunities. Dis-

(1865)

enchanted with large Eastern cities, where factories had blighted old neighborhoods with soot and slums that bred disease, they joined the westward migration by railroad, canal boat, and turnpike. For some, the Industrial Revolution had begun to lose its luster as early as the 1850s, when the newly organized labor movement started to press for reform of exploitive factory practices. But workers had patriotically rested their grievances for the duration of the war. With peace at hand, they revived their cause.

Similarly, foreign policy required attention. Fighting for its life at home, the Union for years had neglected international affairs. While Secretary of State William Henry Seward deftly managed to prevent European countries from aiding the Confederacy, a few took advantage of the Civil War to expand their territory in the New World. Violating the Monroe Doctrine, troops of three nations—England, Spain and France—in 1862 occupied Veracruz, Mexico. The British and Spanish soon left Napoleon III's armies to occupy Mexico City and to establish Archduke Maximilian as emperor. Busy preserving the Union, President Lincoln was unable to combat these outside incursions. After the war, however, the United States pressured Napoleon to remove French forces. Also, following nearly ten years of negotiations with Russia, Seward acquired a large tract of land near the North Pole. When finally Alaska was purchased for two cents an acre in 1867, it was branded "Seward's Folly" and "Seward's Ice Box."

Emma came of age with her country. She was twenty-one years old when the war ended. A well-bred young woman, she lived at home with her parents, surrounded by an affectionate circle of friends and relatives. She taught Sabbath School at the First Baptist Church as did her father and her brother, William, who also served as secretary at the school. Visits with Susan, other relatives, and friends as well as social activities around Cambridge continued to occupy much of her time. She read letters from her brothers in the West, recounting economic hardships, difficulties of resettling in a new community, and one, about a friend from Cambridge who had been killed by Indians. Perhaps Emma saved their letters because through them she could live vicariously. Ned's and Alfred's assorted experiences were certainly very different from her own, protected life.

Of marriageable age, Emma and her friends entertained a steady procession of suitors. They took pleasure in the company of gentlemen and appeared to enjoy writing about their romances, yet these young women were in no hurry to marry. Perhaps they cherished this time, which was likely to be the most carefree period in their lives. Certainly Emma, contemplating Susan's situation, had little reason to rush into marriage. She knew that taking a husband meant forfeiting considerable autonomy. More frightening to many women considering marriage, however, was the prospect of numerous pregnancies with repeated risk to their lives in childbirth. Better to tarry awhile, making sport of romance.

Genteel society abetted romance with discreetly arranged opportunities for flirting and meeting suitable prospects. New leisure entertainments added variety to traditional social and religious events. Croquet, the subject of Emma's next letter, was the first postwar game imported from England. More than a sport, it served as a social occasion that brought men and women together in an out-of-doors activity. Some ladies fretted that hoop skirts got in the way of certain shots and critics berated the garden entertainment as frivolous; nevertheless, by the 1870s croquet was so popular that candleholders were added to wickets for night-time playing. Emma often played croquet. This invitation was written in a neat black hand on creamy linen note paper.

> Cambridgeport
> July 7, 1865
>
> Miss Barbour:
>
> A croquet club has been formed by a few young men of your acquaintance, and we should be happy to have you join us.
>
> We shall play this evening in Leeds lot on Franklin St. at 6 o'clock, if pleasant, when we hope you will favor us with your company.
>
> Truly yours
> Geor. W. Clapp.
> Sec. Protem

The invitation was mailed and delivered within Cambridgeport; the envelope indicates that postage was at a lower rate. Before the invention of the telephone, such "drop letters" were an efficient and convenient way for people within a community to maintain ties, or to conduct a courtship.

Emma probably wrote to Maria about George Clapp's invitation to play croquet. Maria, in turn, told about her feelings as well as the invitations and men in her life. Visiting Mount Holyoke in South

(1865)

Hadley, Massachusetts, Maria explained why she thought it best to leave Washington for a while. The fashionable resort she chose—the first house built on any summit in New England—accommodated about twenty-five guests, promising them "pure air, and clear spring water. . ."

Although she had yet to inform her Washington friends of her broken engagement, Maria unburdened herself to Emma. It undoubtedly comforted her to tell Emma the details of her unhappy romance with the dashing young doctor. He may have been John E. Herbst of Pennsylvania, the surgeon commended by Brigadier General John W. Geary of United States Volunteers Commanding Division for "the eminent degree of energy and efficiency manifested . . . upon the field at Gettysburg."

> Mt. Holyoke
> July 18th, 1865

Dear Emma:

It has been a long time since I have heard from you, and I know that it is I not who owes you the letter. I have written two letters, both are safe in my writing book, and should have sent them but the contents were not entirely true, how funny you will say, but so it is. I thought I would wait for a day longer so as to give you the whole and have thus far left your nice letter unacknowledged. I have been busy though as a bee and have had little or no time to myself except at midnight. Then I felt duty bound I should get as much rest as I could. The last four months seem like many years so much has been embraced in this short time. I don't believe I can give a history. I tried in my other letters but the next thing something would happen so that I could not send them, so I will give you general accounts. Aunt Josie gave you an inkling of what was going on—she thought. I was engaged and so all my friends think who don't know positively from me—I believe I wrote you about meeting at my friend Mr. Delano's a young Dr. I had heard of him before most glowing accounts the family all went to Mrs. Southworth's and met him there one evening but I was sick at home, consequently had considerable curiosity to see the marvel with such handsome eyes when they came home—The next evening I believe I was gratified; Mr. Pierpont read one of his poems at Mrs. D's and the Dr. was invited—he did not say much to me and I looked as much as I chose. I never dreamed I should see him again, only perhaps occasionally. we invited them all to call together and all came—then he came alone once a week, then twice a week, then every evening until I thought it was time to be on my guard. I think he is a nobel man but not a Christian, he is rather skeptical and I have come to the conclusion that he is not the one for me—We are good friends however and he calls quite often now. I have been to many places with him and he is an excellent escort. Educated, very highly respected, stands high in his profession being head surgeon of the Sanitary Commission. Everybody admires him (a little aware of his superiority)—I think perhaps he may come to the Mt. this summer for a few days—he seemed to think he would when I left home —he was to have accompanied Ronee, and myself as far as N. York City. You will see how my time has been occupied in the evening—Oh! haven't I seen sights lately. I went to Richmond with a large party and was gone five days. The trip down the Potomac and up the James was delightful only the sad history of the battlegrounds was constantly before me. We only spent one day in the city of Richmond which was enough amid such horrible sights. I went through Libbey saw Castle Thunder and Belle Isle. Visited Jeff. Davis home but they would not let us in —went through Vice Pres. Stevens house and saw where Gen. Lee lived. When we passed by two ladies came to the windows and closed the inside shutters. —I like the city very much if it had not been rebel—the officers and men wore their grey uniforms through the streets and looked impudent enough. The party went to one of Gen. Pierpont's day receptions. We had a very pleasant trip. Dr. was my escort and he was very kind. Two weeks ago we took another excursion down the river sixty miles, we're gone all night and arrived home at six the next morning rather tired out but had enjoyed the sail very much. Emma, what a change in public affairs within a little time. That horrible night when the President was assassinated is still fresh in my mind—we did not know what to expect next—first the account of our President, then Sec. Seward and many false rumors—and we expected the city would be fired—It was worth a year at my former residence in Washington to be there during all the victories and the sad time that followed—And the day before I came away the four criminals were executed. I would like to be there when Jeff is tried—When we returned from Richmond we stopped two hours at Fortress Monroe, City Pt.

(1865)

saw where Jeff was confined. Also spent an hour and half at Mt. Vernon I don't know when I have felt such a quick sacred feeling steal over me, the birds in the trees softly chirped and the whole seemed holy grand—one very beautiful custom is followed that of tolling the bell on every vessel that passes the place—We saw the key of the Bastile and many old articles of furniture which were used by Washington.

I have been on the Mt. two days came north by the Atlantic down the Chesapeake and along the coast to N. York—the trip was very quiet they said but I noticed I was pitched head first out of a chair when I was reading quietly—R. was quite sea sick —I a little—I must stop now as I have five letters to write and I expect they have about given me up. I have not written anyone for a long time. Remember me to all—Hattie is very happy in W. with much love and <u>ever</u> your sister

Maria

Write soon—

Although she lived in Washington and her father was employed in government, Maria had difficulty learning what was happening on the night the President was killed. To add to the confusion, at almost the same time Lincoln was attacked at Ford's Theatre, Secretary of State Seward was shot at his home.

Washington buzzed with conspiracy rumors. Many Irish and German Catholics had emigrated to the United States in the 1840s and 1850s, and anti-Catholic sentiment surfaced in allegations of a "Romish plot." In some quarters there was talk that Secretary of War Edwin McMasters Stanton, who was in danger of losing much of the power he had amassed during the war, including his own secret police force, may have plotted to take over the government. The most popular explanation held that the assassination was the work of die-hard Southern slaveholders.

A conspiracy trial convened on May 12 and eight civilians were brought before a special military commission. Soldiers had shot and killed John Wilkes Booth on April 25, but seven men and one woman were charged with conspiring with the actor to assassinate the President, Vice-President Andrew Johnson, Lieutenant General Ulysses S. Grant, and Secretary of State Seward.

Their trial, one of the worst miscarriages of justice in United States history, lasted six weeks. Some of the defendants were implicated in a plan to kidnap the President, but their complicity in the murder was based on circumstantial evidence. Nevertheless, anti-Southern sentiment triumphed and all eight were found guilty.

Before appeals could be filed, the sentences were carried out. At the sentencing on July 6, one defendent was given a six-year term; three, life in prison; and four were sentenced to hanging. The executions were held the next day in the courtyard of the Washington arsenal. The execution of Mrs. Surratt, the first woman sentenced to death in a national court, prompted outcries from the press and the public, denouncing "judicial murder."

On the other hand, President Jefferson Davis, who "symbolized the solemn convictions and tragic fortunes of millions of men," served only two years in prison after his indictment for treason. Horace Greeley and other Northerners raised bond in 1867 and Davis was released on bail. No trial was ever held.

As the conspiracy trial indicated, the schism between North and South did not end with the war. Many Northerners shared Maria's outrage at recalcitrant Southerners and *The Cambridge Chronicle* of August 12, 1865, urged the President to keep control and to continue martial law.

Still, Maria benefitted from country living and the company at Mount Holyoke.

Northampton, Ms. Aug. 65
Thursday Evening

My dear Emma:

I am all alone in the parlor—all the people have retired and I am sitting up to send a few words to my friends. I received your good letter. I had a great feast reading it. I was so lonesome that day and it came like a good angel to me. I shall only be able to write little tonight for I have little to say and little of time, but you shall know & understand that Maria Morse loves you just as dearly as ever and wants to see you very much but cannot spair the time or <u>money</u> to go East. I came North this summer on account of <u>my health</u> and am very much stronger than when I came. I have had a delightful time—go somewhere every day and yesterday returned from a visit in Springfield, only a few miles from here. Mrs. Bradley who has been staying at the Mt. two weeks wanted me to visit her very much and as I had a pass on the railroad I concluded to go. I did have a delightful time saw everything of interest and was much pleased with the city. I have been boating on the Conn. river once & go again tomorrow. While in S. I played several games of Croquet, which you spoke of in your last. I like it very much & should carry a game home had we room to play. You must have delightful times. Next Wednesday I start for home and am dreading it very much. I go by way of Albany and down the Hudson—that will be very pleasant. I will write you all about it. I must close now as I have more to do before I can retire—and now my dear Emma you will still love and remember your friend & sister Maria as she loves you. I have hoped you might visit me in Washington and do not give it up entirely now—do you not think it possible? Oh if you only could, I should promise as good a time as you ever had. Now goodnight my sister Emma.

Yours Maria

I haven't your letter down stairs & will answer it more particularly next time. Love to all. Hope Ned is better.

After the war, the Industrial Revolution treated Americans to a new commodity: leisure. Until factories established the six-day workweek, most people, especially farmers, worked seven days a week. With spare time, pleasure travel on turnpikes, canals, and railroads became popular. Steamship companies responded to the increase in tourism by adding excursion trips to their regular routes and by publishing illustrated guides to regions they served. Such amenities as electric lights and running water were added to ships while hotels and homes were still using candles and kerosene.

When Maria went boating on the Connecticut River, she probably enjoyed a steamboat excursion. She also mentioned that she used a pass to ride the railroad to Springfield; earlier, she had used a pass to go from Washington to Baltimore. Railroads often gave passes to employees, to good freight customers, and to insurance companies, among others. For a time, railroad passes were so common it seemed as if more passengers rode free than paid a fare. "Carrying the freight" kept them profitable and added another Americanism to the language.

While Maria was returning to Washington, Emma and her brother Ned set off for another visit with Susan. Emma had hardly left Cambridgeport, however, before her mother wrote with a curious request.

Cambridgeport
September 15, 1865

My dear Emma

We were very happy to hear of your safe arrival at Sues by telegraph, and I suppose you will be surprised to receive a letter before the usual time, and will laugh at me perhaps when you find out my object in writing. I want to know where you could possibly have put the cage, that you cleaned up so nicely after your bird died. I have hunted the house from garret to cellar and could not find it, the day I went to Aunt Rebecca I called on Mrs. Kingsbury she showed me her birds, she has five cages of them and some cages had five birds in them. Small cages, she said she had been trying to get a large cage. I told her our bird was dead and she could have our cage as well as not, if she could get it from our house, she said O I would come out on purpose, and offered to pay any price for it, I told her no, her Father gave it to us and she might take it and use it as long as she wanted it and yesterday she came out and Lo! it was no where to be found, I was confounded! I did not know what to say. After hunting with Mary and Alfred's help, we could not find it anywhere poor Ellen had to go back without it. Mrs. Lewis has lost two more of her birds, and has two sick. I went over there with Ellen because one of her birds had had sore feet and she wanted to know about it, but to begin and tell you of home matters, after we left you we took a car and went to see Sarah Dickman. She seemed very much pleased to see me, and while I was there Mrs. Vinal called and brought some peaches, with Mrs. Holmes compliments. Sarah inquired after Sue and the family and then I thought I had forgotten to send that beautiful little shoe or needlebook I was real sorry, I could not stay long as it was most supper time but told her I would come again she has nearly lost the use of the arm that she hurt when she fell and has suffered greatly with it, but think it is getting better, the next day though I did not feel quite well I thought I would go to Aunt Rebecca, and was glad I did as I felt much better before night we saw the balloons go up, and up quite near her house, aunt Horton came with aunt Mary Anne in the morning she had been taking a new medicine, as she did not feel so well and it had the very bad effect upon her, when I got there she was asleep on the lounge in fact she could hardly keep her eyes open all day, then she suffered such pain she said if there had not

(1865)

been so many there she should have had a good cry, it, she thought the next best thing would be to ask me to let her come home with me, so soon after supper we got ready and came home, she is very poorly indeed I have carried all her meals up to her since, and waited on her as I did before she was not off the bed yesterday nor today until most three o'clock, she is some better today but looks bad. Mr. H. is also with us, so I am not quite so much alone as you thought I should be, it is well perhaps I did not come down instead of you He thought of going to N.Y. today but could not get ready, he thinks he should not like to start for home unless there is a more decided change for the better, aunt has received some more Photographs, one of Mr. Dennet, which I took to be Edward he has no wiskers nor beard or even Mustach and he looks so like a boy I told aunt I was looking for a great man, with a great full beard and Mustach, so I said I suppose it was Ed I did not admire his looks, one of Julia and another of Eliza Jane, which she meant for you, it is taken the style of yours and they are thought to look something like yours, I saw the girls in the Croquet field last night, Ellen and Miss Snow, Alf Whitney and Mrs. Munroe and others were there. I hope it is not so warm down there as it is here this morning is said to have been the warmest morning we have had, I keep hoping it will be cooler, tell Sue she must not put herself out for you and Ned but enjoy all she can. Alf has gone to Midway for Mary this afternoon, he expects to come home with her to morrow morning she is going to her Mothers to stay over the Sabbath, did you tell me where your class book was I have not looked much for it perhaps I shall find it, but I must close, since I commenced Mrs. Clark and Addie have been in, and brought some grapes, then I sent back some pears you know what I said but I must say good bye. as Mary is going to get some bread for supper and will put it in the office. with much love to all from Mother.

The Fourth Annual Exhibition of the Cambridge Horticultural Society was held on Wednesday, Thursday, and Friday, Sept 27–29. Perhaps Mrs. Barbour and the other women were exchanging their produce in preparation for the judging. When Mrs. Vinal visited Emma's mother, she brought peaches. Mrs. Clark and Addie gave Mrs. Barbour grapes and, in return, she shared her pears. The *Cambridge Chronicle* noted, "Seldom has it been our fortune to witness so much variety in any exhibition of Pears, as was there presented."

The reporter continued. "Of grapes, there was a great variety; as they lay in rich profusion upon the tables, in tempting show, we could not refrain from thinking of the advantages that would accrue from a more general cultivation of the vine, and hoping for the day when every house will have its trellis for ornament as well as the gratification of the appetite."

Meanwhile, Alfred and Mary had left their farm and temporarily were making their home with the Barbours.

In addition to her mother's letters, Emma received mail from Albertine Tarbell, who referred to Emma's boyfriend Will Whitney as "the Capt." It would seem, from her remarks, that he was a prankster.

Cambridgeport
September 30th, 1865

Dearest Emma,

Your kind letter was gratefully received, but I hardly dare make an attempt to answer it to night but I am going to try—but please excuse me if I am not very brilliant for it is almost 11 o'clock and I am terribly tired and sleepy. I hardly know what to write first, I have so much to say and have not time to write half, for it will make it quite late. I am glad to hear you are enjoying yourself so nicely also that Ned's health is improving hope he has got over his cold ere this. Well, I suppose you would like to know what we girls have been up to since you left. Well that will be hard telling. One day Julie & I went with Alice and her folks down to Chelsea beach. We started bout 11½ o'clock and reached home about eight I think. We carried our own lunch, parts of us went into the water. We had a splendid time, cannot enter into the particulars. "Croquets" is so-so—Have been out several times. a week ago to night Alice, Julie, Willie, Capt. & myself had a game, after we got through we girls went down street, of course we invited the Capt. to go with us, he asked if we would treat him to some peanuts, but he thought he wouldn't go, so for the fun of it, we proposed for each of us to buy one of those five cents packages of peanuts and leave them at the house—we did so, we left them at the door and gave the bell a pull and ran—He took it all in good parts but I assure you we have had some fun over it. This afternoon Alice, Mary, Mrs. Munroe, Capt. and myself with an extra ball played, while we were playing Capt. took a package of peanuts out of his pocket

(1865)

and put it on the fence remarking whoever hit the stake first should have them, but after a while for fun I took it and put it in my pocket. Alice was the first to hit the stake, so when we all got through the Capt. told me if I would give mine up to A. —he had another one he would give me. I finally did after he had [handed] all the rest a package he gave me one. I began eating them and soon discovered a pin stuck through the outside but upon looking at it again I found there was nearly a dozen in it. I presume you recollect the joke about the pin, do you not? I assure you I went at him well then. Albert & I went over there last night after meeting and played a game of parlor Croquet I like it ever so much this evening we were invited again with Alice & Mary—had a grand time especially coming home— When we were getting ready to come home I said I was tired, Capt. took it up and asked if he shouldn't carry me home in a wheelbarrow, I told him yes (not thinking he meant it) and the first thing I knew he came to the door and said it was all ready, and sure enough it was, so I got in and then he told Alice to follow suit—and he carried us together as far as her home and left her and then brought me home, it was sport. Ella followed him on behind with the rest, he went on the double quick during the evening I told him I had accomadated him by coming over to play and he must do the job I was intended to do if I had stayed at home. He wanted to know what it was, I told him it was to write a letter to you. Ahem(?) he said he should say no at once. Dont you feel bad, but as he left me at the gate, he said "remember me in your letter" I told him I would. Yes, I have been to the Mechanic's fair, went last Tuesday it was very good. Nellie hasn't been very well for the past few days has stayed at home from school part of the time. No Emma my Christian friend has not arrived. I do not expect him. I had a letter yesterday and he said he was as busy as ever if not more so—We had a call today from Mrs. Charles Morse also Charles Markham & T. Hovey was here and spent the night last Thursday. T— is going to be married next Tuesday at 11 o'clock. I cannot write any more for I am so sleepy. I am ashamed to send such a looking letter. read all you can and guess the rest. All send Love. Remember me to Sue. Hope I shall see you soon—

<blockquote>
With lots of love from your true friend,
Albertine
Good Night.
</blockquote>

Albertine had a good time at the Mechanic's Fair, an exciting spectacle. According to the Cambridge Chronicle, many "labor-saving and rapid moving machines" were exhibited, showing "the progress made in application of science to art, and the adaptation of machinery to the various pursuits of life . . ." The Mechanic's Fair envisioned a future "when articles of use and luxury shall so abound, that all may be supplied with the necessaries, and the elegancies of life."

Back in Washington, Maria appeared less optimistic about her future as she confessed to a terrible sadness.

Wash. Oct. 27th 1865

My dear Emma:

I have been trying to write you ever since I arrived home but have been so busily employed that I did not have time. My visit North did me a great deal of good. I gained twelve pounds and got quite a faint pink in my cheeks. I did not like to leave the Mt. [Holyoke] I believe that I am a regular mountaineer. I was sorry when I found the time had come for me to start that I had not gone East. I was really disappointed. I felt that a year ago I lost all I had gained on the Mt. and returned worse than I left home. My health was miserable in the early summer and I knew that I had another year of teaching before me and I must not lose one particle of strength gained. Flesh is not strength and I had only been teaching one month and I was laid up sick enough. For five weeks I have been at home and went day before yesterday for the first time. I had a physician and he says no more school so I resign my position at the end of this month. I am so sorry when I see the dear little faces around me but it is so hard to look after sixty and give each the proper attention. I don't know what I shall do now—something I imagine for I cannot remain idle—I wish I had a good teacher to take my place. I must tell you about my journey home. I started with Mr. Dwight from Springfield and went to Albany at the rate of fifty miles an hour—I almost held my breath part of the way but we arrived safely. We went to the hotel in A. and then out to see a little of the city before we took the boat. I liked what I saw very much—think I would be contented to spend a few weeks there. In the evening took the boat and such a lovely night seldom occurs—our sail down the Hudson was delightful. I wished it had been by daylight but that was impossible as I had to meet Ronnie and Florence in N. York in the morning. My companion

(1865)

was pleasant too. He is a theological student at Andover—quite earnest. I think I wrote you about him on the Mt. I was glad of an opportunity to go that way as I had never been and had always had the greatest desire to see those banks so celebrated. The steamer was quite a study for me. I was never in so beautiful a boat before—it is the quietest in the world I was told. All the staterooms had been sold and I put Mr. Dwight in great trouble by sleeping on the floor. He worried enough and it was quite amusing. I did not think then but it did put him in rather a peculiar position.

We found Washington dusty and dirty. I am getting a little tired of it. I have until this summer felt that I had rather be here than anywhere else but isn't it strange our whole family feel just the same. Ronnie never left home with so much reluctance. Since the war has ended everything seems rather dull. We miss the morning call and the hospitals are all closed. Our family is alone now. All the boarders have gone. Mr. Whitaker begged to come back after his return from the North but everything is so high that it is impossible to live. I want so much to go North somewhere to live anywhere outside of Washington. This Winter though I expect will be very interesting in Congress. You cannot imagine how strange it seems to have a whole house to yourself. I do like it. Father and Mother have been home almost two weeks from their tour—they enjoyed it very much. I did want to go with them so much. They have seen sights. I told Mother I wished I could look with her eyes and see the things. Everything was pleasant—no accident and they were going almost constantly for five weeks. They quite fell in love with Grand Rapids where Mr. William Hovey lives.

Mr. Williams spent the evening with me about a week ago and we enjoyed it much—don't I wish I could be in your place for a little time and feel how it would seem to be appreciated and thought as highly of as some people I know. Don't feel flattered dear Emma for I know you deserve all. He did speak beautifully of you and didn't my heart feel full for you are my own friend. I wanted to laugh and cry both but didn't know which to do. I felt though if I could only see you I should decide very quickly.

He said there was a report that G. Clapp was very solicitous and I enquired about W. Whitney. He said he didn't know. They were all very much interested in you.

Mr. Williams told us what poor health Ned has. Your note

about it and how sad—so young—. I had hoped rest would be beneficial. Do you think he is in a decline? It hardly seems possible he looked so strong. I remember a few years ago he was very unwell—didn't you think he will recover again his strength? I hope so—

What an interesting S.S. Class you must have and what a responsibility. I have no class now but think of going [to] this Bible Class. I have been out of the habit of studying the Bible for so long it will be a great benefit and pleasure to me to begin. I remember how much my Mother used to study and read. Emma I so often think of her with her Bible in her hand during the last part of her life. I often gaze into her eyes in the large photograph and wonder if she sees and knows about her daughter. I must say I am glad she is out of suffering and trial in that happy happy Heaven.

Dear Emma I thought when I began this I had many pages full to write but I soon say not. There is nothing happens of any consequence now that will interest you. I think of you often in your home and wish I could be you. I am so sad all the time. It seems as if God's hand was upon me I have tried and tried to be cheerful and happy but the Lord is teaching us some lesson. What it can be I do know not. I live by the minute it seems to be —often longing for it to pass. I feel condemned but God knows and will help me. I often feel like writing you but am so sad. I think I will not trouble anyone. It will do no good and only make you unhappy. You must not say anything to anyone, but do pray for me. I need your prayers. I could tell you much but cannot write.

With much love always
Your true friend
Maria

Remember me to your family and write as soon as you have time.

This is all the paper I have this evening and don't know when I shall get down to the Avenue for more so I thought I would send it.

Maria judged it worthy of comment that nothing untoward occurred on her parents' trip. Railroad sleeping cars, designed by George M.

(1865)

Pullman, made such extended touring easier in the United States, but travelers still confronted many dangers.

The Western Railroad, which Maria probably took from Springfield to Albany, had recently installed brakes in all its cars. It was the first to do so. Riverboats, such as the one she rode down the Hudson, were no safer. In 1865, 1700 people died when the steamship "Sultana" exploded on the Mississippi River.

Maria's traveling companion, Melatiah Everett Dwight, was a fairhaired twenty-four-year-old, who enjoyed traveling and, after his graduation in 1866 from Andover Theological Institution, spent two years abroad. His college yearbook pictures shows a young man with brooding eyes and the frail, poetic look that women of the period often found attractive. He previously had studied medicine in New York and in 1864 received his M.D. from Bellevue Hospital Medical College. Parsons College, Iowa, also awarded a Doctor of Divinity degree to him in 1906. Despite precarious health, he remained active throughout his lifetime and from 1902 to 1907 served as editor of the *New York Genealogical and Biographical Record.*

He died September 14, 1907 at Mount Holyoke, where he had been born. His obituary stated: Reverend M. Everett Dwight, for many years until recently a prominent Congregational clergyman of New York City, died of heart failure yesterday while visiting at the Prospect House on the summit of Mt. Holyoke. He was sixty-seven years old, and a son of John Dwight, whose donations to Mt. Holyoke College and to Hadley Library made the family well known in that section. He leaves a widow, three sons, and two daughters.

Notifying the seminary of Dwight's death, a classmate wrote, Dwight was "a noble and generous man, in later life very wealthy and a large giver to all good causes."

Susan, too, attempted to be a good neighbor. But sometimes, as she informed Emma, her efforts were not appreciated.

Damariscotta Oct. 29th 1865

Dear Sister

I have not time really to write in but am snatching a few moments, the baby is awake and being temporarily amused with my button box. I have a very dull pencil, and dont expect to write much of a response to your very interesting letter, but I will do the best I can. I have had a busy week and feel glad of Sunday to rest in though I have not much leisure even then, but it is a change. Monday I washed and cleaned a little Tuesday I ironed, and as the baby was fussy, I went out in the P.M. and made one or two calls. I took both the children with me! First I went over to Cynthia's to see if she could come and sew for me the rest of the week. Finding that she could I went into Mrs. Hiltons, to see if I could get an overcoat pattern for Allie. I succeeded in doing so, and had a very agreeable conversation with her, I felt as if I wanted to do some good, and I thought I would go and see Mrs. Harrington, as she is not well and is nervous and low spirited, they say. I remembered how I used to feel and I thought perhaps I might find her alone, and get a chance to say a word or two to encourage her to be steady and try to do right. Everybody is down on her and then she has Mary to deal with who is a dreadful trial. I found when I got there that she had been having a hard battle with her for Mary in return for some reproof had just flew at her, and scratched and kicked her in the stomach, and tried to bite her. Marcia was there and saw it done. Mary has had some such spells before, and Mrs. H. of course tried to defend herself but the story was that she abused Mary. I cant tell you how it was, I suppose the truth is hard to get at. Of course, she was so much excited that I could not say much to her, she had the marks of M's five nails on the back of her hand it was all bleeding. The next day I heard it reported by her enemies that she said I called frequently to see her. I have only been in twice before, and once then on an errand, but the neighbors hardly any of them go there. I do not of course care to be intimate with her, but if a person has no encouragement to do right and relives the past, they wont be inclined to try. I want to give everybody a chance, but I must own I felt rather dismayed from trying to do good in that quarter. Mary is getting very unmanageable and has been quite insane several times. I think it hardly safe for two such to be together, but it is not my affair. Wednesday W.H. went to King's Mills and staid all night. Cynthia came and staid till this (Sunday) morning. She is very slow, and I had rather a tedious time she asks questions and talks most all the time, and in such a low tone that it is most impossible to hear her, especially when the children are in full blast (which is most of the time) It was stormy and I had them in the house, we sat out in the kitchen, we keep a fire all day, and I have my little work table by the new window and it is real pleasant and cosy. We eat out here, and it saves me a great many steps. She made two pairs of pants for Allie, and partly two waists, and part of a vest for W.H. She

(1865)

carried it home to finish. about all I did was housework and a little cutting fitting and mending. She hasn't much gumption about planning anything, and if I did not keep a sharp look out would have spoilt the things. Her sewing is too poor, but she is faithful and honest and her conversation is sensible, after all I enjoyed her company and I guess she had a pretty good time. I gave her some cold meat and bread to carry home with her. She is a poor forlorn creature, she says all her friends have died, and she is so lonesome. She lays awake nights thinking about it, and she is poor and has to work hard, and gets cheated and abused all sorts of ways. I pitied the poor thing I can tell you I hope I shed some light on her pathway.

Monday—I could not write any more last night so I finish today. I have been washing and cleaned 2 shelves of the sitting room closet. The baby is not very well and I did think of putting off my washing but W.H. and I managed so that one of us tended him while the other was working. I did not get done quite so soon, but I had a small wash this week. both the children have got dreadful colds two or three nights last week I went to bed with the goose oil all fixed, and once I had to get up in the night and give Allie some medicine for fear he would have the croup. He is better today and I have let him go out of doors the first time for three or four days. Charlie has a bad cold and his little mouth is full of canker his mouth is running all the time. He has got two stomach teeth through and one eye tooth. He was not well at all the last week. I tend him all I can. some of the time he is pretty cross. He rests quite well nights so we get our sleep.

I got a very pretty sack pattern for an overcoat, but I don't like to cut it till I know what they are wearing. also his new suit I wish I could tell how to make it. If you could get a chance to ask Julia about it before anyone writes again I should think it a favour. I can't find out much here about such things, but no matter if you are busy. I dont think I can make either this week according to present appearance. Oh how often I wish you or Mother were nearby to help me fix and plan, though you and I didn't accomplish much but we had a good time. I want very much to come home to Thanksgiving (ours is the 23rd) but W.H. thinks the weather and travelling will not be fit. I feel every year as if I wanted to be there perhaps we never shall all get together again, and I have been away so long. But I must try to be contented here, we both feel blue to stay here all winter, but I think we ought to be thankful for a home and such a good one too. there were lots of things in your letter I would like to speak of but I have not time. I enjoyed your descriptions very much. The Capt. seems to take his time. Well I am glad if you can have [undecipherable]. Have you seen Jimmy R. lately. I wish I could see little Eddie. I think of him a great deal. I hope he is getting to be less troublesome. Did Alfred go to housekeeping again. I wish I had some of his paper collars. When I come home I mean to get some. Give my love to Mary & Julia. I wanted to give you something when you were here, but I knew you would not take it. I was sorry that I refused to take anything from Jimmy on your account I should have given it to you but a wedding has given me the opportunity. Dont say anythng about it. I can spare it as well as not and you helped me a great deal. I wish I could do more for you. Since the prices have raised so high I have had to leave out the eggs from my Johnny cake and also to cut off other luxuries. You came in a lucky train But you did not come for the loaves and fishes. But I must leave off. I believe this letter is full of nonsense, but I must have something to keep off the blues. We still think a great deal about Ned and hope he will be led aright. I send much love to all the family and yourself from Sue

Susan hoped to be at home in Cambridge for Thanksgiving, but she was not sure of the date. Although the United States still did not celebrate any legal national holidays, in 1863 President Lincoln had issued a proclamation focusing the country's attention on Thanksgiving as a day of observance for federal employees. Thereafter, the separate states enacted laws making it a legal holiday, either on the third or fourth Thursday of November. Not until 1939, when President Franklin Roosevelt deferred to the pressure of merchants who wanted a longer Christmas shopping season, was Thanksgiving universally celebrated on the third Thursday of the month. Soon after, however, Congress passed a law that set the observance for Thanksgiving Day as a legal federal holiday on the last Thursday in November.

Holidays were a special time, a respite from chores, much appreciated by nineteenth century Americans, whose work-week was long and arduous. Susan often commented about her endless household tasks. Each day was assigned a job. Blue Monday, so-called for the bluing used to get clothes white, was followed by ironing on Tuesday. In this letter, Susan wrote about ironing, an especially tiring chore. Usually, two or more heavy irons were used alternately. While one was being used to press, the others sat on top of the stove getting hot. Since the iron was all one piece, the handle heated up, too, so housewives used potholders. In 1871, nineteen-year-old Mary Potts of Ottumwa, Iowa, patented "Mrs. Potts' Cold Handle Sad Iron" (sad is an obsolete word for heavy or solid). It came in a set with three irons and had a detachable handle, eliminating the need for potholders.

In spite of Susan's impression that "the Capt." was in no hurry to declare his intentions, he and Emma soon were betrothed. Upon learning of Emma's engagement, Maria was ecstatic.

> Washington
> Tuesday Nov. 14th 1865

My own dear Emma:

Now don't give all your heart to that gallant Captain. I want a little corner. Your happiness has indeed made me very happy I only wish I could express in words what I felt on receiving your letter—Just three weeks last Sunday, I remember the day well. How I would like to shake you a little for not telling me sooner, but you didn't say anything about when the wedding was to come off. I want you to understand your sister gives her free consent, and approves of your proceedings very "muchly". Don't I remember the talk coming home from school seven year's ago, and didn't we have nice times. But if those were nice times what can these be for my dear friend. But I wondered Father asked first thing when will she be married I said Oh! it is too soon for that but I don't know. Shouldn't I feel provoked if three weeks after that great event a letter should come stating the fact. I should have to wait longer time than that for you would be busier than you ever were before—now Emma Barbour you must send those cards as long before hand as is possible or I will not be ready and as they say here right smart provoked. What a pleasant time you must have had at Sue's—was Jimmie Randall the hunchback who used to live in Cambridge?

But I cannot think of anything but your engagement—How did you feel—Nonsense just as if you would write me but if I could only get hold of the child wouldn't she be glad to tell. And the Captain is kind noble and solid as we always supposed but improved since I have seen him—I really would like to renew the acquaintance—I feel almost a stranger. When you get settled down won't your old maid sister come and see you with her kniting no crocheting and her pockets full of candy if need be—

Your matter of fact subdued way amused me a little—I don't believe you look as subdued when the Captain appears as you write—I wouldn't think of your past experience except to profit —Let a little of the rosy tint color your future and if ill comes accept it—May no dark clouds rise over my dear Emma. You need not say anything about Mr. Williams being too complimentary or what ever you may call it I shall believe just as much as I choose.

Now many thanks for your kind words—no one can help me but God himself. I wish I could feel always near Him. I do trust in him but I get too easily discouraged I know—I was very unwell when I wrote but since then I have in a great measure recovered. I feel better for being sick. No more side ache since then to speak of. Dr. Verdi has given me medicine and it helps me. I have felt well for several weeks but may be on my back next week. I have still my school. The Trustees were unwilling to give me up until they could obtain another teacher and I keep on. —beside this a young lady comes twice a week to recite to me an hour. and I have one music pupil twice a week. I have made quite an effort to get scholars in music for a week past and only one has come as yet. If I could get twenty Goodbye to school with a good relish—Still I should be sorry—

I should be able to attend Congress occasionally and be at home during the day—Mother & Father are well. they are glad to hear of your happiness and both send love—I told Ronnie & her face looked glad I assure you. Flory is attending one of the best schools here—she learns very fast. Hattie is at home—quite well. All send love I wish I had more to write but I cannot think of anything but the best news which I have written. I seldom go to the Avenue now and so we have only our own family do not hear or see much—

I have fixed up my little room and put a stove in it. Ronnie & I take a deal of comfort evenings studying reading & sewing together. I intend continuing my French & music if I ever can get time.

My kindest regards to all your family and I would congratulate Capt. Whitney on the prize he has won

Your friend ever,
Maria

(1865)

If Maria succeeded in attending Congress, she heard debates on the complicated issues of reconstruction. Like President Lincoln, President Andrew Johnson emphasized a conciliatory plan. He wanted to accept back into the Union the government of every Southern state that disavowed its act of secession, repudiated the Confederate debt, and ratified the Thirteenth Amendment, which prohibited slavery. When Congress convened in December, however, the Radical Republicans, led by Senator Charles Sumner and Representative Thaddeus Stevens, gained control. They deemed the President's program too lenient and refused to recognize the reconstructed Southern governments or to seat their delegates.

13
(1866)

With the war years behind them, Emma and her family instigated major changes in their lives. Personal goals had been put on hold for the duration; peace gave people permission to resume their private lives.

Emma had accepted Captain William H. Whitney's proposal of marriage, but a loss intruded on her happiness and the excitement of her engagement. While rejoicing in her own good fortune, she mourned the death of a former classmate. When she wrote to the young woman's parents, Emma enclosed a photograph of herself along with her note. Her friend's father gratefully acknowledged Emma's condolences and expression of sympathy.

(1866)

119 St. Marks Place
New York Jan.13, 66

Dear Emma:

I cannot sufficiently thank you for complying with the request I made for your miniature. The likeness is an excellent one and it will be kept by Mary's Mother and myself as a precious rememberance of one of the dearest of our angel daughters friends. Mrs. Alden is stopping for a few weeks with her sister, Mrs. Allen, at the corner of Hilliard and Brattle street. We shut up our house at East Cambridge last Wednesday morning. God Bless you dear Emma for sending us such kind and loving words relating to dear Mary. Could I follow the impulses of my heart I should write you a long letter telling you how deeply the affectionate interest which Mary's classmates took in her while living and which has found expression since her death, has touched our hearts but time and business duties will not now permit.

    I shall not fail to call and see you as soon as a favorable opportunity offers and more fully thank you for complying with my request relating to your picture, and for your kind quick letter, these I can express in written words.

    Please remember me affectionately to Lizzie Wellington, and through you I would thank the dear girl for her letter, which came to us a short time since at East Cambridge.

    I shall send your letter and photograph to Mrs. Alden by todays mail.

Yours, gratefully
& affectionately,
A. Alden.

Maria penned a long letter to Emma and after much small talk, revealed the reason for this missive as well as her recent melancholy. It is significant that although she had not seen her friend for six years, Maria chose to divulge her painful secret to Emma.

Washington
Jan. 25th. 1866

My dear Emma:

I do not owe you a letter but feel just like writing you—I did not say what I wanted in my last and have thought ever since, I would write again. I often think of you in your happiness and wish I could see you. I feel almost as if you were slipping away from me and that Captain friend was getting the prize. I haven't let you go altogether and he need not expect it. I imagine you attending lectures, skating, sleighing and having a good time generally. I am glad glad for you—I wish I could only visit Cambridge and witness some of your happy times. The North is the place after all for cultivation and improvement and enjoyment too. This winter seems very quiet, so many of the officers and soldiers have returned home—the streets look almost deserted. I have had a very quiet time—have not been away from home to spend the evening for two or three months—quite a contrast with last winter when I went every day somewhere and not one evening was spent alone—I feel real lonely sometimes but think it is all for the best and try & look cheerful and it don't "require much" effort. Changes must come with time and the last year has been one which can never be forgotten.

If I could only see you—I wonder if you are the same Emma in appearance (the heart I rest sure is the same) have you grown older or has love and happiness kept you sixteen? They tell me I have grown older and I feel so—it seems to me if I could run wild for a year I should breathe in enough of the pure air of Heaven to last me years. I am well though and do not complain but one cannot help wishing sometimes—I must tell you what a treat I have had recently. Henry Ward Beecher lectured at the Capitol about a month ago and mother was fortunate enough to obtain tickets which were given out at twelve o'clock when father was at his office and she was obliged to get them or go without. Ronnie tried too but did not succeed—they had all been taken a few minutes before she arrived. I came home from school full of anticipation and rushed "Yes. —two—" My countenance fell I assure you, two would not admit five and I thought my case hopeless. I said it was too bad but it must be all right. I went up stairs again to attend to a music scholar and trying to choke the tears down which would come. I did make up my mind to be resigned though—After the lesson I found Mother again and asked a little more minutely and at last she had to confess she had indeed bought five—I did feel happy enough for I had never seen the man or even heard his voice and I had longed for the time to come when I could—Well this is a long story—I went and heard—It was very very interesting and I believe I have written you what a passion I have for such

(1866)

gatherings at the Capitol—I looked my fill that evening—it was the first time I had been to the Hall this year—A week ago I heard Speaker Colfax give his great lecture "Across the Continent"—This was another great treat. There is no course of lectures this winter. I forgot one Concert I attended in Georgetown. Sarah Whitaker and her father accompanied me. Miss Butts a young French lady was the prima-donna—she is a most beautiful singer and promises to surpass the celebrated singers of the country. I have had quite a number of feasts come to count them—My school I still keep and ever expect to—Professor Bailey of Yale the great Elocutionist has been in Washington and the Trustees of the school invited him to give some instruction to the Teachers. We all assembled every afternoon for a week and he lectured and heard us read. The exercises were very interesting—He kept us quite merry by his anecdotes. We all learned much and got quite rested only teaching half a day. The nervous headache is an accompaniment of the school.

Must tell you about my Christmas and new Year's. I had quite a nice present from my pupils. A handsome china cup and saucer very heavily gilded—a pocket book worth two dollars—a bottle of Lubin's Extract—two quires of paper with envelopes and some pretty houseplants. It was all a surprise to me except the saucer which one little boy had to hint about. New Year's was dreary and rainy—We had several callers but did not feel much like receiving this year. Ronnie prepared a great surprise for her boys. She called upon the parents of ninety-six boys and told them privately of her surprise and they all assisted her by contributions. It was a Christmas Tree and each boy received a present from their parents on the tree, the school room was lighted with candles and also the tree. nine candles over each window and door—the room beautifully trimmed with Evergreens and "Merry Christmas" over the back part of the room. After Santa Claus had distributed the presents, refreshments were passed around to the whole company and scholars—of ice cream—A very nice time and the scholars knew nothing of it until they entered the room and found it all illuminated and trimmed. I wished so much I had been able to prepare such a surprise for my school but it was at the time I was feeling too unwell and had as much as I could attend to out of school. Our Sabbath School also had a Christmas Tree and Festival for the scholars—I spent the night at Georgetown but understood it was very merry—I have heard some news today—do you call it good or not—The old church is burned to the ground. Now I imagine you will have a new church very soon—What a great cause of rejoicing. Our new church is progressing rapidly and the handsomest in the city—Amos Kendall has already given $100,000 and about two thousand remain to be paid by the ladies for furnishing. The carpets are already bought and the vestry finished we have been worshipping there for about three weeks and expect to go above by the 1st of March

Emma, I hardly know what to write you about the great change in our family. I felt when I wrote you before as if I could not say one word to you but you must not think it was because I did not trust and love you just the same but it was all so fresh and heartrending I could not find words or thoughts and so uncertain I did not dare write. I cannot tell all now—probably you have heard much, how much I don't know. I wish you would give me some idea. Hattie now is in the Insane Asylum and very happy there—I went to see her two weeks ago and she said in parting "Maria I have been here six weeks tomorrow, and it only seems two weeks" I was surprised and pleased that she was happy, but I felt too sad to leave her there under lock and key. She has acted very strangely for about a year but particularly this last summer. It sometimes seemed almost impossible to be in the house with her—we had often remarked that she must be insane but did not feel competent to judge as she was always a strange child from her birth. She was to have been married last Sept. but I got her to postpone it until January for many reasons which then seemed good. Father was very much opposed as Brainerd was very young and Hattie only eighteen—Just before Father and Mother arrived she took that strange freak into her head of running off. I was the only one at home when she went and never suspected her intention. You cannot imagine my feelings. I cannot tell them when I found her trunk gone. Father arrived the next day, after she was found and persuaded to return. She was very sullen for two weeks after her return and then she became quite sick we thought threatened with the Typhoid Fever—she thought she was going to die. She had two of the strangest visions I ever knew. I went up to her room right from school and she opened her eyes from a nap and stared around very strangely and she commenced laughing. I did not know what to make of it—at last she said "I have had such a funny dream I wonder what it means—I saw Mother and she seemed an angel—a bright star was in her forehead so

(1866)

bright I could not look at her face only it was mother—She had the Bible open in her lap and sitting here on my bed beside me she took my finger and placed it upon a passage of Scripture but the star shone so brightly I could not read it—I tried and tried but I could not. She then closed the book and looked at me pityingly—and I awoke" Hattie seemed impressed that she was not going to recover but still she did—That night again she had a second dream—She seemed placed within a large field and it was very stony and rough—Near by were two figures one dressed in white and the other in black—The white seemed called "Life" and the black "Death"—They told her to run and the one who caught her would possess her—She started and ran Life almost caught her but she ran on, and then Death came nearer and she stumbled and Death caught her—She was much distressed when she awoke in the morning—But from that time I never saw a greater change in anyone—She seemed perfectly lovely—no one could be more affectionate or kinder to each of her family—the contrast was so great that our confidence returned but rather wavering. We really hoped she had repented her course and was trying to redeem the past. But our hopes were short lived, in three weeks she was again missing. Father went again in search and found her and placed her in safety. He then called a meeting of Pastor and Deacon and the other leading members of the church. He laid her whole life before them and they decided unanimously that she must be insane. Three physicians were called and they gave certificates of insanity—It certainly seems so but yet I can hardly believe it she is so pretty in some things. Emma if you have not known of this before please do not circulate it—I know not how much is known North it is all too sad to be a subject of gossip.

I have just returned from the Prayer meeting it seems as if God had sent this upon us for our good—I believe I have been led to think more and I trust my faith has grown stronger—I do need more strength though and I trust my dear friend and sister will pray for me. Will you not.

The people of our church have been very kind they all loved Hattie—she was a general favorite and they sympathize with us strongly—There are very interesting meetings held now every evening this week several have found Christ precious to their souls and quite a number are enquiring the way. Mr. Howlett our pastor is a very devoted Christian. I am in the S.S. now as a scholar—in Mrs. Buell's class whose husband was missionary to

Greece. She is also Florey dayschool teacher—a very intelligent Christian lady—I enjoy the Sabbath morning much and take great pleasure in preparing the lesson—it is so long since I have been scholar I really enjoy it one day in the week. I would like to hear all about where you worship and how you do now the church is burned. I hope to get North and spend most of my time East next summer. I have never felt a greater desire than now to go home again. I am looking forward with a great deal of pleasure—My school is doing nicely now and I enjoy it notwithstanding my occasional murmurings about the confinement. Now I have had a good part of my say—don't you think it rather a long say? I shall look for a letter from you ere long—Remember me to my "to be brother" and all your family—We are all well and alone (without boarders). I sometimes wish we had someone for it would be a little livelier. Goodnight Sister, Maria

It is doubtful that the congregation of the First Baptist Church in Cambridge joined Maria in rejoicing when their wooden church was razed by a fire, attributed to an overheated furnace, early Monday morning, January 22, 1866. One woman recalled, "Something pathetic was there also in the fate of the bell, which rang its own knell, ceasing only when the rope connecting it with hands of men outside, was burnt away. It rang nightly at nine o'clock, the curfew, until that old custom, borrowed from feudal times, ceased among us." She also rememberred the last time the "patriotic organ" had been played: to render "America." Within the year, the church was rebuilt and the new sanctuary was dedicated on Christmas Day, 1867.

Maria noted that clergymen as well as physicians were consulted to determine whether Hattie was insane. Contemporary treatment of mental illness often hinged on religious attitudes towards The Fall and the Will of God. Although the biblical view of the insane as people possessed by demons had been discredited, clergymen considered guilt and sin basic in matters of morality and mental health critical in determining accountability. Individuals unable to distinguish between right and wrong, however, could not be held responsible for their actions. The concept had been translated into law and adopted by courts in the United States shortly after 1843, when a case in England established the McNaughton test—the ability of an ordinary person to understand the difference between right and wrong—as the criterion for an insanity plea.

(1866)

Psychiatry was a nascent specialty without a name. In 1843, Dr. William Sweetser used "mental hygiene" to describe treatment and many physicians in England as well as the United States adopted the term. Nevertheless, some physicians continued to practice bloodletting to eliminate the impure vapors believed responsible for insanity. Others thought strong emotions were harmful and insisted that religious fervor, such as excitement at a revival meeting or an evangelical service, could precipitate madness. Many regarded insanity as a physical disorder, an irritation of the brain, analogous to stomach indigestion. In spite of the range and number of theories, by 1866, mental illness was generally treated as hereditary, somatic, and incurable.

Asylums evolved from almshouses. Confining mental patients, especially poor people and immigrants whose customs sometimes seemed peculiar, resulted in crowded and unsanitary conditions in public asylums, where care was primarily custodial or residents were enlisted as a source of cheap labor. Privately owned, corporate asylums, such as the one Hattie appears to have been committed in, catered to the upper and middle classes. Maria's letter—in which she slipped into the past tense when speaking of Hattie—poignantly discloses that insanity, viewed as hereditary and incurable, was a social stigma.

Maria enjoyed a respite from family problems at her school's elocution sessions coached by Mark Bailey. After his graduation from Dartmouth College in 1849, Bailey married and taught at Yale. Subsequently, the couple left New Haven and traveled throughout the South, where he taught at various institutions. Eventually, he and his wife returned to New Haven and he held the post of instructor of elocution at Yale for many years.

Professor Bailey was typical of many young men who, after the war, moved around the country, from community to community, following professional opportunities or searching for land on which to settle. In the era of the self-made man, men often traveled widely to see what they could make of themselves. In spite of success stories that wafted East, however, it was difficult to pick up stakes and to begin again in a new place, far from supportive family and friends. Emma's brother Ned, and later Alfred, went west and discovered it was not all they had anticipated.

No doubt, Ned would rather have stayed in Cambridge. He went west in search of financial opportunity so that he might marry his Georgie sooner. Despite experience as a boarder, when he was a traveling salesman before the war, he now fared badly in a furnished room. Writing to Emma, Ned tallied his woes.

Cincinnati O Feb. 6, '66

Dear Sister Emma

You were very kind to write to me and I didnt mean to let so long a time pass before answering your letter, but numerous things have prevented me from writing sooner. Before I came here I had been very pleasantly situated both at Cleveland and Columbus but when I got here I found it more difficult to obtain a boarding place. I found one house where I could have a room and board for $20 a week but that was a little too steep for me. I have finally settled down here but as I dont feel at all satisfied with my quarters don't consider myself settled exactly either, for I am constantly on the lookout for a better place. I was obliged to get a room in one house, and board at another, when I hired the room I thought it was quite a pleasant one, there was a young law student occupying it at the time, but when he went out he took a great deal of the furniture, saying such was the arrangement made with the landlady. I couldn't do anything for it was the only room I could find, but I didn't like it much. I pay $15 a month for the room besides paying for fuel I consume, it is on the first floor front, is large and airy and cold as a barn. I have a rousing fire in the grate which has been burning about three hours, and now I can see my breath a few yards from the fire. The room is not well taken care of, the sheets are not clean, the water pitcher has the handle broken off, and the two chairs, although covered with crimson plush, are so old that it is dangerous to lean against the backs for fear of a fall, as I write this I have the back against the bed-post, and the table drawn up in front of me. I suppose I am fastidious but as I have been so used to having things nice at home I feel the contrast very painfully. I pay $5 a week for board, and they set a very good table, but I couldn't room there, if I could I should be all right for that is a very nice place, it makes me feel terribly homesick, but I suppose I must stand it awhile longer. I called on Mr. Ellis today at his banking-house, he appeared to be glad to see me invited me to his house to tea, and I promised to go this evening, but I felt quite unwell at night so concluded not to go, shall some other time. Parker Hovey is here selling a patent broom. Sunday A.M. we went to church together heard sermon on the Miracle of the

(1866)

healing of the leper, minister described the loathsomness of the disease very graphically, after enumerating its symptoms & progress, summed up the whole description by saying that if a dead person could be resusitated after having lain in the grave two or three weeks, and made to walk about we could on seeing it get a correct idea of the person thoroughly impregnated with the leprosy, he then compared its loathsomeness to that of sin in the eyes of God—& in the P.M. we went to a mission school at the west end of the city, it is a very large school and very well conducted, although not quite as well as ours, their average attendance for the last month has been 350—In the evening I went alone to the 9th St. Baptist, sermon on the judgment, after the services there were nine young ladies and gentlemen baptised, it was a very impressive ceremony, and made me feel as though I would like to have been one of them. I am very much interested in the subject of religion and wish I could make the promises of the bible mine. I do pray that such may be the case. I have much more I would like to write but as I am pretty tired and dont feel very well guess I must stop, the weather has been very cold here ever since I came, about the coldest of the season they say. Write me soon as you have leisure, my love to all and regards to the Capt.

Ned

I thought I had my stencil with [me] but on looking in my trunk for it dont find it ask mother to send it by mail to this place if she can find it.

Ned

Cincinnati was ideally suited to Ned's pursuits. Above the Ohio River, surrounded by beautiful hills and terraces, the Queen City of the West was a gateway to the South as well. Not only a river port bustling with the traffic of huge side-wheel and stern-wheel cargo and passenger steamers, Cincinnati also was a railroad center. By the 1850s, it was the largest pork-packing center in the country. An earnest and well-connected young man, if he listened well and kept his eyes open, was in a position to benefit from many business opportunities.

Like Ned, Susan and WH were on the move, too. Not by choice, however. Apparently, worshippers at Damariscotta's First Baptist Church desired a more dynamic leader. As a graduate of Harvard

College, the Rev. Evans had been expected to achieve a distinguished pulpit. Sincere and hard-working though he was, however, he failed to develop the melodramatic preaching style, popular in his day. Indeed, the *Massachusetts Baptist Year Book 1895–99* noted: "His ministry, while not exciting curious attention, had two marked virtues; first, it always tended to strengthen and establish in the faith all candid Christians, and secondly, it prepared the hearts of the unconverted with a substantial basis of belief when gathered in under the ministrations of others. He was able happily, to count some souls to shine in his future crown, but his main calling seemed to be to edify by well-prepared and instructional teachings." His unflinching rectitude, too, may have offended the hard-nosed merchants and tradespeople of Damariscotta.

Waldeboro Monday May 7th

Dear Sister Emma

I know it is a long time since I have written you, but I have been very busy and have had to content myself with writing where when and to whom I could. You have been pretty well employed too I should judge at home. I am glad the children are getting along and better of the measles. I hope mine will escape, at least till I get a settled home. Well I am through at last and a homeless wanderer. You can hardly have any idea of what my feelings were when I went through my empty rooms each dear by some association, and thought it was to be my home no more. But such things must be and we must be reconciled I trust I am. I staid with Mrs. Hutchins after Monday till Friday. She paid me every attention, and the girl's took care of the children a great deal of the time so that I got along very nicely with my packing and moving, but it was a great job I am glad it is over. We had two men 2 days packing and matting the furniture and Mrs. H and I packed 4 trunks. We had to make more calculations on account of the change of seasons and pack for summer & winter both. This is about the worst time of the year to move. Then the house was to clean all over. I expected to come here Wednesday but instead I had to walk one or two miles for a woman to clean house, tried 3 unsuccessfully. then went home and Mrs. H. and I cleaned till night, after tea I hunted again and Mr. Berry sent a woman the next day so I had two. They finished the house Thursday night I was coming here that night but the stage was crowded and I had the sick headache so i waited till Friday

(1866)

and came at noon. I got pretty well tired with so much packing and cleaning, but I am resting now after a fashion—Mrs. Marshall has company besides us and we are stored rather thickly but the company is agreeable and it seems a relief to get away from D—it was very unpleasant for me to stay there alone—WH is in Great Falls now but I expect him at Scotta tonight and he will probably come over here tomorrow. Next Sunday he is probably engaged in this State and a week from today he is coming to Boston I suppose there are 3 boats from Bath now. they go every day fare one dollar. They are going to have a railroad to Wiscasset I believe—I hardly think I shall come to Boston with him but I cant tell till I see him and know his plans I will write again the last of the week, but you need not make any calculations on seeing me at present. I do not know whether WH has any definite idea where he shall settle—but he will soon be in Boston and you will have all particulars from him about places where he has been—I rather hope to stay in this state though I hope it will be in a more accessible part. I have lived here so long that I have in a measure got used to Maine ways—but I want to be in a place where we can be contented and do good. I am enjoying myself here, have freedom from care and hope to rest and do a little sewing. Mr. Nugent was here today he wants us to go up to his home and stay awhile—We have been washing this forenoon and after dinner we all took a ramble in the woods after Spencer games we had a really nice time—But I shall have to stop writing now for I am depending on someone to carry this to the Office—You cant tell what a relief it is to get the care off me awhile—I think of you all at home and want to see you. but I cannot tell how soon I shall come—I am glad Eddie is better but I am afraid he is cross & troublesome. I hope mother will not get sick with so much care. I shall try to write again soon. I am sure I dont know now where to tell you to direct my next letter but if I dont write please send it here—

> Goodbye yours in Last -
> Affec, Sue
>
> Love to your <u>beloved</u>—

WH's next parsonage took the Evans family to Cape Cod, Massachusetts, where once again Susan busied herself, turning their temporary homestead into a cozy oasis among strangers. Although remote and sparsely settled, the place had advantages—it was closer to Cambridgeport and more accessible to family visitors.

Hyannis July 4th

Dear Emma.

I suppose you will be wondering what has become of me, but I have been so busy I have not had time to write before. I had a large wash Monday, and in the P.M. & eve had a number of callers. Tuesday I spent the day at "the Port" which is about a mile from here. I spent the day at Dia Sanders I had a splendid time it is a nice place there in the summer, but in the winter many of the families shut up and live in the city. just now there are summer boarders and visitors who make it very pleasant. I could have had a house there, and should have enjoyed it much better than here. I could have bathed every day and have had nice neighbors but it would not have been convenient for W.H. and I try to remember that we did not come here to enjoy ourselves, but have a work to do.

Yesterday I ironed and in the P.M. attended the S. Circle. I had a pretty good time, though I felt rather lonesome and strange. There is some good society here and some not so good. I have no neighbor that I care much to mingle with. The people seem pleasant and cordial but I have not found the Hutchins nor Mrs. Hilton yet. I feel the need of a friend to go round with me. I am so far from the village that I cant go out much, and I have a good deal to do. However, as we shall move so soon, I shall not do any more than is absolutely necessary. I have just as much as I can do to get through my work with the interruptions I have. Today is the glorious fourth and I have a feeling of homesickness decidedly it is so quiet here. A good many have friends come from the city to spend the fourth, and I have wished you and Capt. were here. Some are goin in the woods and some are sailing. Last night W.H. met Sam Crosby and another fellow who were going out fishing. He invited him here today but he thought he should be out fishing. W.H. did not know him at first. We have been out picking green peas for dinner and Allie has a flag a man lent him and I am going to try to get him some torpedoes or something to amuse them this P.M. I guess I shall go to walk. If I only had some one to go with me I would go every day. It is about half a mile to the shore from here.

(1866)

Last Sunday I took Charlie to meeting in the forenoon he was not so good as before he did not speak but was very uneasy. In the PM I got a girl to stay with him, and W.H. preached his inaugural and we were received into the church. Rev. Mr. Chase of this place made the address. It was a solemn day to me, and I felt much overcome. I had the sick headache when I got home and did not feel able to write.

I was so glad to get the letter from father and hear that Mother was better. Tell her not to try to write and I will write just the same to her. I hope she will go away and get recruited soon. You must excuse me now for I cannot get any more time to write. Ive got to get my dinner now I shall not be able to write as long letters as I want to nor tell you half I would like but all in good time. I dont expect much from home while you are so busy, but I want to hear often if only a few lines is better than nothing. I wish youd ask father to send me a pen one of those golden ones if he has any. This is a horrid thing, but the best I can do. This isnt much of a place to buy things not half as good as D.

I would write evenings but I get so tired I am glad to go to bed. It is very cool here most of the time. Good bye in great haste with much love,

Sue

Should be glad to see anyone from home anytime.

About the time Susan moved from Damariscotta, Alfred was on his way to join Ned in the West. Meanwhile, Mary and their son Walter, born May 17, 1865, remained with the Barbours in Cambridgeport, which may be the reason Susan suggested Emma would be too busy to write long letters. Alfred stopped in Cleveland and Columbus, Ohio, before settling in Tremont, Illinois, where he found work as a bookkeeper for Ingalls Spalding & Co., a retail business. In May, he'd written to his mother, "I feel as well contented here as a person can be who has left so pleasant a home, such kind parents, such a dear wife and baby and so many friends . . ."

Apparently, like Susan, Alfred felt homesick and had a hankering to be home on the Fourth of July. That day, underlining the date for emphasis, he wrote to "the family circle" and told his father, "I am spending my independence day flat on my back in bed, with you all in imagination . . . taken down Sunday eve with Diarrhoea and dissiness, and have had all the symptoms of Typhoid fever with perhaps a slight touch of it. I have not been able to leave my room since and with the exception of about fifteen minutes yesterday have not been off my bed. I sent to Peoria yesterday and got some medicine of Dr. Cheever, but it dont seem to help me as I wish, yet I am very comfortable and have every attention I can desire. I suffer more with my head, and this pain across my waist or in the region of the Liver or Kidney than any thing else—extreme weakness. I do not wish you at home to feel at all worried about me, for I am in no way dangerous, and Ned is taking good care of me and filling my place at the store. Everybody is kind & doing all they can for me. I dont want any thing said to Mary about it, for I have written to her just how I am and dont want to have her feel worried."

Susan and her mother were not feeling well either. Susan's neuralgia seems to have been aggravated by the ocean air. Nevertheless, she offered to take Eddie back so that her mother, who suffered with tuberculosis, might recuperate in the mountains of New Hampshire.

Hyannis   August 7
Wednesday

Dear Sister Emma,

I meant to have written you yesterday but was too busy. I found I had quite a wash and as we did not begin early, and I did not feel very well it took me longer than usual. It was very hot and is so today, but a cool breeze came up at noon and at evening a fog, which made it quite comfortable. Today I feel much better and ironed all the a.m. I thought I would only do a little, but made out to do all but my dress—which I shall do tomorrow. I thought of you and Mother and thought you would have a hot time of it. I was glad you didn't, either have to do it alone I hope mother got home safely and felt rested. I looked for a letter today but did not get one. Thought likely you were too busy. There were two men here today to see the house. They seemed to like the appearance of things here. The man who now occupies our future house has engaged another and is fitting it up to move, so we may move very soon and we may not move till fall, all is uncertain. If we only stay this month out which is quite probable, I don't much care. Slong as I've got to move, still I would like to put it off till it is a little cooler. Tell Mother I think my arm is better, though it hurts me some to sew or write on anything that I have to curl up my fingers to do. It is worse in the morning, and better in the P.M. My knee is rather stiff, but I

(1866)

save it all I can. Yesterday P.M. I mended a number of things and cut the childrens hair "fighting out". They feel much better for it and look so too. Yesterday they were cross and quarrelled all day, today they are more amiable. There was a cunning little kitten came to our house day before yesterday, the children are delighted and though they use her pretty hard, she seems to be fond of them. I shall keep her, if no one claims her, she is maltese and white. I have put Charlie to bed every night since Mother went away, and left him. He cried a good deal, but I did not mind him, after a while he went to sleep. I'm in hopes to break him in by & bye. W.H. took a walk down to the Port this P.M. I think very likely he will stay to tea, hope be with him. I shan't have to make any fire. Last night I thought I'd got to bake bread, when luckily a baker came along and I got bread, buns & crackers. He calls once a week and has everything in his line. The day that I went down to the depot I bought a hoop skirt, which would be about $1.25 in Boston I paid 1.75—I could not find but one pair of boots that fitted me, they were Balmorals and were 2.25. I got a pair of neckties for Charlie & paid .75. I could not find a check, nor anything suitable for Charlie's dress. There is no assortment here, and what there is, is dear. I think it would pay to go or send to Boston. When I got home, I found two of the upper wires in the skirt broken (probably doing it up) I found also that a peddler had called, who very likely might have supplied me. It was too far for me to exchange the skirt and indeed I saw no other that I liked. I made two calls and walked home, one on old Mrs. Parker, and on Mr. Parkers wife. I fancied I was not very cordially received. I learned afterward that old Mrs. P was one of those who voted against WH. By the way, she is mother to that Mrs. Hallet whom Alf hired his house of. Young Mrs. P. seemed very sad and as she was almost a perfect stranger I could not expect much from her. They had no hope scarcely of him, but think his brain is softening. When I came home I met a lady at the gate, who had called 3 times and found me gone every time. She would not come in so you see I had rather hard luck. I felt lonesome and thought I would go [to] Mrs. Sherman's found she had gone out, Mrs. Loring had company, young Mrs. Snow was out. So I sat down at home and read a paper. I missed Mother very much indeed. But I was glad for your sake she was on her way home for I know you had had a hard and lonesome time and I know she would not feel contented to stay away any longer. She was thinking about you all the while she was here. I think you did splendidly. I was sure you could and would cheerfully for her sake and I feel very thankful to you it was a great favor to me for she did much for me (though I did not wish her to, but she would) I would not have sent for her for my sake, but hoped she might gain by the change and I think she did seem much improved when she left, though she was sure the air did not agree with her. I tried to do all that would make her comfortable and contented and think I've nothing to reflect upon. I hope she will go to N[ew].H[ampshire]. in August for I think she will be very much disappointed if she does not. If you can get Eddie down here, I will take care of him rather than not have her go. I will do anything. But I must leave off writing now as I have to go to get my supper soon the children are getting witchy I will try to send a list of things that I want and if you go shopping you can perhaps get them. I want a little dress most of all for Charlie, but I am not in a great hurry. The breast pins I want the most, they have some here quite pretty for 1.25, but I think I could get one for .75 at that Court St. store. This was very much like your black one that Alf gave you. I don't know as I can send any money in this letter but I will pay you soon, Dear Emma. I was very sorry I could not do your work any better but I had not used my machine much since I came and was out of practice and then I could not see very well. I did the best I could and wished it 'twas more. How is Capt. ? Suppose he is taking his vacation and you are feeling lonesome. No matter, you'll have him all to yourself by & bye. What a long letter give my love to all much for yourself from S.E.E.

In spite of painful stiffness in her arm and fingers, as well as trouble with her eyes, Susan seems to have used her new sewing machine to prepare clothes and household articles for Emma's trousseau, sending the items home to Cambridgeport with Mother Barbour. Still, Susan apologized to her sister. The stitching did not meet her own stringent standards. "I did the best I could," she said, "and wished 'twas more."

14
(1867)

Day by day, Susan endeavored to fashion a satisfying homelife for her family in Hyannis. She learned to cope with the idiosyncracies of her stove and well. She contended with windows that slammed shut on steamy days when she wished for a breeze, then rattled threateningly when assaulted by the ocean's winter winds. By their reputation and her experience, she discovered the tradespeople and peddlers who were reliable. When she met W.H.'s congregation and her neighbors, some of them became friends. Meanwhile, cooking, cleaning, and childcare suffused the rhythm of her life. And, if there was a spare moment, she wrote her letters or sewed, sometimes for Emma's hope chest.

In his own way, Alfred, too, was adapting to new circumstances. His first Western winter tested his stamina and persistence.

Tremont, Ill.
February 16th, 1867

Dear Sister Emma.

I am almost as long in answering your letter as you were in writing to me. I have however been quite busy with my family as well as official duties and have not really seen the time to spare. I have however to day a place where I can steal a little time, which I will improve. We are completely out of the world this week, no mail, bridges down and roads almost impassible. On Tuesday last it began to rain and has kept it up until this morning, the Snow and Ice melted and raised the creeks, and rivers so that East of us on the Mackinaw and Sugar creek, Prairie of Mud Creeks, the water came down in such torrents that many bridges are gone, and in some places for one or two miles on a stretch the water covers the roads to the top of the fences, making it next to impossable to travel, several bridges are down so that we have had no Eastern mail this week, the stage not being able to come through, on the other hand to Peoria, our stage due Monday could not get through on account of bridges being down between us and Delavan, but yesterday they came through Pekin and thence to Peoria, then out here and brought us mail from Peoria, but none from Chicago or North and East, as the Railroads were blocked by their bridges being washed away, so we know nothing of Eastern affairs. On Wednesday morning George having Banking business which he wanted me to do for him in Peoria and some goods to bring back I started with our teamster in the team, we got out about 2 miles and found the bridge over Dillon creek almost flooded, the road leading to it was covered with water covering the fences and roaring down with great fury, we were afraid to venture over as it looked as if it were being undermined so with others who had assembled there we turned around and came back, then we decided to take the light-buggy and go up north to Morton about 4 miles and see if we could through there. I started fully rigged and equipped for any emergency, Rubber suit and Saddle in case I got where I would have to ford a stream, or swim, to leave one horse and the buggy and go on

(1867)

horseback with the other horse. I however got along very well, had to ford two rather rough looking creeks (swelled so that they were nearly 1/4 of a mile wide) and arrived safely in Peoria about 1/2 past 3 in the afternoon. I finished up my banking business and what other business I had to do, when it was so late I did not dare to go back that night, so I put up at the Hotel and waited till morning, when I started, and arrived home about 2 o'clock P.M. the roads were awful, mud 6 to 10 inches deep and as much as we could do to get along at a walk with two horses, we hope the roads will be better next week, it is cold now and freezing and may make good travelling——there has not been such a flood for 22 years before. In one place one of our Farmers had 20 Horses out in a field, the water came up so he could not get at them, there happened to be one place where the ground was rising and here they all collected making it sort of an island there they remained for three days, with nothing to eat but cornstalks left standing in the field, the roads are so bad that we have hardly any trade and business is awful quiet. Yesterday it was warm and springlike so much so that we had a Thunder storm, to day it is cold and windy and freezing fast, the changes are very great and trying so that we all have colds, though not unwell any of us. Baby seems the sickest his stomach teeth have not yet come through though they look as if they would come every day, he dont make any fuss about it though and behaves well about it, we have two girls this week to help Mary. one is a sister of our girl who is staying with her just for a little while, so that this week she gets along nicely. Ned is well and I think stronger, he does my <u>farm</u> work when I am away, he is real handy and will I hope <u>be real</u> strong this spring. we hope we may get some letters by the first or middle of next week as it makes it rather lonesome. But I must close as I want to do something else now, give love to all the folks, from us all. I dont know when you will get this letter, as we have no prospect of any mail yet. I shall try to write to mother tomorrow and to Sue in a day or two, give Kind regards to Will (W.) and remember your bro. Alf

Alfred worked hard to establish himself in Tremont, not only because he was ambitious, but also because he wanted to prove himself to his parents. The previous summer, he had visited Ned to determine whether "the West" was the place for him. Stories of self-made men who took advantage of opportunities in the new land to accumulate wealth regaled the folk wisdom of the times, but Alfred may have voiced misgivings about the prospective move. In a letter dated July 17, 1866, he had written to his father, "I felt bad and thought your idea was that I was of a roving disposition not contented to settle any where . . . It was that remark of yours which caused me to feel that you had not confidence in me to use sufficient judgement." Then, as if to certify his sincerity, Alfred continued, "I have decided to stay here, bought me a house, and am now fitting it up shall be on about the first of Sept for my family and goods."

According to plan, he returned to Cambridgeport. Mary and the baby were ready and the threesome started out almost immediately for the return trip. On September 5, Alfred wrote to his parents from Albany that he had safely completed the first lap of the journey and thanked them for their hospitality towards Mary and Walter. Appreciative, and mindful of his responsibility as the eldest son, he wrote, "Remember, now we have a home, it is ever open to receive you to all its comforts, and should any thing happen, we should only be too happy to give you its privileges. Write me if Emma does not get well soon."

Three days later, Alfred's family were the houseguests of Mary's aunt in Chicago. Alfred wrote home, "Very providentially I did not leave on Tuesday as I expected, for if I had I should have been on that train which was wrecked on the N.Y. Cent. R.R. just east of Rochester a terrible accident, however, we view it only as an additional proof of God's care over us, and in his bringing us all here in safety and comparatively good health. We were all quite tired out did not see Niagara falls because it rained so hard we did not dare to take baby out."

Mary and the baby remained in Chicago, while Alfred arranged the house in Tremont. On September 12, he wrote to his mother, "Here I am at last in my new home, though not a single article of furniture has come over yet . . . I am very heartily welcomed here by all my friends . . . baby was not well at all, his diarrhoea was bad . . . we had the Doctor . . . Mary wants to come here Saturday and I have consented but I dont hardly know how we will get along the roads are so bad that I am afraid I cant get my furniture over."

On September 16, he penned a hasty note. "Mary & Baby arrived here safely last night, very tired, and baby quite unwell. the roads were very bad mud up to the hubs of wheels and raining . . . baby is not well, cant keep any thing on his stomach, he throws up

(1867)

his milk, all curdled thick like cheese . . . We have had a hard time getting our furniture over and the roads are so very rough and muddy that it will cost me near double to get my furniture over . . . If I had any idea of the magnitude of the job I dont know if I would have stayed East and not tried the western clime."

A week later, he was more sanguine, writing, "We are comfortably situated in our new home. Mary and Baby are better in fact pretty well, except tired from the effects of the journey we have succeeded in getting a nice girl . . ."

No sooner was Alfred settled than he had another problem—his employer talked about closing the business and moving away. Nevertheless, when Ned had a relapse of a longstanding lung ailment, most likely tuberculosis, Alfred didn't hesitate to take his brother in and nurse him back to health.

A fire of suspicious origin destroyed the store where Alfred worked and Mr. Ingalls told insurance investigators that Alfred was the last person in the building, having worked on accounts until one in the morning. Interrogated by authorities, Alfred quickly established his innocence. Indeed, the investigators concluded their meeting by offering him a job. Alfred accepted and assumed the duties of an agent of the Phoenix Insurance Company of Hartford, Connecticut. In the back of his mind he entertained the idea that after Ned recuperated, the agency might be a good business for someone who was not too strong.

Meanwhile, hearings were held that revealed Mr. Ingalls's precarious financial position and cast doubt on the amount of inventory for which he had made insurance claims. Through it all, Alfred stood by his employer. No criminal charges were filed.

Tremont, Ill.
June 4, 1867

Dear Emma

Three times I have set out to write to you, but have been prevented by other matters. Ned has been quite sick with fever and confined to his bed for just a week now, but is getting better now, feels a good deal better now, the Dr. was over yesterday and said Ned was getting along as well as could be expected now, and thought this might help his lungs. I have just as much as I can do now. I work part of the time on the building and then taking care of Ned doing my chores and my garden to look after George now talks of giving up here and going some where else, where, he does not say but I suspect his wife and her brothers are trying to get him to go to Springfield, as her brothers are in business there, and she likes more style than there is here in Tremont. Things look awful squally here, and although we are going ahead with the building yet it is mixed about George ever doing anything here again, he will have to lay out over $2000 before he gets the old building in good order, then it will cost him 4 to $5000, to build the front, and I fear he will never be able to do it, however I am not going to complain or fret (if I can help it) but wait the course events shall take and try to be patient. I sometimes get discouraged and awful blue, but I think it is right that I should be here, to give Ned a home and the care he now needs and try to rest content with that. Ned is improving now and will I hope in a few days be up again and around. Mary is not over and above well, the hot weather wilts her down very much. Baby appears well, and is real good boy he cant walk or talk yet.

I was very busy yesterday all day acting as clerk of Election, we had an Election for Judge & Clerk of Circuit Court and as the town clerk could not attend the meeting they came for me, getting in office early aint I?

I was sorry I did not write for Mother to come out and make us a visit during the Anniversaries as the fare was down, but I did not think of it, do not know as Mother could have left her family though I should think with Sue & yourself you might carry on the establishment.

I must now stop writing & go home help Mary get dinner (as our girl is away) and then work on the building this P.M. Tell Father we thank him for the papers as it keeps us posted on Cambridge affairs, more than letters. Everyone says well I suppose Georgie told you this or Emma told you that or Father or Mother or Grace and so we dont get the whole news out of any. Mother and father generally give us news and there are snatches in others, dont be afraid of telling a thing twice. Goodbye love from us all

I am your aff Bro.   Alf

As her wedding day approached and she busied herself with necessary preparations, Emma may have started writing shorter letters to Alfred, hence his complaint about not receiving all the news.

(1867)

In September, she was in Hyannis, visiting Susan. Perhaps the sisters sat together chatting and sewing. Emma required sheets, pillowcases, and personal items, many of which were embellished with embroidery. It is likely that Susan, as she often did, offered advice and probably some recipes.

When Will Whitney, back in Cambridgeport, wrote to Emma, he told her how he was preparing a foundation for a cottage and their marriage.

Cambridgeport Sept. 10th 1867

My Dear Emma.

I thought I would try a letter on a sheet of letter paper, as I am tired of commencing new lines every fourth word. It is Tuesday evening and I am in my chamber feeling as though the bed in front of me might feel good. My hands are very stiff for I remained at home yesterday and to-day, and have been shoveling, carting bricks in my hands & using the trowel spreading the concrete both days. We finished this to night; and I am heartily glad of it. Now I know we have a good foundation both in the kitchen and new dining-room; one which the rats cannot undermine. I shall let it remain to dry a week or ten days, when it will be floored. We have decided on a change in regard to the finish of the front entry, or rather mother and Mr. Thayer wish it, and I yielded. It is this, we will not have any door at the head of the stairs but they will be open to the light and view; where the old door was will be an arch over the stairs across the entry; thus the entry will look larger than before; the stairs will be pleasanter and lighter; but there will be nothing to prevent one from falling down if they do not see the opening (as in the evening). This will necessitate a new woolen carpet for the front entry and stairs up and down. The new stairs are ready for travel and mother, having passed down and up, pronounces them strong and easy. I am really glad the work has gone on as well as it has thus far now I feel that I can say what I want in the morning, and go in town, and not loose any more time. It has been threatening weather for several days, save Sunday, so that I think work has not been very brisk at the office.

I think it is about time I acknowledged the receipt of your letter of Saturday. I received it on Monday, about 3 o'clock. I think you gave me a splendid letter notwithstanding your illness, and I am grateful to you for the effort you made and for the result. I made quite a call on your father and mother last night after meeting. Your Pa had been at home about an hour. I hope this letter will find you better, and more able to enjoy your visit.

I could not help thinking as I read your letter how selfish and unsympathizing I must appear in your eyes, because I do not enter into your feelings entirely as you regard our marriage and subsequent life. For I must confess I do not regard your scruples of incompetence, as having any foundation save, perhaps I ought to say, what anyone has in entering on any new and untried undertakings. It may be that I do not, cannot understand you. I am conscious that selfishness is my besetting sin, and it may blind my eyes to the reality of your position. But believing that the title with which you addressed me in your last viz: "My loving Will" is a just one I promise you that I will do my utmost to forget myself, and that you shall not bear alone any trouble in store for you; nor find any cause for discouragement in the life, you are willing to enter, and in which I anticipate so much enjoyment, so far as I am able.

We had a fine meeting last night, though (it sprinkled) not a great many were present. The tall brother, a friend of McCoy and the loud singer (I can't think of his name) gave us an account of his experience, which was very interesting. From the time of his awakening to his union with Tremont Temple Church was several years, during which he was urged several times to make a profession, but could not as he did not believe himself a Christian, though he took part in meeting and taught in Sabbath Schools in different places.

Ella has been at work in Jordan and Marsh's sewing with the Ricker girls for two days. I don't know how long it will last. I mailed a letter to you yesterday a.m. and a Chronicle . . .

From your "loving Will"
Wm. H. Whitney

After the war, William Henry Whitney worked as a civil engineer, so he was familiar with building principles. His comments about the changes in the house, however, suggest that Emma may have acquired an interfering mother-in-law.

On the other hand, Will enjoyed a warm relationship with Emma's family and, while she was away, the Barbours welcomed his visits.

(1867)

At Home Sunday Evn'g Sept 15th

Dearest Emma;

I am sorry now that I did not write Friday after the reception of yours of the 11th but from what your father said Monday evening, and your own unsettled mind, I thought you might return Saturday. But on my early return from town I found the next best thing, another letter from you for which "all thanks". In your first you ask about Mr. Mason. If his giving us two more excellent sermons to day is any sign, he has "recruited" if not "wonderfully" at least sufficiently. I hear nothing about a house for him. His subject this afternoon was in continuance of that of last Sunday P.M. on "a conscience void offence" and with R Ch. 2 Cor. IV 3&4.

The carpenter has been busy all the week and things are progressing favorably. I do not favor a change in the front door. I suppose you refer to removing the side lights and door and replacing my light in double door. It would be an improvement surely in looks, but as our door does not show from the street and not much from the court in Summer I guess it will get along with a coat of paint. Our closet in the sitting room is not injured much; the floor is cut off in front of the door and more shelves substituted, and in under the stairs the safe takes up part of the room. I expect the ceiling in our spare room will be repaired. I have spent all the time since Tuesday in Boston, so that nothing has been done (save what the carpenter has done) but yesterday Frank took hold of furring and lathing the new room and I helped him a little at night. The news of your expected return on Tuesday gives me great pleasure I will gladly make it my business and pleasure, to meet you at the depot, and if there is time take tea with you at home. I have an engagement of a week's standing that evening at the Chapel. The Young Men's Association meet at eight o'clock and generally stay late, as I am President I feel compelled to be present. I am sorry, but the next night is Wednesday and we have no meeting on account of the Association at Somerville.

I planned to call at your house Friday, but mother had a little job she wanted me to do, so I was compelled to put it off. And by waiting till last evening I had more news to communicate. Your father was just about starting for the P.O. to get the letter he expected from you, but concluding after hearing mine that there was none, he gave it up. I don't know as I ought to tell you, but I found a great change in the appearance of the dining room. They had just finished papering the room with a light paper, which gives it a very cheerful effect. I read to them parts of both your letters, and I think they were glad to hear from you even thus, second hand. They joined in your arrangement for Tuesday. This P.M. as I was comming home from meeting on passing your gate, Eddie ran over and barred the way, stretching his arms across the sidewalk, and your mother and father from the gate joining in his expressive invitation; I gladly availed myself of it and took tea stopping till meeting time.

Your brother Will was much disappointed Saturday in receiving a letter from Manchester saying that his wife would not return until the middle of next (this) week. He and Mrs. A had been working hard cleaning up the yard and house and your ma had cleaned up also expecting her return yesterday. Mrs. Munroe brother has lost a child dying last night. Mr. Ingalls is here and your father was expecting him to call this evening. They have not had a letter from Alf. this week. Georgie has a picture (recent) of Ned in which she says, he looks poorly. There is a report as yet not very certain that Arthur Hodges has been killed by Indians in Montana. The telegram is of a business nature to Mr. Williams, and he is not absolutely certain of the identity.

We have had a cool pleasant day and good attendance at the S.S. Your father got Mrs. Tosliff for your class again.

Mr. Charles Morse has been here all day; his father is still low and he thinks will not recover.

Mrs. Manson has been here also. Miss Lottie Valentine has not returned yet, at least I have not seen her. Did you see in the papers the notice of the marriage of Lieut. Maj. Butler to our friend Miss Lothrop? At the rehearsal Saturday Mr. Roberts said he intended to start something that would interest the young folks in singing more. Thursday evening I attended a meeting of my old company "A" about twenty five were present, the purpose being (and it was carried out) to organize and meet occasionally to talk over old times.

The lesson in the S.S. today was the continuation of the narrative of Christ's appearances. next Sunday we finish the book.

The subject of the readings the last Sabbath is "The Price of our Redemption".

I noticed our ivy today, it is growing nicely. We have a few

(1867)

grapes ripe (Concord) and our peaches are just ripening and it will be lucious if they are not stolen from us. With remembrances to your relatives, I am your loving Will.

Alfred wrote to alert Father Barbour that George Ingalls was on his way East and might try to borrow money to reopen his business in Tremont.

"You had better perhaps talk with him a little," Alfred wrote, "and find out what he is doing in the way of getting started again, and how he makes his payments if you can in an indirect way, so as not to appear too inquisitive, because if he pays all or attempts to he will have to start again with entirely borrowed capital or goods on Credit. . . . If you see he is going ahead again on a sound basis (i.e. as sound as he can under the circumstances) you might offer to pay him $100 or $200. of the money you were to loan me, and the bal in 30 or 60 days. If he does not say anything about it, I guess I would not offer . . ."

Ned tried to establish a business in Illinois, but experienced financial reverses. In a letter dated May 17, 1867, he asked his father for "some fancy labels for cologne Hair Oil, Pomades &c. Alf thinks you might get them of your friend Mr. Barry at L. Prangs in Boston, the nicer the style of label the better the article will sell . . . I will be very greatly obliged to you, send them by mail if it don't cost more than $1.25 otherwise by Merchants Union Express, as that is their price for a small pkg."

Ned experimented with various health and beauty aid preparations, which he pronounced, "quite good, equal I think to Preston & Merrill's, also some very good Blk Ink, if you send the labels by Express I should like a gallon of Salid oil for making hair oil Webber says it costs about $1.50 I cannot get it here."

A relapse of his illness prevented Ned from carrying out his business plan. In a long letter dated July 12, he listed his symptoms: "the least exertion upsets me, my head cracks away with fever after which come the night sweats, my cough seems . . . a little worse." Discouraged, he unburdened himself to his father. "Of course now I wish I hadn't done anything about manufacturing the Extracts etc., for I am unable now to complete the unfinished work and carry on the business . . . if I go away I must leave the things I have made and the money I have put into materials here lying idele, [sic] and shall of course be unable to pay you the amount of the bill of drugs at the time it becomes due, all these things trouble me . . . I thot I was doing write when I commenced the enterprise and thought 'twould prove successful. Now will you tell me what to do."

Apparently, Father Barbour successfully reassured Ned, urging him to make getting well his first priority. In appreciation Ned expounded, "I cannot tell you how much I thank you for your words of sympathy and encouragement." In August, making plans to seek out a more healthful climate, Ned wrote, "I have a quantity of Extracts I made up, which I shall try to dispose of before I leave. I have also the greater part of the Oils from Rogers & Lawton on hand, having used but a small quantity of them. These things will not spoil, and if I do not use them now I may have a chance to at some future time."

Forgoing Alfred's offer of help, Ned decided against working as an insurance agent in Tremont. Rather, he made up his mind to head for the great Northwest, where he hoped to improve his business opportunities and health. His girlfriend Georgie was in Cambridgeport, however, so in his absence Ned asked Emma to play Cupid. Perhaps because he couldn't afford to buy his sister a present, he didn't mention her upcoming twenty-fourth birthday.

Minneapolis Minn. Nov. 11, 1867

My dear sister,

I am here on my way for the pine regions, I have enjoyed much in seeing and being with mrs. Leeds and Col. the Col. is pretty feeble. I hope he is going to get better but I'm afraid, his mother is doing everything for him that can be done, it was good to see her familiar face and feel that she was so recently from home, it did me a sight of good. She has been making me a nightcap of black and white plaid flannel to wear in camp 'tis just what I want, and several other things she is doing just exactly as mother would do them if she was here.

I leave here this P.M. for the pines. I expect it will be a pretty rough, cold ride, between 40 and 50 miles by stage and lumber wagon before I get to the Settlement from which I start for the woods. how far I have to go after I get there I can't tell. I look for a pretty rough life this winter, but I shall try to take care of my health and hope that it will not only not be injured but that 'twill be much improved.

I'm thinking of you all at home continually and of course wishing I was there but I must wait until it seems prudent near time I want to see you all very much. I hope Alf has been successful in working up his lock and that he will make lots of

(1867)

money out of it. he and Mary have been very very kind to me. I can never repay them, but I do feel grateful from my heart to them, and hope sometimes I shall be able to show it.

I feel rather anxious about Father on account of his losing his office. Hope he has got his new appointment for I know he'll not be contented unless he is busy.

How about being married, you haven't written me about it yet?

Now, Emma I want to ask you to do a favor for me and I know you'll do it. Georgie's birthday comes 19th this month I want you on that day to go to the greenhouse on Main Street or the one on Harvard Street and get a bouquet and carry it to Georgie as a birthday present from me. I enclose $1.50. get the nicest one you can for the money, I don't care that it shall be very large, but I want it made of fine fragrant flowers with long stems so that they'll keep long as possible. I've no doubt you know just what I want and I leave it with you to get just such an one as you'd like the Capt. to bring you. Will you do this for me?

I haven't had much leisure since I've been here so haven't written before. give my love to all the folks. My health is improving tho' I have a little cold on hand just now. The weather is very cold here, really like winter and the ground is freezing fast.

Write me where you can and direct Jerrets' Mills, St. Croix Co. Wis. with much love I am your brother

Ned

America was a nation of improvisers and tinkerers so it is not surprising that Ned commented on Alfred's interest in devising a new lock. Even Abraham Lincoln, having whittled a wooden model of a steamboat with "adjustable buoyant air chambers," in 1848 acquired a patent.

Ned set out for the Northwest expecting the worst. He wrote to his father, "I appreciate your good advice about allowing the unhealthy degradation of camp life to influence me . . . I know and feel that I am going among a class of men who are vulgar, profane & reckless . . ."

Yet shortly after arriving at Camp Taylor in Wisconsin, in December 1867, he revised his opinion. He wrote to his father, "There is comparatively little profanity and real gaiety considering there are so many men together alone by themselves, the crew has the name of being the most orderly and well-behaved one in this vicinity."

In the same letter, he described his room. There were "large cracks in the floor, and door, and there's lots of air coming in all the time . . ." He continued, "The cook who sleeps in our shanty turns out about four in the morning and starts his fire, about five the teamsters get up and feed their teams and at six breakfast is ready and all eat, after which about daylight all go to work, dinner at twelve, work stops at dark, and then supper, after, the evening is spent in various ways according to the tastes of different ones in the main shanty they have a rousing great fire in the middle, on two sides of which the length of the room are long benches without backs, called the "Deacon's seat," on these the men sit and listen to songs or stories from different ones in the company, the songs are generally ballads in which some long story is told and they are listened to with considerable attention. In our camp the men are a little different class and of an evening, read or play checkers, card playing is not allowed in camp at all neither is any whiskey allowed about the premises. I occupy my evenings mostly reading . . ."

"Sunday in camp is a day of general repairs, choppers and swampers make their axe-handles, teamsters fix their whips and mend harness, and everybody whose clothes want washing or mending do it Sunday, with them it is the day for odd jobs of all kinds, of course I don't like to see it and do nothing of the kind myself, it is a kind of established custom and the men do it for want of other occupation . . .

"Now for what we eat, we have a first-rate cook, and he makes first-rate bread, pies and sweet cake, we have baked beans three times a day, and they are the genuine Yankee beans, they bake them in a 'bean-hole' 'tis a deep hole just in front of the fire-place in the large shanty, the ground is heated all the time, the beans are put in it in a large iron pot and then the hole is filled and the pot covered with hot ashes, they bake all day and all night and are splendid in the morning, we are having no meat at present but pork, but after a while shall have fresh beef and venison, potatoes we don't have, they would freeze here it is so cold, have no butter, and no milk or sugar for the tea, use molasses on the bread have tea every meal, no coffee. I confess the fare don't quite suit me but if I can only get well that won't make much difference."

He described his duties, for which he was paid $2 a day plus room and board. "My work isn't arduous at all now, tho' I shall have a little more to do when there comes a little more snow so that the trains can haul bigger loads, at present, I can go to the landing once a

(1867)

day and scale all the logs hauled in a day in fifteen or twenty minutes, then I have to figure the contents, keep camp books and the time of the men, all my day's work can be done in an hour and a half, but by and by I shall have to be on the landing most all day."

15
(1868)

*E*mma's friend Ellen Stone went to live in Waltham, Massachusetts, nine miles west of Boston on the banks of the Charles River. She told about the view from her front window of a cotton factory, the first in the United States. In 1814, when it opened, this factory was the most modern textile mill in the world. For the first time, all processes in the manufacture of cotton cloth were accomplished under one roof. The red brick building, which harnessed water from a small falls for its power, was the brainchild of Francis Cabot Lowell. By memorizing the parts of machines he saw in England, Lowell cannily evaded that country's ban against exporting machinery or its plans, and transported the Industrial Revolution across the Atlantic Ocean.

(1868)

Waltham Jan 30th

Dear Friend

You may have wondered why I have not written before, but I thought I would not do so until I had been to Sabbath School. I don't find Waltham like cambridge, but I suppose I shall like the place better when I see more of it, as I have not had a opportunity yet.

The street we live on is called Pine Street, somewhat retired, but very pleasant, I should judge, in summer.

The steam cars run pretty often here; the railroad is but a few steps from our house, the cars can be seen very plainly from our sitting room window, particularly the Watertown Branch. The cotton factory is situated near us.

Now I will describe to you the church and Sabbath School both are small and very unlike in appearance the spacious place that I have left. The name of the pastor is Bacon. he is newly married we saw the notice of his marriage in the Watchman and Reflector some time before we left. He is not a very young man by any means, yet he is not nearly so old as Mr. Mason.

The singing is conducted by a choir. I miss congregational singing very much.

I did not join the Sabbath School until last Sunday. It commenced at one o'clock. I went over there with my little brother. I entered the vestry, and seeing a gentleman walking about, I stepped up to him, asked if he was the superintendent, he said he was; I then told him that I had brought my little brother to join the infant-class; also, I should like to join the school, myself. "I should like to have you," said he. Then he took our names. I told him we had not lived long in this place; that we came from Cambridge, what Sabbath School we attended.

I seated myself with Henry until it was nearly time for school to commence, then Mr. Draper (the superintendent) conducted H. to the infant-class, me, to a class of young ladies some of whom I should judge are a little older than myself. The teacher, (if the class had one) was not present, so mr. Draper took the place of one. The lesson was in the tenth chapter of Acts. beginning from the 31st through the 36th verses. I enjoyed Mr. Draper's explanation of the lesson very much. I understood before hand, that he is an excellent man, and for one Sabbath, I like him very well indeed. My thoughts would that day go back to the time when I used to be in the Cambridge Sabbath School, and I would wonder what you were saying to the girls. I wondered also where the lesson was you were explaining about. Oh, I want to ask one little favor of you, that is, if you can without any inconvenience, get me a card containing the lessons for the year. If you will, I shall be greatly obliged to you for your kindness. Each Sunday I can read over the lesson for that day and think of you and the girls and wonder what you would be saying about the lesson.

Mother sends her love to you and your mother, also to give hers to Alfred and Mary the next time you write to them.

Remember me to the girls, also, to your parents.

Believe me yours
sincerely
Ellen M. Stone

P.S. Please direct your letters to the care of Hemble & Hastings 69 Commercial Street Boston because I shall get them sooner and it will be more convenient.

The Reverend Albert M. Bacon was pastor of Ellen's church, The First Baptist Church in Waltham, from February 1, 1867 to March 31, 1869. His tenure was short, according to church records, because "Mr. Bacon was a 'western man' and did not fit into the quiet tastes of New England. One woman, returning from a church service, remarked, 'All we want now is footlights.' He was a combination of sparkling fervor ammounting to brilliancy at times and inferiority with commonplace illustrations at other times."

On the day that Ellen wrote, Emma's Aunt Harriet issued an invitation for Emma and Will to visit on their honeymoon. Although marriage was the high point in a woman's life, it was considered a wrenching experience for a young woman to leave her family circle —even if she were only going to live on the other side of town as was Emma. Wedding trips, therefore, customarily included visits to the bride's relatives.

Jersey City January 30th 1868

My Dear Emma

Your Aunt Margaret desires me to answer yours of the 28th which reached us in good time, notwithstanding a 3 day snow and rain storm, it found us in the enjoyment of our usual health, and all at home busy sewing. She desires me to say she

(1868)

will only be too glad to see you, and will feel that her spare chamber will be highly honored with a bridal party. Mrs. W. says the conditions are "if you will play his music", so if you think you can comply— "come on"—it is nothing difficult, all who play the piano can play on the melodian. Alfred and Gustovus W Jr. played on it so do not hesitate to come on that account, for you know, your uncle is full of mischief. Last week Friday N. & G. called on the Misses Russels. Mrs. Y.C. said "Her husband had a letter from the Capt. II setting the time of the wedding the middle of February," M. asked if he said anything of a bridal tour, "she said no you were too steady people to conform to the customs of the world." hence our joyful surprise, we shall count the time, M. can hardly wait. she is very glad the Russels cannot receive you, else we should not see so much of you.

Your Uncle and Aunt went to a wedding on Tuesday Evening of this week over to "Green Point". She probably remembers the bride, though at the time she visited Ravenswood she was a small child, her parents were very nice Welsh people, by the name of Jones, the bride was Miss Ellen J. She may remember that whatever you said to the old folks they invariably answered, "sure".

The sun is shining very brightly today and we intend to go to N. York this afternoon to hear Rev. A.B. Earle who is laboring with the 5th Avenue Baptist Church.

Your Aunt M. has just come into the parlor where I am writing and wishes me to say that she does not see any "boldness" to excuse, but will be always hoping to see you or any of our relations or friends from "down east" How does Eddie stand the loss of his Aunt Emma? or doesn't he realize it?

The letter of your Aunt Norton's to which G. referred in your Mother's last, I found commented on only, in the Watchman & Benefactor of January 23. It expresses Mr. Gayden's mind exactly.

Give my love to all who take the trouble to inquire for me, Mrs. Little, Miss Elizabeth Davis in particular.

Love to every member of your father's numerous family.

From your
Aunt Harriet
297 S. 5th St.

Emma's World

Emma Sargeant Barbour and William Henry Whitney were married in her parents' living room on February 18, 1868. Neither Ned nor Alfred were present. Ned was at a lumber camp in Jewett Mills, Wisconsin, working as a bookkeeper, when he wrote, "The very day I came was the day sister Emma was married . . . if I hadn't come, I shouldn't have known anything about it until the whole thing was over, and I should have been very much disappointed as it was I got your letter with the information as to the time, and with the prices of her dresses in it, at about half past five in the evening, so I had just about time enough to get ready for the wedding, tho' differences in time between us is about an hour and quarter, so at 1/4 of 7 with us the ceremony was going on. I read your letter to Mrs. J and showed her the dresses and we talked about the wedding for about an hour, she seemed much interested, she said she was married in just such a white alpacca trimmed with satin of the same color (that is if you call white a color) I enjoyed the wedding very much tho' not so much as if I'd been a little nearer . . . I liked all the dresses very much particularly the green, and the pearl silk the bridal dress of course took the lead. I think twas very kind of Will to furnish it. I am glad to think Emma had so many presents, but I want a complete inventory of them and who each one was given by. you say there were about sixty but you name only about half a dozen . . ."

Neither did distance dull Alfred's interest in the wedding. Despite his troubles, which included heavy debts, business setbacks, and sundry physical ailments, he regularly wrote to his parents. On February 23, he had plaintively remarked that he missed their letters, but understood the reason they hadn't written. "I have known your time was fully occupied in getting ready for the wedding and getting Emma ready. how much we have thought of the dear girl and how many times we have spoken of her and wondered where she was, what she was doing and how much She was enjoying herself. I suppose now that she has gone you begin to miss her and perhaps feel lonesome but how pleasant it will be to have them so near you. and how pleasant it must be to them to be so near home, one does not realize what it is to be away from home until they have tried it. We wish Emma much joy and happiness in her new life . . ."

Epilogue

*P*ines and hemlock shade the final resting place of Emma Sargent Barbour Whitney at Mount Auburn Cemetery in Cambridge, Massachusetts. On a gentle drumlin adorned with marble statuary and impressive memorials, a simple, waist-high, squared column of granite in the center of the Whitney family plot bears her weather-worn name, along with her loving Will's, and the faded dates of two of their infants, a boy and girl. In death as in life, Emma dwells eclipsed by many noted persons—Mary Baker Eddy, Amy Lowell, Julia Ward Howe, Charles Sumner, and Winslow Homer, among others—whose final resting place is also America's oldest garden cemetery. In such company, her gravesite at 1401 Asclepias Path rarely warrants a second glance.

Emma was forty-five when she succumbed to breast cancer. Will survived her by twenty-one years, but never remarried. Throughout his life, he was active in veteran's organizations and in 1896, at ceremonies celebrating the fiftieth anniversary of the incorporation of the City of Cambridge, he addressed public school students on the subject of patriotism, euologizing the military heroes for whom Cambridge streets are named.

Emma and Will had a daughter and a son, who survived them. Clara Mabel married Arthur Pevear, an insurance broker, the son of the Reverend H. K. Pevear at Emma's church. At first, Clara and Arthur lived a few doors away from her parents. Later they moved back into the family home at 105 Chestnut Street, probably to look after her widowed father. Clara was sixty-one-years-old in 1932 when she died of colon cancer, survived by her husband and only child, Dorothy. Dorothy never married. The first member of the family to obtain a Social Security number, she had a job as a clerical worker and devoted herself to caring for her father, but he survived her by four years. In 1963 at the age of ninety-one, he died in a Waltham institution. Dorothy was fifty-nine when she died, like her grandmother Emma, of breast cancer.

Emma's son, Charles Fuller, who joined his father's civil engineering firm in Boston, married Laura Haverley of Watervliet, New York. They had no children. In 1913, he and his wife moved across the Charles River from his home in Cambridge to 284 Summit Avenue, Brighton, where he lived until his sudden and fatal heart attack in 1944 at age sixty-nine. He was probably the last member of the family to own Emma's letters, since they showed up at an antiques market about the time his widow moved from Brighton. Laura survived Charles by fourteen years, residing for the last nine years of her life at The Baptist Home of Massachusetts, Newton, where her husband's uncle, Alfred Loring Barbour, had been a trustee, clerk, and president.

In spite of many false starts, Alfred finally did achieve the business success he craved. Unfortunately, Mary did not live to share in Alfred's accomplishments and prosperity. Not long after Emma was married in 1868, Alfred and Mary, "depressed in health and business," sold their Illinois farm and returned to Cambridge, cashing in their hopes for the west. Mary died in childbirth in March 1871, when their second son, Robert, was born. Alfred, who adored her,

Epilogue

was devastated. Father and Mother Barbour, supportive as always, stepped in to help rear his motherless boys.

In July 1871, a grieving Alfred, accompanied by his son Walter, journeyed to New Hampshire. He hoped to benefit from a change of scene; he knew he needed to gain some perspective on his life and to formulate plans. Boarding in Newport with a Mrs. Goodrich, he took pen in hand and, from his room overlooking the common, poured out his anguish to his mother.

"The sense of my loneliness comes over me with terrible force, the fact that the dear, cheerful little wife who so devotedly loved me and whom I delighted to care for will never be with me again on the Earth that the craving for her love and tender care can never be satiated by her in this world, it is hard, very hard for me to bear, I do not murmur or complain, for God knows what is best for me, I know she is happy and it is a great comfort to me, but I am selfish, I feel the loneliness, and know how great is my loss. I know I have a rich bounteous store of love and sympathy in you my dear Mother, and in Father and the multitude of friends I have, and an unbounded store in Christ, but in my human weakness I crave the loving care of that tender little wife who for ten years has so carefully ministered to my wants and leaned upon me . . . I often feel bad when I think of the weight of care which you have upon you, in assuming the charge of my little ones, and fear it is too much for you . . . I hope when I return I may in a measure be able to take some of the care or labor from off your hands . . ."

In time, Alfred did rebuild his life. He returned to Cambridge, assumed responsibility for his sons, and worked diligently to establish his insurance business. He met Josephine (Josie) M. Smith, daughter of Professor Eldridge Smith, who was for twenty-five years master of the Dorchester High School in Boston, and fell in love again. Alfred and Josie were married in 1874 and had three daughters, Mary, Grace, and Ethel. Grace, who married John Carlyle Davis of Kansas City, Missouri, settled in Hartwell, Ohio, but her sisters remained in Massachusetts.

Good fortune never blunted Alfred's desire to do good deeds, and with financial security, he became a propertied and prominent citizen in Newton, where he lived the last twenty-five years of his life, active in many civic undertakings. In addition to being secretary and treasurer of the Cambridge Mutual Fire Insurance Company with an office at Cambridge, Alfred was connected in an official capacity with other corporations. He was president of the Columbia Co-Operative Bank and a director of the First National Bank of West Newton. He joined the Newton Lodge, I.O.O.F and was a member of the First Baptist Church of West Newton, serving as chairman of the Executive Committee. He also was a member of the Board of Newton Associated Charities, and vice-president of the Boston Baptist Social Union. When Alfred died in 1912, he was the much-honored patriarch of a family that included five children and three grandchildren. In his will, he bequeathed to each a token from the many awards he had received.

Ned followed his older brother's example and returned East, too. Living with his parents in Cambridge, he courted Georgia Roberts, daughter of Louisa and Professor Benjamin Roberts, master for fifty years of the Roberts School in Cambridge. As a teenager, "Georgie" had stolen Ned's heart and while he was away, she had written to him, sympathetic to his frequent illnesses and bouts of loneliness.

When he was in Wisconsin in 1867 and a letter was all that he could afford to send his parents for Christmas, Ned explained, "I sent some money in a letter to Julia, asking her to buy something for Georgie . . . I would have liked very much to send something for each and every one of you at home but you know I havent the werewith now . . . I feel sure that you'll not think hard of me because I sent something for Georgie and nothing for any of you except the little ones, you understand my position and hers. You know she is lonely without me, that she is subjected to a good many privations and inconvenience on account of my absence from her and tho' I never make her very valuable presents, my feeling is that by occasionally giving her some little thing, she shall know that I think of her continually, and that my wish is that she may have as much pleasure as possible, and I know she values them just as highly as she would something more costly. She is a dear good little girl, she has been true as steel to me, and I want to show her that I appreciate her." In 1869, Ned married his Georgie. He was twenty-nine; she was twenty-one. Their union was childless.

William also returned to Cambridge. He and Julia quit their farm in Greenfield and moved into a house at 14 Cottage Street. His firm, W.S. Barbour and Hodges, civil engineers and land surveyors, was located a short distance away in the Merchants Bank Building. Apparently, the venture was successful for Ned asked Bill if he could borrow one or two hundred dollars for six months, telling his father, "The reason I wrote to him for it was that I thot 'twould be more convenient for him to let me have it than for you . . ."

When William died in 1889, he was the city engineer of Cambridge, a post he had held for many years. Julia and their two sons survived him. When the older boy, Frederick, born in 1867, reached his majority, he followed in the footsteps of his uncles and blazed a trail west, to Denver. Julia was the court-appointed legal guardian of the younger boy, Edwin Fairbanks, who was only fifteen years old when his father died. Shortly after William's death, Julia, too, went west, settling in San Francisco. Her annual reports to the Massachusetts court, accounting for boarding school expenditures from Edwin's trust, are emblazoned with the gold seal of Alameda County. Later, she put down roots in Los Angeles.

Susan Barbour Evans traveled too, but never as far or as widely as Julia or her brothers. In addition to Maine and Cape Cod, over the years, her husband's ministry took the family to Holyoke, Littleton, North Oxford and Still River, Massachusetts. Susan died in 1889, not quite a year after Emma. She was survived by W.H. and five children: Alfred H., Edwin B., Charles A., Mary E., and Austin E. Long after the Reverend W.H. Evans had died in 1897, their youngest son remembered his father's Sunday sermons and recalled that he was not a good preacher. Growing up, Austin and his sister and brothers had endured several sermons every week, a captive audience as the Reverend Evans completed the circuit from one church to the next. Some Sundays they fell asleep at as many as four different churches.

Austin preserved fonder memories of trips to Cambridge to visit his grandparents. He often accompanied his father to his paternal grandfather's tailor shop. Among the customers Austin met in the shop of William Henry Evans, Sr., was Henry Wadsworth Longfellow. While waiting for a pair of cuffs to be sewn or his waistcoat fitted, the poet enjoyed reciting verses to young Austin and jiggling the youngster on his lap.

In 1885, Emma's mother succumbed to "consumption"; she was seventy-eight. Emma's father lived another five years, surviving all of his children, save Alfred. A loving and thoughtful family man, he had drawn his handwritten will years before. When he died at age eighty-five, it's provisions were sadly outdated. He had left his entire estate to his wife for her life use. Whatever remained after her death was to be divided: one fifth to son William Sullivan Barbour of Cambridge, civil engineer; one-fifth to son Alfred Loring Barbour of Cambridge, now secretary of the Mutual Insurance Co.; one-fifth to daughter Emma Sargent Whitney, wife of Wm. H. Whitney of Cambridge, civil engineer; and two-fifths to daughter Susan Elizabeth Evans, wife of Rev. William H. Evans, residing in Holyoke, Massachusetts.

"I think my family will appreciate my motives," he wrote, "in giving to their elder sister, a larger portion of my estate, as her family is engaged in the noble work of Saving Souls and will not probably receive sufficient income to educate their children as they should be educated and I commend the family to their tender care and attention.